D0868851

The Man
Who Ate Toronto

THE MAN WHO ATE TORONTO

JAMES CHATTO

Memoirs of a Restaurant Lover

Macfarlane Walter & Ross

Toronto

Macfarlane Walter & Ross

37A Hazelton Avenue

Toronto, Canada M5R 2E3

Canadian Cataloguing in Publication Data

Chatto, James

The man who ate Toronto

Includes index.

ISBN 1-55199-025-3

1. Chatto, James. 2. Restaurants–Ontario–Toronto.
3. Food writers–Ontario–Toronto–Biography. I. Title

TX910.5.C42A3 1998   647.95'092   C98-931681-5

Macfarlane Walter & Ross gratefully acknowledges
financial support for its publishing program from the Canada
Council for the Arts, the Ontario Arts Council, and the
Government of Canada through the Book Publishing Industry
Development Program.

Printed and bound in Canada

TO THE MEMORY OF
Joseph Hoare,
without whom I could never
have eaten so much
or so well.

✍ CONTENTS ✍

≈ ACKNOWLEDGMENTS ≈

AS A JOURNALIST, I have been very fortunate in my sources. My sincere thanks to every chef, cook, restaurateur, maître d', sommelier, bartender, waiter, runner, and busboy who took time from the labours of the night to answer my questions, argue with my conclusions, and teach me about their professions.

Much of the information in this book first appeared in *Toronto Life* magazine, disguised as feature articles, columns, or restaurant reviews and verified by absurdly over-qualified researchers: Veronica Cusack, Charles Rowland, and Eileen Whitfield. Profound thanks are owed to them; to the editors who assigned and worked on my food and wine stories over the years, Marq de Villiers, John Macfarlane, Stephen Trumper, Anne Collins, Charles Oberdorf, and Michael Totzke; and to all my other friends at the magazine who have exerted a civilizing influence over a wayward freelancer. My greatest debt, of course, will always be to my friend and mentor, Joseph Hoare, *Toronto Life*'s food editor for thirteen years, to whom this book is dedicated.

Some of the food, wine, and travel articles commissioned by other magazines have also served as ore. For those words, I must thank Elizabeth Baird at *Canadian Living*, Matthew Church and Anna Kohn at *EnRoute*, Trevor Cole at *Destinations*, David Wheeler at *Convivium*, John Hatt at *Harpers & Queen*, Kathleen Fitzpatrick at *Departures*, and Malachy Duffy at *Food & Wine*.

For their help with this book, I am deeply grateful to my editors at Macfarlane Walter & Ross: to Jan Walter, to Barbara Czarnecki, peerless arbiter of syntactical truths, and especially to John Macfarlane, whose trust, encouragement, and perspicacity were equalled only by his patience.

Above all, I would like to thank my wife, Wendy Martin, source of all energies, and our children, Joseph and Mae, the most entertaining and forgiving of dinner companions.

James Chatto
May 1998
Toronto

A percentage of the author's royalties from this book will be donated to the Ford Martin Fund for the Welfare of Children Suffering from Leukemia.

R ESTAURANT CRITICS? Twenty-two years
ago, when I worked briefly as a waiter in a
wine bar in London, England, the whole idea of
them seemed deeply unfair. What gave some blasé
little clique of freeloading journalists the right to
dismiss the achievements and threaten the liveli-
hood of hard-working professionals they had
never met?

I asked Mike, the chef, as he chopped the
red cabbage for the house salad. "What I say," he

grunted, without taking the cigarette from his mouth, "is fuck 'em."

When he showed up at closing time to empty the till, I put the question to Steven, the manager. He smiled. "It's all part of the game, my dear. The price of free publicity. Some of them know what they're talking about, some of them don't. You just hope they're hungry and in a good mood when they come in."

For a decade or so, as a reviewer and columnist for *Toronto Life* magazine, I have earned my living writing about restaurants, and my perspective has changed. From the other side of the table, I can see that restaurant critics do serve a purpose. We alert the public to hypocrisy, pretentiousness, carelessness, and cigarette ash in the cabbage salad. We can help the uncertain fashion victim decide what is hip and what isn't. Eating out far more often than any chef, we see, or think we see, patterns of taste, the coming and going of influences and ingredients. We know enough about food to be able to tell when a fried egg is burnt or slimy or tastes more of old skillet than mother hen.

I no longer think that criticizing restaurants is unfair, but I have to concede it is impudent. Ask any chef or restaurateur. Disguised as anonymous members of the paying public, we secrete ourselves in some corner table for two or three hours, open our senses to what transpires, and then measure the evening against the yardstick of our own particular tastes and experience. It is, by definition, a wholly subjective process, but when the review appears in print, it can seem as if sentence is being passed from a position of godlike objectivity. This piece of fish was overcooked; that combination of vegetables did not work. The music was too loud, the service too distant or too attentive. In the court of the restaurant critic there is no room for clemency, no acknowledgment of mitigating circumstances, and only occasional recognition of an alternative aesthetic.

The restaurant columnist, however, has a different agenda. For me, the meal is only the beginning of the story. When a chef puts strawberry sauce on his spinach I want to know why. I try to find out if it's part of some avant-garde culinary manifesto, an act of revenge by a line cook who has just been given his notice, or simply a tragic cry for help. Because the restaurant business is only incidentally about food. It is really about people – some of them artists or entrepreneurs, others journeymen, cynics, or genuine eccentrics, one or two of them rogues. Every serious restaurant is an expression of intent on the part of its creators, a balance of values and compromise, an attempt to establish a brief but vivid relationship with the person who walks through the door. The whole exchange may be conducted at a subconscious level, but without that human dialogue, a restaurant is simply a place to eat.

Dining out in Toronto is a much more complex activity than it was when I first came to Canada, twenty-one years ago. The city had an earlier bedtime then, and slept more soundly. Jet-lagged and hungry, I prowled the midnight streets looking for dinner, but all I could find was a vending machine in the underground depths of the Royal York Hotel selling plastic-wrapped submarine sandwiches, clammy, insipid, and indigestible as putty. All this changed in the 1980s, when restaurant-going became the city's favourite pastime. What had been an occasional treat was now a regular, even fanatical recreation. People with money and confidence discovered the glamour of restaurants and began to use them as social venues to a degree that would have astonished their parents. They revelled in the novelty of exotic foods, the names of obscure ingredients, and indulged themselves in shameless games of wineupmanship. Having learned the names of chefs and restaurateurs, they followed them round the town, leaving a large slice of their disposable income in a succession of extravagantly decorated rooms. It was flash, fun, and frivolous, and by the time the recession brought it all to a crudely abrupt halt as the decade ended, restaurants and restaurant-going had changed in this city forever.

At least, things had changed for the well-to-do, for people living above the arugula-iceberg line. Just where that cultural and economic division occurs in our particular society is a moot point, but it is certainly close to the summit of the demographic pyramid. Toronto is an affluent city, but unlike the cities of Europe, we have no demanding bourgeoisie with the gastronomic sophistication to sustain a deep second echelon of restaurants. Beneath our top two or three dozen, the level of expertise drops rapidly, and it would plummet but for the safety net of quality provided by the city's ethnic restaurants. Ingredients are also a challenge. Almost every imaginable foodstuff is available somewhere in Toronto, but not always looking its best. Anyone who has tasted a tomato, a peach, or a sprig of basil close to the Mediterranean, a properly hung game bird in England, a saltwater fish at the seaside, a tropical fruit in the tropics, will know that when it comes to raw material we are often forced to settle for the second-rate.

That said, I believe it is possible to eat out as well in Toronto as in any other major city in the world. Over the years, I have experienced the most imaginative and delicious cooking of my life here, at Nekah and Lotus, and I could nominate ten more establishments that have matched the quality, professionalism, and consistency of any European restaurant I know. The achievement is all the more remarkable because it has happened without the benefit (or the constraints) of a rich fine-dining tradition. The pinnacle of our restaurant industry is small, incestuous, and excessively fashion-conscious; it is also fast, complex, and fascinating, a hybrid growth with roots in all the world's cultures. In a single generation, we have evolved from prime rib to sushi of foie gras with icewine jelly, all at a breakneck pace. I count myself lucky to have been along for the ride.

Walking home from a good night's work, footsteps echoing along the city's dark backstreets, my habitual game is to trace the genealogy of the meal I have eaten: where this waiter worked before, where that cook learned his trade, who has started importing such excellent venison into Toronto. I try to relive each texture and flavour and silently recite the professional restaurant-goer's prayer of gratitude: We thank you for the daily resurrection of the appetite, for saving our ties from coulis stains, for letting us steal the menu without an embarrassing scene, for expense accounts. Lead us not into obesity, and deliver us from cholesterol. For thine are the breath mints, etcetera.

Eating out remains an unpredictable adventure. The evening may be wonderful, it may be mediocre; often it will be both. But even when the service is grim and the food inedible, the fascination remains. Going to a different restaurant four or five times a week has not diminished my pleasure in sitting down at a table, be it made of wood, marble, plastic, Formica, or glass, hidden by butcher's paper or draped in stiff white linen. You settle yourself, look up expectantly, and wait to see what will happen next. The waiter approaches. You are in a theatre and the lights are dimming to darkness before the play. He hands you a menu. The curtain rises.

STEAK OUT

THE FIRST TIME I came to Toronto I fell in love. Not with the city, in some coy and figurative way, but with a beautiful young woman of twenty, literally, passionately, feverishly, complacently, utterly. I did not woo her in restaurants (though these days I do, from time to time). We went out for a meal only once, on our first date, to Sunday lunch at the Hazelton Lanes Café, and it was a gastronomic fiasco. She ordered a spinach salad; neither one of us ate a thing.

Falling in love in a city will always improve its image in your personal gazetteer. Even before I met her, however, that month in Toronto seemed to sparkle with a peculiar glamour. It began with the ride from the airport, swooping in on the Gardiner Expressway, the shining blue lake to the right, big glossy American cars cruising alongside the limousine like dolphins pacing a boat into harbour. At one point I looked ahead through the haze and caught my first glimpse of the city, towers of white and gold floating upon the horizon, a twenty-first-century vision of the New Jerusalem. I expected the magic to end, but instead it persisted day after day, week after week, while the sun shone perpetually.

June 1977 is the most significant of many debts I owe to my godfather, the actor Robert Morley. He had written a play called *A Picture of Innocence*, and starred in it, as a happily married, happily transvestite high court judge. The highlight of the piece came at the end of the second act, when he entered dressed in a white ballgown and diamond tiara, carrying a white ostrich fan and looking uncannily like the late Queen Mary. After such an apparition, Act Three was an inevitable anticlimax. I think this was already clear during rehearsals in London, but Robert was confident he could rewrite it on the road, during the long tour that would culminate, if all went well, in a West End opening.

Toronto lay halfway along that tour, an improbable intercontinental detour between Birmingham and Bath. As assistant stage manager, lowest of the low, I had packed up the props after the last performance in Birmingham and seen them loaded safely onto the truck – a rainswept, blustery night's work. On our first sunlit Sunday morning in Toronto, I arrived at the Royal Alexandra Theatre assuming I would unload them, but instead our company manager took me aside. He explained that Canadian Actors' Equity, the actors' union, forbade me to lift a finger this side of the ocean. I could come in every night and stand in the wings, checking that every prop was in place, but otherwise my duties as ASM were to be handed over to the Royal Alexandra's own stage management team. By way of compensation, I would be paid Canadian Equity rates, which worked out at roughly three times my usual salary.

I stepped outside to mull over this extraordinary information. The sun beat down on the broad, dusty, deserted streets around the theatre, on the empty parking lot next to the new concert hall, on the spire of the CN Tower presiding over the silent morning. In those days, the Sabbath was a day of rest in the entertainment district – almost. Someone had set up a card table on the sidewalk outside the theatre. A dapper, black-haired man in his sixties, dressed in an immaculate white suit, stood beside it like a carnival barker, waiting to sell tickets for future shows to anyone who might happen to come into view. Our company manager had told me his name was Honest Ed Mirvish, and that he owned the theatre, the block, and a whole village elsewhere in the city. He saw me and raised his hand in a greeting. "Welcome to Canada," he said.

MY GODFATHER liked Toronto. He had friends and relatives here, and a loyal following who still recalled his success at the Royal Alexandra five years before in *How the Other Half Loves*. After that triumph, he had written about the city in one of his books, about the spartan dressing-rooms in Ed Mirvish's theatre and the good steaks in his restaurants at the other end of the block, about the New City Hall, Niagara Falls, Muskoka dachas, and a nightclub in Yorkville that boasted the only naked chef in the world. But the one remark in the book that all Toronto seemed to remember, and to have brooded upon ever since, was a casual observation that each time he went to dinner in someone's home, the hostess served lasagne.

"Really, dear," he said to me over breakfast in the Royal York Hotel's coffee shop, raising his eyebrows and spreading his huge soft hands, "you'd think they had more to worry about than that."

Underemployed as an ASM, I had plenty of time to devote to my other role, accompanying Robert to publicity functions, most of which seemed to end with a meal. I had been eating with him in restaurants for as long as I could remember; I wish now I had been more attentive to his wisdom. Robert's knowledge of the ways and wiles of restaurants was equalled only by his love for them. He had a talent, famous among his friends, for finding the best place to eat in a city he had never visited before, setting off on foot from the hotel, guided only by instinct. He could predict a menu from the awning above the sidewalk, or guess a chef's nationality from the size of his artichokes. And he could gauge a restaurateur's attention to detail from a single glance at his dessert trolley, for he had learned to read carts as a hunter reads the tracks of his prey, with more than the eyes of hunger. He was wary, for example, of any establishment that parked its trolley too close to the door: however welcoming the glint of glazes, there was always a danger of street dust peppering the flan. He was alert to bistros that piled the top shelf with gâteaux but offered inadequate crèmes and mousses below: a sign that the place was uncertain of its volume of business. It was also his view, quite current in those simpler times, that the quality of cooking in an Italian restaurant could be precisely judged by the excellence of its almond cake.

As restaurant critic for *Punch* and *Playboy*, Robert enjoyed his reputation as an international gourmet but was far less interested in food than in the people who cooked, served, and consumed it. He never forgot that the purpose of a restaurant is to give pleasure to its customers, not kudos to its owner or chef. Above all, he despised pretentiousness and snobbism, seeing them as a kind of bullying, and burst many an egotistical little bubble with his tongue or the nib of his pen. Recently I was talking to Harry Barberian about his restaurant's glory days in the early 1970s and mentioned the evening Robert dined there with Rudolf Nureyev.

"Robert Morley?" Barberian slapped his thigh and rocked back and forth with laughter. "He drove me crazy! Shall I tell you what I did to him that night? It was late and he wanted to go back to his hotel, so he asked me to call him a cab. I said, 'I can do better than that.' I led him outside and said to my chauffeur, 'Take him home in the Rolls.' Robert's pompous as hell! He says, 'I never ride in a Rolls-Royce.' At the same time, the garbage truck pulls up. I know the guy who drives it. I give him a beer every night. I said, 'Here's a movie star, the hotel's on your route, please take him home.' The last I ever saw of Robert, he was climbing into a garbage truck."

My godfather would have enjoyed the adventure. He was insatiably curious about people and no doubt questioned the garbage truck driver at length about his life and family, his job, his prospects, his politics. Robert's own Shavian socialist views frequently took strangers unawares. They assumed from his accent and lifestyle, and from the parts he played, that he must be a top-hat Tory, and they attempted to ingratiate themselves accordingly. Forever mischievous, he would let them wander as far to the right as they wished to go, paying out rope until they had all they needed to hang themselves.

I think Robert liked Ed Mirvish. He admired his drive and the legendary rise from rags to riches; he understood the purposes of his showmanship and the public persona of the uncultured, bargain-mad salesman. He himself had long ago mastered the useful art of self-caricature. The one area in which he thought Honest Ed went a little too far was in his parsimonious attitude to backstage decoration at the Royal Alexandra. There had been no chair in the star dressing-room when he played *How the Other Half Loves*, and he had been obliged to pull weight with management to have one brought in. Removing his makeup after the last performance, he was interrupted by two stage-hands who wanted to take it away again. It all came too close to a lack of respect for the traditions of the theatre for Robert to be entirely amused.

"I'm a storekeeper," offered Mirvish by way of an explanation. "I don't know the traditions of the theatre."

Then again, Honest Ed was capable of setting his own theatrical precedents. It was his generous custom, for instance, to treat a visiting company to a meal at one of his restaurants. Our own invitation came on the day after we arrived. Attendance was obligatory. And so it came to pass that my first experience of dining out in Toronto, indeed, the defining gastronomic moment of my introduction to the New World, was shrimp cocktail and steak, mashed potatoes and peas, at Ed's Seafood.

And to think I almost missed it. We were asked to convene at six o'clock, an hour I did not then associate with eating, and the summer sun still burned hot upon the sidewalk. So I left my jacket in the theatre, never dreaming that a formal coat and tie could be de rigueur at a place with a name like Ed's. The English have a morbid fear of being underdressed, and I blushed as if I were naked as I stammered my explanations to the maître d' at the door. He must have been used to such scenes. Obliging hands brought a clip-on tie and helped me into a tentlike dark blue blazer that smelt strongly (and reassuringly) of dry-cleaning fluid. Feeling like a turtle in a borrowed shell and looking like a nightclub bouncer, I finally made my way to the table, where Ed Mirvish was already entertaining the company with his softly spoken, well-rehearsed stories.

"I'm a storekeeper," he was saying. "What did I know about restaurants?"

Enough to know that they go with theatres like cheesecake with cherries. King Street West was Desolation Row in the early 1960s, when he rescued the venerable Royal Alexandra from a proposed transformation into a parking lot. The neighbourhood was rich in automobile body shops and abandoned factories, but there was nowhere for people who came to his theatre to eat before the show. So he bought a mill-construction warehouse at the end of the block and turned it into a restaurant.

For advice on the looks, he called in professional decorators. They suggested he pull out the old posts that supported the ceiling, and offered to do the work for him at $2,500 per post. Too expensive. He kept the posts and festooned them with the photographs he had unearthed from a room in the theatre, thousands of pictures of actors who had trodden the Royal Alex's boards since its curtain first rose in 1907. Then he added the Tiffany lamps he had bought as a job lot years before. Red carpets, stained glass, statues, antiques – every inch was dressed as if for a Viennese operetta or a New Orleans bordello –

and outside, a façade of marquee bulbs and framed press reviews: Ed's Warehouse began to take shape.

For advice on the menu, he called upon Harry Barberian, and also on Benny Winbaum, whose meat supply company, Vaunclair Purveyors, provided the city's steakhouses with top-quality raw material. They suggested he offer only one item: roast beef. "I hate roast beef," said Mirvish, "but it was very popular, and they said you could serve a lot of customers quickly with roast beef. Other people told me, 'Ed, you can't have one item in a restaurant. And what will you do on a Friday? The Pope says you can't eat meat on a Friday.' But soon after I opened the restaurant, the Pope changed his mind. So that was a help." For vegetables, Mirvish decided to stick to mashed potatoes and peas. "It's amazing how many people like mashed potatoes and peas." Looking for staff, he turned to his own organization. Yale Simpson would run the restaurants; Tony Falaco, then the guy in charge of the parking lot at Honest Ed's plastics factory, was given the job of chef – positions they hold to this day.

The antithesis of Toronto's sober, self-deprecating personality, the empire of restaurants expanded. First a downstairs room, serving steaks. Then the steaks moved up to bolster the beef, and the downstairs room became Ed's Italian. Later Ed's Seafood was born, then Ed's Chinese, and lastly Old Ed's, in 1979. One hundred and ninety-two seats became two thousand, with a model laundry and an in-house bakery to fill every basket with bread rolls. Every year, a thousand coachloads of customers drove in from the States to add to Ontario's numbers, all dining at Ed's, then walking next door to take in the show. A captive audience.

"But what do I know?" he asked. "I'm a storekeeper. Bargains are predictable. Theatres and restaurants are risky business. That's why I don't give up my day job."

WORKING IN THE THEATRE displaces a person from the normal timetables of society. The same effect is reported by chefs and waiters, a feeling that their lives are being lived to a rhythm distinct from the beat of the city, like a permanent case of jet lag. Leaving the Royal York Hotel around ten every morning, I could not help but notice that the sidewalks were virtually empty. The traffic was a roaring torrent, but the few pedestrians I saw were tourists, looking down at maps or craning up at the towers of the downtown core. On days when Robert had no need of me, I walked down to the lake and took the ferry across to Wards Island, catching some rays on an empty beach beside the glittering lake. My only glimpse of busy Toronto came in the late afternoon, when I walked from the hotel to the theatre, a couple of blocks away. Then the sidewalks were jammed with people, all very well dressed and well groomed, each with a brief-case, moving swiftly in predetermined patterns. They seemed never to speak or smile. Their faces were set in clear-eyed visionary frowns, like the idealized workers in Bolshevik poster art. Here too, although in a different way, *das Kapital* was clearly the driving force.

Ever since the sartorial trauma of that first meal at Ed's, I had worn my white suit and tie at all times. I was prepared, therefore, for the company's second meal out. This time our host was Gino Empry, the Royal Alexandra's publicist, and the venue he chose was a steak-house called Carman's Club. By now the show had opened, to politely dismissive reviews, the critics as bewildered as the audience by the failure of the third act. Robert rewrote it frequently, rehearsing the new material every morning. To perk things up, he introduced a pantomime cow into the plot, but in spite of its capering antics, the cast remained demoralized. Perhaps Empry thought more steak would strengthen our resolve; perhaps it was just that Carman's was one of the few restaurants in the city that stayed open for dinner after a show.

After the sumptuously kitsch extravagance of Ed's Seafood, the equally eccentric ambience of Carman's seemed no more than par for the course. Old Masters hung beside pictures painted on velvet, innumerable objets d'art shared mantel and shelf space with pewter and brassware, beer steins, flagons and goblets, all agleam in the dim penumbra. I was beginning to take it for granted that top-notch Toronto restaurants served little more than steak and Caesar salad, in surroundings that combined the resources of the Royal Opera's prop room with the decorative taste of a Las Vegas casino lobby.

It was a dramatic setting, and Robert rose to the occasion. Having toured in his youth with such giants as Sir Frank Benson, Russell Thorndike, and Glen Byam Shaw, he understood the role of the star in sustaining company morale. He had picked up the murmurs of dissatisfaction from two of the senior actors who were peeved at so much extra rehearsal, and had seen the first symptoms of mutiny as they tried to develop a following among the rest of the cast. That night, one of the not-so-young pretenders decided to make his move. Over Carman's preliminary pickles, feta salad, unctuous garlic bread, and Kalamata olives, the rebel began a subtle display of name-dropping and anecdote, hogging the limelight, discreetly challenging Robert's position. Over Carman's delicious, garlic-rubbed, charcoal-broiled striploin, the tales became more involved, the delivery louder and more theatrical, his part in each story more central. With the famous Black

Forest cake, he embarked on a yarn that warned of the dangers of changing a script too often during a run. It was then that Robert finally picked up the gauntlet. I don't know how the conversation suddenly brought it to pass, but somebody mentioned Rudyard Kipling. A hush fell over the company. Everyone turned to face Robert. Quietly, and with the most poignant feeling, he was reciting Kipling's poem "If," at first to the actress beside him, and then, without breaking stride, to us all. Spellbound in the silent restaurant, we listened, caught up in the subtle rhythms of Robert's voice, the psalmlike cadences of the poetry, the message of loyalty, hope, and triumph over adversity. When it was over at last, nobody spoke, but a sort of satisfied sigh went up from the table. There were tears in some eyes, adoration in others. The rival said not a word as the waiter approached with the bill. Robert had timed his move to perfection, a coup de théâtre that was also a coup de grâce.

"HOW WAS THE STEAK at Carman's?" asked John next day. John was a Canadian of my own age who worked backstage at the Royal Alexandra and had assumed all my hands-on duties. To him I had passed on the only secret of the theatre that I knew and he did not: how to make slim, crustless, English cucumber sandwiches (a crucial prop in Act Two) that would not slip apart in the actors' hands or curl up under the lights. He was a willing apprentice but seemed more at home with a hammer than a butter knife.

I told him I had enjoyed the steak very much.

He nodded. "I guess it's a change from boiled meat."

Pressed to explain the remark, John said he had always felt sorry for the English, with their unending diet of boiled meat and gravy. I tried to correct his mistake, but nothing I could say made the least impression. As a boy, he had listened to stories from relatives who had served in England during the war, and had even heard of a song, "Boiled Beef and Carrots," that boasted about the horrific British cuisine. He was glad, therefore, that I was finally getting used to properly char-broiled steak. Now there was one last step to be taken in my belated culinary education: to taste the ultimate tenderloin, cooked on his own barbecue in his own backyard. The whole company was invited.

Though pity was the reason he gave for the party, civic pride was also a motive. John, I suspect, felt that our little downtown beat was giving a false idea of Toronto as a cold, impersonal city, and he wanted to show us its sterling, generous heart. It is true that we hadn't had much of a chance to explore the hinterland north of King Street, though several members of the company had already made private expeditions – some of the gentlemen to an innocuous gay discotheque called the Wunderbar, up on Yonge, some of the ladies to the locker room of the McGill Club. Other actors who had been billeted in an apartment-hotel on Charles Street East told of a French restaurant called La Chaumière, just across the street, but its hours coincided with those of the theatre and no one had eaten there.

So one morning we drove away from the neighbourhood I knew, up Jarvis Street and the unknown territory of Mount Pleasant, then east along Eglinton, deep into the tree-lined residential suburbs of Scarborough. Robert, alas, was not with us – he was taping a television interview with that prolix prince of the chat show, Brian Linehan – and some of the other actors had decided to stay in their hotel rooms to learn the latest version of Act Three, but there were enough of us present to show John we valued his kindness. We sat in the sun in his small backyard, drinking beer out of bottles, while he cooked his steaks at the barbecue, expertly and with considerable flair.

To John, steak was the ultimate foodstuff, and he took enormous pride in its preparation. As is the case with many Canadian males, barbecue was his single area of culinary expertise, and the act of donning the apron, with its curious echoes of Freemasonry, carried the sanctity of masculine ritual. Steak was his North American birthright, the same meat his father and forefathers had relished, the protein of pioneers, the food of possessors. Red-blooded, ungussied, big, it had all the qualities John valued in a man as well as a meal.

The rise of the Toronto steakhouse during the late 1950s owed much to the backyard barbecue. Men who couldn't tell an artichoke from an almond liked to know what they were eating. When they dined at Le Baron on Church Street and watched a young chef called Harry Barberian grilling a well-marbled slab of New York strip right there in the dining room, they felt comfortably in control of the situation. There was no French to mispronounce, no foreign gastronomic mystery to threaten and confuse, just formal, solicitous service, a décor their fathers would have recognized and approved, and steak.

FORTY YEARS LATER, steak is still with us, and so is Harry Barberian. In 1996 I spent a morning beside him, up in the private dining room above his eponymous restaurant on Elm Street, looking forward to lunch and talking about those pioneer days. Le Baron was not the first steakhouse in Toronto. That honour goes to the Sign of the Steer, Hans Fread's place at Davenport and Dupont, which opened around 1950. It was popular, but the steaks there were pan-fried and then branded with a poker to mimic the marks of the grill. When

Frank Kiss opened Le Baron in 1955, and customers tasted real, New York–style char-grilled meat, Fread's days were numbered. "Time had passed him by," mused Barberian, turning the pages of an oversized scrapbook, "but he didn't realize it, and blamed the world." Impeccably dressed in a blazer, white shirt, and cravat, Barberian turned out to be an encyclopedia of restaurants gone by. A bout with throat cancer made speaking frustratingly difficult, but his memory was as sharp as a steak knife, backed up by a personal library of clippings, reviews, and carefully photocopied obituaries.

"I learned to cook from my mother," he began, "and she had a brilliant training. Brilliant! It was during the First World War. Allenby and the British are sweeping up against Turkey; the Armenian massacres are on. My mother is a schoolgirl in a convent in Turkey. One night, three men arrive at the door, seeking sanctuary. They're Abdul Amin's three chefs, Armenian Christians. Years before, they had been allowed to go to London and train at the Savoy under Escoffier himself. The convent takes them in and hides them. They have nothing to do, so they teach these thirty young convent girls how to cook. My mother was one of them.

"Soon after the war, she and my father came to Canada and settled in Brantford, Ontario. Later they were joined by my father's mother, and her story was stranger still. The Turks had a way of killing Armenians. They would take the old and the very young deep into the desert, and leave them there to die. My grandmother was 66 when they came for her. Three years later, she shows up in Yokohama, Japan. She had made her way on foot across Afghanistan, India, China. She died in Brantford at the age of 106."

By then, Barberian had moved to Toronto. His training was in time and motion management, but he had worked in several Ontario and New York restaurants. The year 1955 found him running a hot dog stand in Grand Bank, Ontario, when two friends showed up one day with a message. A man called Frank Kiss wanted to open a steak-house in Toronto, like the famous old places in New York. He needed a chef, and someone had recommended Harry.

"At that time, there were no more than half a dozen restaurants worth mentioning in Toronto. There was the King Edward Hotel – everyone went there for lunch. There was a place called De Cosimo's, and Angelo's, which became Old Angelo's. Oscar Berceller had Winston's, where the press and the actors went. The only French restaurant was La Chaumière, and of course there was the restaurant at the top of the Park Plaza, where Mary Millichamp was the chef. The suburbs? Jack Kent Cooke's Le Cabaret on St. Clair Avenue West was it. So Frank Kiss opened Le Baron, and I cooked the steaks right there in the dining room. A brilliant idea."

Barberian's memories of the opening night included a guest list – names that meant little to me but that left an abiding impression of Le Baron as some kind of Rick's Café Américain from the movie *Casablanca*. The tables were filled with recently arrived immigrants from Europe, all of whom had just opened restaurants or were about to. There was Imre Martin, who was in the construction business and also owned the Patria restaurant on Spadina: he used to boast that he had spent the war years as chauffeur to the Japanese ambassador in Budapest. Nearby was David Copeland, a movie producer, and his friend the Contessa Charlotte, who opened Les Cavaliers on Church Street. Both were rumoured to have been wartime secret agents, though no one was told on which side. At another table was Colonel

Dewhurst, who ran the Concerto coffee shop at Bay and Bloor – the Len Deighton novel *Funeral in Berlin* was apparently based on his life – and Imre Finta, who had the Moulin Rouge on Dupont and was later charged with war crimes, although the case never came to trial in this country. According to Harry Barberian, all of them claimed to be war-ravaged Europeans, but they seemed to have enough money to open up restaurants.

Le Baron survived this strange début and quickly became successful. So did Barberian, and after a couple of years, he decided to try something on his own. Looking for a location, he found a recently vacated coffee shop on Elm Street, in a historic cottage dating from 1860. "There was a well-known brothel next door, but I didn't care. I took the lease and opened in 1959, as a steakhouse with twenty-six seats. The rest is history."

So Barberian's was the third steakhouse in Toronto? Not quite. A few months earlier, Carman's had opened its doors, co-owned by a young Greek chef, Athanasios Karamanos, who had changed his name to Arthur Carman when he moved to Canada. He cooked in restaurants and hotels in Montreal, and then for a year in Toronto, at Diana Sweets on Bloor Street, before he found partners within the Greek community prepared to help him create a place of his own. The location was a handsome nineteenth-century house on Alexander Street.

Carman had noted the popularity of Le Baron – Barberian said he had even tried to find work there – but his restaurant was no imitation. Sensing that his clientele, so fussy and critical about the way their steak was prepared, would nevertheless be just as happy to leave the ordering of the rest of the meal in somebody else's hands, he decided to minimize choice on his menu. Order the meat, and the rest of the meal just appeared: eight dishes ranging from olives and garlic bread, rice or potato, through to dessert. The idea worked. For the first eight years, Carman did his own cooking, grilling the well-marbled, garlic-seasoned Alberta steaks over charcoal in the traditional Greek way, mixing the salad dressings and making the sauces himself, sautéing clams, garlic, and oregano in hot olive oil and tossing them with pasta in a Hellenic version of spaghetti vongole.

"I introduced garlic to North America," he told me once. A slight exaggeration, but no doubt there were many Torontonians during the 1960s who first tasted the stinking rose at Carman's.

Where steakhouses were concerned, however, the decade belonged to Harry Barberian, on points if not quite a knockout. Flamboyant, loquacious, he was already a minor celebrity when he left Le Baron, and he quickly became the darling of the women's pages in Toronto's newspapers. Food journalists soon discover which restaurateurs will smile for the camera and offer a pithy, quotable opinion on demand. In no time at all, Barberian had bought the adjoining half of the old building on Elm Street and invited interior designer Jouke van Sloten to turn the whole property into a retro patrician shrine of panelled wood and evocative Canadiana. Van Sloten had worked on Le Baron and would later design a cluster of other steakhouses for the city, establishing an Old World, dimly lit mood that customers came to expect whenever they stepped out for steak.

Perhaps from watching the rise of Winston's, owned by his friend Oscar Berceller, Barberian saw the value of encouraging a showbiz clientele. Frighteningly long lines of credit were extended to publicists such as Gino Empry, enabling them to wine and dine visiting stars. An intimate upstairs room was furnished so that tenderloins could be chewed and swallowed in something approaching privacy, but somehow a press photographer always appeared before the meal was quite over. And when the time came to leave, no matter how late, Harry's Rolls-Royce and chauffeur were waiting outside to whisk the celebrity back to the hotel, unless it was Robert Morley.

"The rest is history," he said, slapping his scrapbook shut. "A couple of years after I opened my first restaurant, I opened another, Harry's, on Church Street. The Rolls would take people back and forth between the two. I also took the lease on the building that became Tom Jones, then gave it to one of my managers. It opened in 1966, struggled the first year until it got a liquor licence, then did well. My chefs, my managers, when they left – with my blessing, and my management systems – all did well. At one time, every major steakhouse in Canada could be linked back to us. And remember, I was also a consultant." He pulled a book from his shelves and showed me the handwritten inscription: "To Harry, he taught me the restaurant business in ten minutes," signed by Ed Mirvish.

"The roast beef at Ed's Warehouse was my idea. Serve it rare today. If it doesn't get eaten, serve the same cut well done tomorrow. At the opening party for the Warehouse, Ed turns to his manager, Yale Simpson, and says, 'Harry won't take any money. Get him and his wife a matching pair of Cadillacs.' I said to Ed, 'What do I do with them? I drive a Silver Shadow Rolls-Royce. I can't come down to Cadillacs.'

"But you get tired. I eventually sold Harry's to the Martin brothers from Paris, Ontario. As manager, they took on a waiter from the King Edward Hotel, called George Bigliardi. I advised them to make him a shareholder. Years later, in 1976, Vern Martin calls me up. He says, 'This kid, this ingrate, has found out the seafood restaurant opposite is for sale. He wants to open a steakhouse across from me.' I said, 'I thought you sold part of the business to him.' Vern says, 'We never got round to it.' I said, 'Has he taken the lease yet?' He says, 'I don't think so.' So I told him to phone Bigliardi quick and sell him Harry's. 'Don't let him open across the street or he'll kill you. Because he's the guy that's there every day. He knows the customers.' Well, Bigliardi opened. He's still there, and Harry's isn't. It went through a number of hands and eventually closed.

"It was just about the same time that I sold this restaurant. One day, two boys from Montreal came into town – Bob Hanson and his partner Weir Ross. They said they wanted to buy Barberian's. I gave him a price for a twenty-year lease, never thinking he'd pay it. He paid it. Never put your own name on a restaurant. You sell it to someone else, they keep the name, and it hurts too much whenever someone does something stupid."

A knock on the door interrupted the monologue – a waiter, asking if we were ready for lunch. Barberian put a hand on the waiter's arm.

"What happened on this day, two years ago?"

The waiter thought for a second. "You took back your restaurant?"

"Thank you. That's right."

In 1976, having sold his restaurant to Hanson and Ross, Barberian left Toronto for Florida, where he continued to work in restaurants, acted as a consultant, and fought his battle with cancer. Eighteen years later, he returned. Steak and steakhouses had fallen from grace. The restaurant that bore his name was floundering.

Barberian settled the last two years of the lease out of court and resumed his reign.

He beams at me. "It's been thirty-seven years and two and a half million steaks since we opened. I've kept the paperwork. You can check it.

"Now, what would you like to eat? I recommend a ribeye. True steak lovers enjoy a ribeye. And plenty of my cabbage. I got the recipe from my cousin, who was a major in the Turkish air force. In the Middle East, officers in the air force are very highly exalted. He decided the cook in his mess was no good, so they sent for a chef from Marseilles. That's where the recipe for my cabbage comes from: Marseilles via Istanbul!"

The cabbage was delicious: cooked through but still crunchy, anointed with lemon juice and masses of pepper. The steak was a little treatise in honour of meat, exceptionally tender, beefy, seasoned only with salt and pepper, its rich juices freed by the heat of the grill and shared through the succulent gradations from crisp, dark surface to blood-red heart. Barberian watched me closely while I ate, enjoying my appetite, while he sipped coffee and toyed with a bowl of mushroom soup.

"You picked your moment to come back," I suggested.

ALTHOUGH THEY NEVER ACQUIRED the legitimate patina of history that gave credibility to their New York equivalents, Toronto's steakhouses developed a reputation for butch sophistication and an important place in the city's foodscape. Then came the eighties, and that cachet faded away. Driving past some quarter-century cow palace on my way to the latest Cal-Ital opening, I would mutter, "Good Lord, are you still here?" In an era that adored novelty, steakhouses dared not change: to do so would jeopardize what business they had. Critics and food writers ignored them, or else chastised them as expensive and old-fashioned. And also unhealthy. Cholesterol was the demon du jour, and red meat its vehicle. It made no difference when Canadian farmers developed beef that was leaner. The diet-conscious still stayed away, while the steak lover grumbled that a good marbling of fat was essential to the flavour and tenderness of his favourite cut.

So, who kept the charcoal glowing? Every couple of years, some foodie would venture into the candlelit lair of the carnivores and discover a clientele of tourists and out-of-towners, Americans and Japanese with a reverence for beef, Europeans seeking a North American experience. There were also the folks – some of them Rosedale or Forest Hill millionaires, others once-a-year restaurant-goers from the suburbs – who still equated a pound and a quarter of beef with a good time, who slapped their bellies at the end of the meal and felt that they had dined well. It was a masculine customer base with jock overtones (why else were so many steakhouses clustered around Maple Leaf Gardens?) and a complacent sense of loyalty. Many of George Bigliardi's battalion of beefeaters had crossed the street from Harry's, as Barberian had predicted. They stayed with him through thick and thin. Carman kept his own clientele, so did Hy's and Bardi's, and so did the House of Chan, that curious, clublike anachronism on Eglinton Avenue West where the Chinese food is inedible but the steak and lobster are bona fide contenders; so did all the survivors. Steak aficionados are a profoundly conservative species. When they find a place that cooks the meat in precisely the way they like, that fulfills their own backyard barbecue criteria, they become customers for life.

Such established patterns, however, do not explain the sudden resurrection of steak in the mid-1990s. First, restaurateur Bob Sniderman finally conceded that his American-style dining room, the Senator, was a steakhouse, and started using the term. Then the Ruth's Chris Steakhouse chain ventured north of the border and opened its first Canadian franchise in the heart of Toronto, serving massive U.S. prime cuts, sizzling with butter. And then, in the spring of 1996, there was Michael Carlevale, aiming to rival the city's finest restaurants with his magnum opus, Black and Blue, and basing its menu on steak.

Black and Blue seemed extraordinary for a number of reasons. In some ways it typified the ethos of Toronto's burgeoning cigar culture; in other respects, it didn't feel part of this city at all. I first saw the room when it was under construction, an adjunct to Carlevale's prosperous, fashionable restaurant Prego della Piazza and its chic cadet space, Enoteca. It was already apparent that no expense would be spared in making the vision flesh.

Carlevale is a cultured Bostonian who dresses better than any other restaurateur in the city. He has the requisite ego of the successful entrepreneur and both the longevity and the connections to be counted among the industry's established élite. More interestingly, he still has ambition. With Prego he went as far as he could go within the genre of up-market, consistent, commercial fine dining. Black and Blue, he explained as he showed me around, would exist in the higher realm of "elaborated gastronomy," a fifty-seat room with glistening opulence in the décor, on the wine list, and on the plate. I admired the accoutrements: the arched ceiling, the dim blue glass light fixtures, the crystal and silver, the sanctum sanctorum (an upstairs cigar lounge where the bar is stocked with nineteenth-century distillates). Some months later, I crept back alone for dinner.

An open mind is the indispensable attribute of a restaurant columnist. Your critical apparatus has to be clean of prejudices as you walk in the door. Before you begin to form even a first impression, you must see the place on its own terms and switch into whatever dialect of style the room speaks. Only then can you tell if the restaurant has achieved its intentions.

Black and Blue looked exactly as Carlevale had described it in his imagination. It was simultaneously modern and ultra-conservative, as if some avant-garde Milanese designer had played with the notion of an English gentlemen's club while thinking about the first-class dining car on the Orient Express. Every gleaming surface was made of the finest material; every detail, from the silver bowls of pommes frites to the squares of thick blue art glass that served as plates for the amuse-gueules, was studiedly beautiful. Such obsessive perfectionism tempered the room's masculinity with an undertone of the exotic.

The other customers seemed too busy to notice. A party of businessmen were concentrating exclusively on the glories of the wine list; a brace of brokers, who had removed their jackets according to time-honoured steakhouse custom, were lost in a world of meat. Across from my booth, a lawyer spent the whole evening talking about himself to an uncomfortably bored young woman.

The menu proposed by Carlevale and his long-time executive chef, Massimo Capra, began with a selection of amuse-gueules: bite-sized mounds of pâté, of pork galantine, smoked salmon spread, soft cheese impregnated with walnuts. There was a shyly flavoured consommé with a hint of game and the scent of sherry, an ostentatiously minuscule portion of gnocchi in white sauce with a dab of caviar. Then, startling after such delicate chamber music, a great big steak appeared, beautifully cooked, alone on the plate, and wee jugs of four traditional sauces with which to play.

The juxtaposition of refined, classical European dishes with a classic American steak was a bold idea, more impressive than the actual cooking in those early days, for textures were sometimes pedestrian, flavours uneven. But the mood of the place fascinated me. From the prices on the menu this was unabashedly a playground for the rich, Toronto's ultimate temple to the new aesthetic of red meat, fine wines, and the gastronomic anathema of the Cuban cigar. At the same time, it was so idiosyncratic, so unapologetically one man's vision, that it seemed to stand outside fashion altogether. It was that utter absence of compromise that distanced Black and Blue from the Toronto of 1996.

The revival of the steakhouse had little to do with nostalgia: it reflected a broader contemporary mood. In her brilliantly titled food book, *Offal and the New Brutalism*, English writer Charlotte Du Cann traced a fanciful connection between the rise of Thatcherite Conservatism and the return of offal to British restaurant menus. In Ontario, Mike Harris and the Tories came to power, brandishing macho policies based upon bullish cuts, and simultaneously Toronto rediscovered steak. Young bloods, reared on pasta and grilled fish, became instant experts on the merits of dry-aged, corn-fed U.S. prime. Was it just a coincidence, or is there a link between a taste for red meat and the true blue politics of power?

The first time I came to Toronto, the city seemed to me to be entirely devoted to steak. Twenty years later, cigars and sixteen-ounce slabs of protein were back in vogue, and the devil take the vegetables. As if to underline the fact, on the day after my visit to Black and Blue, I received a letter from the ageless Gino Empry singing the praises of

Carman's. Not that I needed any such aide-mémoire to waft me back to that carnivorous June in 1977.

It is a cliché that actors on tour make a beeline to the nearest pub as soon as the curtain falls and the greasepaint is washed from their faces. We never did find an English pub in Toronto, but we quickly discovered Peter's Backyard, a recently opened restaurant and cocktail bar, seconds away from the Royal Alexandra's stage door. The owner, Peter Skretas, had worked for Harry Barberian, and I dare say there was steak on his menu, but I don't think I ever tried it. Instead, I would nurse a gimlet or a dry manhattan and watch as an occasional couple giggled their way onto the tiny dance floor, where an elderly disc jockey alternated songs by the Bee Gees with that month's inescapable hit, "Copacabana," by Barry Manilow. One of the cocktail waitresses was a young university student, working her summer vacation, and it suddenly became a matter of the first importance to sit at a table where she was taking the orders. After three weeks, I summoned the courage to ask her out. To my astonishment, she said yes, and suggested Sunday lunch at the Hazelton Lanes Café. The rest, as Harry Barberian would say, is history.

2

⊱⊰ GRAND HOTEL ⊱⊰

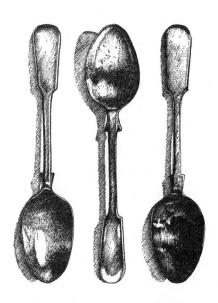

SO I LIED. It wasn't all steak and submarines.
There were sometimes hamburgers, too.

There was, for example, a Big Mac at the
Metro Zoo. My godfather had been invited to see
the animals by a man called Tommy Thompson,
and that morning at breakfast in the coffee shop,
Robert asked if I'd like to come along. As we
crossed the Royal York's lobby from the eleva-
tors, Thompson was waiting for us. He stood at
the top of the stairs that led down to the street as

if he were a climber posing for a photograph on the peak of Mount Everest, legs planted apart, hands crossed on the pommel of a stout walking stick. It may have been a trick of the light, but I swear he was wearing plus-fours and an Eton jacket, a cross between a Scoutmaster and an Edwardian gentleman dressed for a hike.

By now I had grown accustomed to the subtle tilt of surreality that made daily life in Toronto so agreeable and intriguing, so it came as no surprise when the limo, instead of taking us to the zoo, turned in through the gates of Mount Pleasant Cemetery. Robert's eyes twinkled with amusement, but Thompson did not notice. He was sitting beside the driver, engrossed in his own dissertation on the history of the city's founding families. "This seemed a good place to start," he explained.

"And no doubt a fine place to end," murmured Robert.

For the next twenty minutes, the car crept along the sun-dappled avenues that wound between the graves, while Thompson, who we now learned was the Metro parks commissioner and a power in the land, pointed out mausoleums of interest and drew our attention to rare and unusual trees. Ever gentle when in the presence of genuine eccentricity, my godfather responded with suitable oohs and aahs. Nevertheless, there was a palpable lifting of the spirit when we finally left the cemetery and accelerated back into the city of the living. Five minutes later, we pulled into another park.

"And is this the zoo?" we asked.

"This is Edwards Gardens. I wanted to show you the flowers."

We reached the zoo in the end, walked for hours past meadows and up and down steep forested slopes, glimpsed a peacock and what could have been a tiger asleep in its distant den.

"Very nice, dear," said Robert, "but I can't help missing the old zoo by the river. The animals were so much easier for people to see."

By the time we sat down for lunch in the zoo's McDonald's franchise, Thompson had forgiven the remark. I believe he may have felt a frisson of daring self-satisfaction at bringing a famous gourmet to a fast-food outlet, and it was clear that he himself was a fan of the egalitarian convenience of mass-produced burgers and fries, a way of lunch that all could afford and enjoy, no waste of time or money, no foolish airs and graces. Perhaps he expected outrage, or else gasps of admiration at such Space Age efficiency. He seemed just the tiniest bit disappointed that Robert simply took the whole thing in his stride.

Thompson wasn't to know, of course, that England had already been conquered by the tall clown and his brace of all-beef patties. At least once a week during rehearsals in London, Robert had ordered in Big Macs and fries for the company. We would sit around a prop table on the stage in the empty theatre, enjoying our foray into the transatlantic junk menu. Such picnics were fun, but it would be hard to think of a more inappropriate choice than McDonald's for a restaurant in a zoo. Ground-up animals, larded with salt and fat and preservatives ... The keepers take pride in showing visiting schoolchildren the fresh fruit and vegetables they feed to the creatures in their charge, and many a classroom comedian has earned kudos by volunteering to scarf a couple of pellets of vitamin-packed monkey chow. His own lunch should be so healthy.

Perhaps it was Thompson's personality that has kept the recollection of that first visit to the Metro Zoo so clearly in my mind, for the day remains vivid while other, far more lavish meals have faded by comparison. I'm sure I ate dinner at least once in the Royal York, because I remember the ugly cylindrical shape of a bottle of Black

Tower against a stiff white tablecloth, and a plate of something the waiter assured me was a true Canadian delicacy: daine of arctic char, or was it chine of arctic dar? Either way, a watery and insipid little fillet of fish.

We also had lunch at the Sutton Place Hotel. Robert was invited there for the inauguration of a new restaurant, and the hotel's publicity department had worked out a program well in advance. They wanted photographs of his face beside a pig's head on a chaud-froid buffet display, of Robert with a forkful of food, of Robert actually eating. "I suppose they want me to look greedy," he said, genuinely annoyed. "I may be a bore, but I don't want to be a boar's head." In the end, they had to settle for a picture of him shaking hands with the chef. I wish I could remember more about that meal, or even the name of the chef. A few months later, Tony Roldan took charge of the hotel's kitchens, but at the time he was still at the Harbour Castle Hilton. Rumours of the quality of his cooking reached Robert through people he knew in the city, and for a while he considered leaving the Royal York for the Hilton, or for the Windsor Arms, where the restaurant known as Three Small Rooms enjoyed an even more august reputation. But the Royal York was within walking distance of the theatre, and convenience triumphed.

WHAT WERE WE MISSING? Something spectacular? I'm not so sure. By the late 1970s, the allure of hotel restaurants in Toronto was already fading. In their time, they had been the city's principal source of gastronomic sophistication and the training ground for an extraordinary number of leading cooks, waiters, and managers. The Westbury, the King Edward and the Royal York, the Park Plaza, the

Lord Simcoe, the Walker House, and then later, during the late sixties and early seventies, the restaurants of the Windsor Arms and the Four Seasons hotels ... Theirs was the prestige, the power and the glory.

It didn't last. As the 1980s kicked in, that carefully cultivated reputation for formal fine dining, classical service, and consistent performance started to work against the hotels. What had once been an asset became a liability. Their kitchens did not suddenly lower their standards; it was more that dedicated diners-out developed a prejudice against hotels. The old values seemed merely "stuffy" to a new generation of restaurant-goers who prized novelty over tradition, energy over experience, and informality over ritual. Respect for grand old institutions was replaced by the cult of celebrity, but the notion of the chef as superstar had rarely found favour in the team-oriented hotel industry. Very few people who dined out in the fifties and sixties knew the name of the man who fed them. It is only when you talk to veterans from within the business that the heroes emerge, and then one name shines like a diamond. For a crucial nine-year span, from 1957 to 1966, Georges Gourbault was executive chef at the Westbury, a small hotel owned by the American-based Knott group. On the genealogical chart of Toronto's restaurant industry, the sturdiest trunk of all has its roots in his kitchen. And the roots go deep, touching even the great nineteenth-century hotels of Europe, for Gourbault's teacher had been Auguste Escoffier himself.

In Toronto, Gourbault was ten years ahead of his time. He arrived from a Knott hotel in London, England, and immediately started to apply his own standards of perfection to the Westbury kitchen. His brigade there was Toronto's first culinary dream team, and many of them went on to achieve enormous success. Sous-chef

Tony Roldan succeeded Gourbault as executive chef at the Westbury before moving to the Harbour Castle Hilton in 1975. Night pastry chef Horst Fabian, hailed in his day as Canada's finest proponent of the saccharine arts, went to the Four Seasons Inn on the Park as chef pâtissier. Breakfast cook and later saucier Joseph Vonlanthan ended up as executive chef of the Constellation Hotel, a position he still holds and from which he has sent forth countless apprentices who have in their turn gone on to fame and fortune. Saucier Fred Reindl became exec at the Hyatt Regency, later the Four Seasons Yorkville. None of these men, however, was to do more for Toronto's restaurants than a young Swiss cook called Herbert Sonzogni, who joined Gourbault's kitchen as a saucier in 1960.

Over the years, as my ignorance of Toronto's culinary past slowly eroded, I would read Sonzogni's name, or hear it mentioned, often reverently, by chefs who had spent part of their formative youth in one or another of his kitchens. But it was not until 1996 that we met, when I drove out to see him at his farm in the Caledon Hills on a Friday in the last week of May.

After eight months of monochrome misery, Ontario had suddenly flung itself into summer. The sky was an improbable blue, the woods and meadows ripe with saturated colour under a hot morning sun. Sonzogni had given me precise directions – a grey barn close to the road, an orchard of miniature, carefully pruned apple trees – but the fifty-acre property seemed deserted as I arrived. I parked on the gravel driveway close to the house, walked around the lawns that surrounded it, to the edge of the woodland, back to the car. I watched a groundhog make its unconcerned way across the golden dandelion carpet of a neighbour's untilled field. Birds were singing; an occasional car droned slowly by. Then a shout. A figure waved from the far corner of the orchard and climbed onto a red tractor. The far-off throbbing of its engine grew slowly louder.

I was expecting an old man in a straw hat, passing his declining years in the shade of an apple tree. But Sonzogni was only sixty-one years old. He was tall and broad-chested, his lean, limber body as hard as cord. Bright blue eyes glittered in a weathered, suntanned face; his large, strong chef's hands were dark with soil. He had been planting saplings all morning and was dressed for work in old green shorts and a loose-knitted T-shirt.

"What a morning!" he boomed. "What a sky! Glorious! You should see the sunsets we get up here, spectacular purples! And now the days are getting so long. Come and see the house!"

As we reached the front door, a car pulled in off the road – Sonzogni's wife, Barbara, and a small, energetic grandson. Glasses of sweet apple cider appeared as the shopping was unpacked; Sonzogni helped the boy assemble a new fishing rod, every inch the indulgent Grosspapa from some Alpine storybook. He watched them cross the lawn to a pond beside the orchard, then led me into the sunroom.

"So, now. You mentioned Gourbault on the telephone. What would you like to know?"

For the rest of the day we sat there, drinking coffee and beer, eating the lunch of bread and cheese, pickles, and ham that Barbara Sonzogni provided, conjuring names and moments from the past. In some ways, Sonzogni's story was a paradigm, the tale of the lucky immigrant who parlayed his talents into success. In my mind he typified that era when chefs, by definition, came from abroad and made their careers as team players. To him, perhaps, such notions would have seemed too pompous and too vague. It was the details of his past that brought out his laugh and made his eyes sparkle as he repeated important words in his booming bass, emphasizing each one with a fingertip thumping heavily onto the table.

"Quality, quality, quality, quality, quality. That was Georges Gourbault. He had phenomenal dedication. A fanatic. A true professional.

"I was twenty-five when I came here in 1960. Barbara and I had married in November, and we arrived here on December 16th, 1960. It was like a honeymoon. I figured I might as well get here before Christmas, when the hotels and restaurants are still busy and I might be able to squeeze myself in. I had no idea how to look for a job, I hardly spoke any English, but I saw an advertisement in a newspaper for a cook in a coffee shop. I showed him my résumé, my references, but the guy said, 'You're overqualified: we don't need you.' Then I met a Swiss fellow in the streetcar and we got into a conversation. He said, 'Forget about the paper, you go and knock on doors.'

"So off I went on the streetcar: the Park Plaza, the Westbury, taking copies of my résumé, my phone number, my business cards. Gourbault wasn't in, so I left them all with the sous-chef and went on to the Royal York, the King Edward, the Lord Simcoe, the old Walker House. The places that people told me had a name. At the Walker House, good old Ed Linton offered me a job, starting tomorrow, in the butcher's shop. I hurried home to tell my wife and she told me I had had a phone call from Gourbault at the Westbury. I called him back. 'I've got a position for you as a saucier,' he said. A saucier! Much more interesting, and it paid $25 more – a lot of money. So I explained to the Walker House and I started at the Westbury. How long had I been in Canada? Two days."

From the beginning, Sonzogni could tell that the Westbury's kitchen was a place of the highest standards. It reminded him of the Hotel Hecht in Switzerland, where he had trained. There he had paid the chef for the first two years of his apprenticeship, buying his own uniforms and equipment, taking a job in the construction industry to make the necessary money, all for the privilege of slaving for sixty hours a week with free room and board. Only in his third year did he receive a salary: 25 Swiss francs a month.

Sonzogni understood what the Westbury was trying to achieve. For a hotel to make a name for itself, to acquire prestige in a city, the food and the service had to be superb. Forget the bedrooms. Few Torontonians would ever see them. But develop a reputation as a restaurant and word would spread that the hotel itself was great. Then, when people from out of town asked about somewhere to stay, the Westbury's name would be on every local lip.

"He could do whatever he wanted, if it made the restaurant famous. And Gourbault was good! We looked on him as God the Father. He was a very kind person who didn't have to be the crazy chef to earn our respect. Every morning he went through the kitchen, came by your station, shook your hand, said, 'Good day.' And if you had ideas of your own, you could go to him and he would listen. There were no restrictions. We had wine, we had cream, we had butter coming out of our ears! He was not wasteful, but if you needed cream you needed cream. It was as simple as that."

Given the freedom to cook as he pleased, Gourbault consciously broke away from the corner-cutting traditions of hotel cooking. For example, the usual method for sole bonne femme was to make a white sauce with flour, pre-cook mushrooms to keep them white, and then poach the fish in white wine and shallots. Add the white sauce and a dash of cream, the mushrooms with some of their stock, and serve it forth. Gourbault would have none of that. His way was to poach the sole and the mushrooms in very good wine with lots of black pepper. Then the fish was lifted out and taken off the bone. Into the poaching liquid went cream and more cream, no flour at all, while the saucier stirred it over the heat until it was good and thick. A liaison of egg yolks was added, then the sauce was poured over the fish and the dish was finished by glazing it under the flames of the salamander.

Could the customers tell the difference? Gourbault didn't care. It was a matter of professional integrity. There was pleasure, too, in finding ingredients beyond the ken of most of his clientele. Instead of frozen salmon steaks like pink rubber horseshoes, he bought whole fish, filleted them, poached them in a subtle court bouillon, and flattered them with delicate sauces. He made salads of spinach, not iceberg, braised leeks, served lamb that was pink and fragrant, not baked for hours as if it were mutton. At a time when chefs used frozen liver from baby beef, he found a supplier for fresh calf's liver. He even introduced Toronto to fresh Bay of Fundy scallops, the best in the world but hitherto unobtainable. The entire catch was packaged at sea and shipped off to Europe and Japan, but Gourbault found a way of diverting a little into the Westbury. It took him years, but he did it.

On one point Sonzogni was adamant: "Gourbault did not get the respect he deserved. There was his dish Scampis in Love. Where he got the recipe from, I don't know, but he was extremely proud of it. And he wrote on the menu beside it 'Grand Prix Gastronomique.' After Gourbault left, Tony Roldan became executive chef, and he took the credit for it. Look, it's nothing personal. God bless their souls, they're both dead, but in the years that followed, Roldan lived off Gourbault's laurels, and he never corrected people when they praised him for dishes he had learned from his master."

Ancient history, even for Sonzogni. Gourbault moved on from the Westbury in 1966, working for a while at Les Cavaliers, and eventually accepted a position, in semi-retirement, as a consultant at the Inn on the Park. Appropriately enough, he was the founding president of Toronto's Escoffier Society, but outside the circle of his colleagues, his achievements were soon forgotten. When he died in 1976, his family threw out all his trophies and awards. The garbageman realized what they were, phoned the Canadian Restaurant Association, and asked if anyone wanted to save them for posterity.

Sonzogni had moved on from the Westbury a year before Gourbault left, to be chef at the newly renovated Thornhill Golf and Country Club, and he carried his mentor's precepts with him. He was earning a reputation and had bought a house in the area when Joseph Vonlanthan called.

"Joe had been with Gourbault before I joined the Westbury, but I had got to know him a little. He told me someone wanted to interview me for the chef's job at a hotel called the Windsor Arms. The owner was a young guy called George Minden and he had big plans, big ambitions. For a manager, he had brought in David Barette, an Englishman of twenty-five, from the Inn on the Park. Barette had hired Ernest Zingg, and he in turn asked Joe if he wanted to be chef. Joe said no – he had just started as chef at the Canadiana Hotel in Scarborough – but he recommended me. Like him I was young, cocky, energetic, eager to prove myself. So I went downtown to an interview with

Ernest. I was scared. It was a very challenging idea, but I told myself I was too ambitious to get stuck in a country club for the rest of my life. I had bigger visions than that.

"The first thing Ernest said to me was that the Windsor Arms was going to be different. No shrimp cocktail. No prime rib. And I said to myself, 'Yippee! That's right up my alley!'

"Oh God, I'd had so much of that damn prime rib. All through my time at the Westbury, and the same thing at the golf club, we always had to have roast beef and Yorkshire pudding. It's such a pain in the butt! You cook it rare, then somebody comes in and wants it well done and you end up butchering the damn thing. Wrap it in tinfoil and reheat it the next night – three, four, five times. Of course it wasn't good any more!

"And that's how the revolution at the Windsor Arms began. Remember what Gourbault did for the Dover sole at the Westbury. Now take it further. Liberate the cooking from cuisine classique! Use those tremendous skills we had learned, the meticulous training, but break away! There would be no bain-marie station to pre-cook a sauce you could use for that and that and that. Each dish would stand on its own, each one freshly made with its own sauce. And flour is gone. Period. Instead we would make glazes. Much more healthy, much more delicious."

But the Windsor Arms wasn't the Westbury. This time the restaurant had to make money. To compensate for the extraordinary food costs, the prices had to be higher than the city was used to, but that was a risk that management was ready to take. "Peasants Beware!" was the headline of the first write-up Three Small Rooms received, a reference to the hors d'oeuvre riche for two persons: foie gras, caviar, smoked sturgeon served on a silver platter. It cost $24, but the ingredients cost the hotel $14. They made more money on the Dover sole. Food costs for fish were a stable 25 percent.

To the moneyed elite of Toronto, however, it all seemed bizarre and newfangled. Sometimes Sonzogni heard raised voices from the dining room, demands for the dreaded prime rib or shrimp cocktail with ketchup and horseradish sauce. The waiter would suggest an alternative: crevettes marseillaise, the shrimp cooked in their own juices with saffron and herbs then cooled in the shell – but in vain. Often the guest just stood up and stamped across the road to Le Provençal, where shrimp cocktail and prime rib of beef were still on the menu.

Gradually, however, the city became aware that there really were three small rooms down in the hotel basement – the Restaurant, the Grill, and the Wine Cellar – and that remarkable food was being served. "Guess who was eating caviar there, yesterday afternoon," teased the newspapers. "Conrad Black and his cronies." The Wine Cellar, in particular, became the place to see and be seen. Barette and Minden were masters at public relations. They would target the journalists by groups – food writers, fashion columnists, the most influential women writers – invite them in for the whole afternoon, and feed them soufflés and raspberry ice. An old game, but always effective.

For Sonzogni, the glory days had begun. The money was good, $275 a week in 1966, but the real thrill came from the team spirit that bound him together with Minden, Barette, and Zingg. For the best part of ten years, it seemed they could do nothing wrong. Every new restaurant they opened was a triumph, and every young cook, just starting out in the business, wanted to work in his kitchen. Freddie Lo Cicero arrived from the Westbury, via the Credit Valley Golf Club.

Jamie Kennedy came from George Brown College to serve his apprenticeship. Even Joanne Kates, before she started reviewing restaurants for *Toronto Life*, the *Toronto Star*, and eventually the *Globe and Mail*, paid her dues at the Windsor Arms.

"It's true!" roared Sonzogni. "It was 1971, and I had decided to take a month's holiday, to go back to Switzerland for the first time in ten years. Then we lost a pantry person and I didn't have anyone to cover. This girl walks in and applies for the job. A cute little thing. I interviewed her, and Frank Suosmaa, who was the saucier at the time, said, 'Chef, why don't you hire her: at least I'll have somebody in the pantry doing something.' Now, we were very macho in those days. No girls in the kitchen. But the pantry was different. So I said okay. She started the day I left, but she was gone by the time I came back. So she and I were never in the kitchen together."

LIKE ANY GREAT GENERAL, George Minden had a gift for choosing his officers. He was always alert to talent, even on holiday. At Coral Beach in Bermuda, he came across a young French maître d' and liked his manner. His name was Georges Gurnon, and Minden invited him to come to Toronto.

Restaurants had not always been the summit of Gurnon's ambition. After three years at the Nice hotel school, he had trained to be an airline steward and was all set to start when somebody noticed he was colour-blind. He moved to cruise ships and secured a job as first-class steward on the Marseilles-to-Dacca route, but chronic seasickness forced him to quit. So he moved into restaurants, perfecting his craft at Michelin-starred establishments in France before moving to Coral Beach in 1965, at the tender age of twenty-two. What was it about him that Minden enjoyed? A certain discreet flamboyance perhaps, a mixture of Old World charm and professional energy, the infallible memory for faces and names of the born maître d', the conspiratorial twinkle that is still in his eye. Minden set about pitching Toronto, told him that great things were happening in the city, that the future was there.

When he arrived in January 1972, Gurnon's initial reaction to Toronto was one of guarded dismay. The cold was a shock, and though he admired the broad avenues and streets, they were alarmingly empty. The hotel seemed an island of warmth and sophistication. "I could see at once it was a very fine place," said Gurnon. "There was an Englishman at reception who charmed everyone, a wonderful bar off the lobby, called Club 22, where Camilio Deliberato was the great barman of all time. Paul Drake played piano and sang in the evening. A customer called Bill Marshall was always on the pay phone in the corridor outside, doing his show-business deals. It was all very much alive."

Minden had brought Gurnon to the Windsor Arms with a specific project in mind. He knew that Herbert Sonzogni's grandfather was from Bergamo, in northern Italy, and that Sonzogni had grown up with a rare and intimate knowledge of Italian cooking. It was a side of his repertoire that had never been put to professional use, and Minden thought that was a waste. He saw an opportunity to create an Italian restaurant that would break away from the checkered tablecloth, spaghetti and meatballs tradition. The name of the place would be Noodles.

Flash, suave, blatantly modern, Noodles was unlike anything Toronto had ever seen. The entrance, off Bay Street, just north of Bloor, was deliberately difficult to find. Inside, the narrow corridor suddenly opened into a soaring, two-storey space of glass skylights, polished steel, orange tiles ... Architect Blake Miller's design was the antithesis of sober restaurant proprieties. Minden added creative touches of his own – a steaming pasta kettle in the middle of the room – and assembled a team to bring the creation to life. Hans Punzenberger, the talented grill cook from Three Small Rooms, was the chef charged with making Sonzogni's menu reality. Georges Gurnon was the manager.

"It was the Space Age!" he enthused. "Just like *A Clockwork Orange*! So exciting, so big! We were open for lunch and dinner seven days a week and quickly became the great rendezvous for the advertising world and everyone else. People could have a telephone in their booth if they wanted to, but the dumbwaiter was the pièce de résistance. It was enclosed in clear plastic tubing and you could see trolleys going up and down to the mezzanine level, where my assistant, Roberto Tiso, had his own clientele. Sometimes a customer who had had too much to drink crawled in and took that ride for a lark. The city was so surprised by the menu. As well as the Italian dishes, the polenta, the vitello tonnato, we flew in fresh turbot, baked our own bread, had marvellous pastries and the famous raspberry ice from Three Small Rooms. It was a show, high-maintenance, high rent, requiring endless energy, but we enjoyed every minute of it."

Gurnon left Noodles in 1980, but the restaurant lasted a decade longer. In 1985 Minden sold it to the Windsor Arms' executive chef, Dante Rota, who gave it a new lease on life as a straightforward Italian restaurant. His wife, Rina, did a fair amount of the cooking; his son, Carlo, worked there as manager (to Dante's immense satisfaction) and was able to rekindle the sort of customer loyalty engendered by Gurnon and Tiso in the restaurant's heyday.

I first got to know Carlo in 1988, long before he became the CBC's roving palate with his own national television food show, and found him keenly aware of the restaurant's past.

"In the few years I've been here," he told me, "I've been introduced to no less than five teenagers who were conceived in one or another of the booths on the mezzanine level."

Noodles under the Rotas may not have had the same thrust of power and novelty as it did in the 1970s, but its clientele could be every bit as eccentric. There was the debonair gentleman in the smart tweed suit who ordered impeccably, charmed the waiters, calmly paid his bill, and then went on the rampage, smashing chairs and generally demolishing the restaurant. It later transpired that he was an outpatient from a mental institution. There was the Christmas when a well-known downtown hairdresser arrived dressed as Santa Claus. The beautiful young woman on his arm, dressed in the micro-mini crimson of a Yuletide elf, sat on his lap throughout the meal. And there was the quiet boy who dined there regularly with his mother, and then suddenly stopped coming to the restaurant. Six months later he reappeared, no longer with his mother, but wearing her clothes.

For Herbert Sonzogni, the triumph of Noodles was just one in a string of adventures. The next project, in 1975, was the Millcroft Inn, an old mill near the Forks of the Credit River that Minden turned into a luxurious country hotel. By now, however, the extraordinary nine-year ride was slowing down. Resurrecting those later memories, Sonzogni's voice dropped to a growl: "The team had begun to break up. David Barette left in 1975 to start his own consulting company, and that was the biggest blow. Hans Punzenberger came back from Arowhon Pines as chef, which was a great joy, but there were an awful lot of things that didn't really work out with David gone.

"You see, the whole mood had changed. George was spending more and more time away from Toronto, in Switzerland and in England, and gradually, we started to live off our laurels. By the end of the seventies, I realized all we were doing was stopping holes. It was good money, company cars, but I didn't enjoy it any more. Then, in December 1980, between Christmas and New Year's, one of the other partners, Ted Foster, died of a heart attack. Another partner left. Minden had lost interest in it all. I got terribly sore later in life with George Minden. There is more to life than just money, and so much love and care and pride had gone into what we had achieved. In the end I just had to get out, while I still had my good name. It was like a sixth sense that one has sometimes.

"And so there I was. I was very disillusioned. I had no plans. I took a six-month sabbatical with my wife and tried to figure out what to do. In the end, we decided to open our own small restaurant. We found a property in Mississauga and called it Babsi's. My God, it was different. For years I had had 120 employees under me; I hadn't cooked for at least five years. Suddenly I was behind the stove again, doing my own prep, my own purchasing. And here I was working with my wife! Spending all day, every day with her for the first time in decades. That was a huge adjustment, but I loved it. And it went extremely well. In fact, it was the best thing I ever did. Even though we went through a hard time getting rid of it a couple of years ago, it really was the best thing I ever did."

Sonzogni walked me back to my car. As we stepped outside into the silent afternoon, he looked about him, filling his lungs with air.

"The beekeeper's coming by later to pollinate the trees. We have fourteen different varieties of apple here now. Semi-dwarf trees.

"When I bought this place, I named it Bonaria. My grandmother spoke Romansh, you see. We came from that part of Switzerland. When I was a boy of twelve, thirteen, I used to spend the summer on a farm in the high Alps, learning to work rather than being just one more mouth to feed at the family table. That farm was called Bonaria too. So all this is a return for me. A happy return.

"It was hard to leave the restaurant business. I loved it. Loved it! But now I have found my peace."

THE WINDSOR ARMS is long gone now; so is Noodles. The Westbury has become a Howard Johnson's. Like the theatre business, the restaurant industry obliterates its past. The most gorgeous sets, the most triumphant productions are papered over as if they were yesterday's playbills, surviving as a box of menus and clippings in an old man's upstairs room, and as a fading memory in the public mind. We erect no monuments to beloved dining rooms and have devised no empirical method of recording the taste of a meal. Film can capture something of a theatrical performance, but cooking is a transient art form, each little landscape of flavours assembled on the plate with the express intention of instant demolition.

I once believed that the repetition of this Sisyphean act of creativity must have an effect on the psyche of a chef. Eventually, he or she would ache for some expression of permanence, the bricks and mortar of a restaurant of their own, an art collection, children. From time to time, I thought I detected proof of my hypothesis, but no example has ever come close to the vision of Herbert Sonzogni in his retirement, planting apple trees on his farm in the Caledon Hills.

Driving home that afternoon, I tried to superimpose his narrative onto my own memories. Almost at the end of that first, formative month in 1977, my godfather and I had gone to the Windsor Arms for dinner. By then, Three Small Rooms had been eclipsed by the Courtyard Café as the most likely place to see stars of stage and screen. Indeed, there was something of the Hollywood commissary about the huge sunken room with its theatrically tiered seating and girdered conservatory roof. The food was complicated but not spectacularly good. The service seemed fussy without being genuinely attentive, as if the waiter were more concerned with the way the table looked than with his customers' well-being. Robert was unimpressed. "We may be three years too late, dear," he suggested, his eyebrows shooting up, his blue eyes wide with ingenuous innocence. "The waiters who cared have moved on."

Twenty years later, I still hear the same complaint about hotel dining rooms. Impersonal comes right after stuffy when people explain why they try to avoid them. As with any prejudiced generalization, it is patently unfair, and yet ... There is a particularly depressing style of service that seems to cling to second-rate hotel restaurants like the aroma of cabbage in an elevator. It isn't that the waiters lack expertise. Quite the contrary. During the eighties, hotels and steakhouses were the Alamo of silver service, the last stand of the table-tossed Caesar salad, the final farewell of the flambé cart, and those skills have not yet been lost. Nor is it that staff are rude – their manners are as smooth as crème anglaise. But there always seems to be something missing. A willingness to meet the customer's eye, perhaps? Or is it merely lack of motivation? That would be understandable, given job security, union protection, a salary that does not rely on tips, and a menu that may not have changed sinced the Diefenbaker years. Factor in vacuous canned music and a badly lit, windowless room, and that waiterly indifference suddenly makes perfect sense.

Such caricatures do not apply to Toronto's first-class hotels, but it's tough to persuade our citizens of the fact. Hotel restaurants ring few bells in Hogtown these days. Executive chefs and food and beverage managers do their level best to win back friends and reacquire a local clientele, but nothing seems to work, and out-of-town visitors soon pick up on the vibes. Toronto's burgeoning reputation as a sophisticated food city does not help matters. In Asia, and to a lesser extent in Europe, one has dinner in the hotel. To do so here would seem perverse.

Of course, there have been exceptions to this rule. Café de l'Auberge at the Inn on the Park was a landmark in the sixties under chef Georges Chaignet. The precocious Mark McEwan won justified adulation at Sutton Place in the mid-eighties; to this day, John Higgins cooks brilliantly for parties who book the Chef's Table in the King Edward's kitchen. Above all, there has been the example of Truffles, in the Four Seasons Hotel in Yorkville. In the years surrounding its million-dollar facelift in 1993, executive chef Susan Weaver and Hong Kong–born restaurant chef Patrick Lin gave Toronto a dazzling series of menus that combined subtle Asian references with Lin's deep understanding of classical technique. They even made use of that rarest of ingredients, wit, baking a juicy fillet of black bass inside tissue-thin scales of potato, sauced with a frothy sabayon of fish fumet and lemongrass. For dessert, pastry chef Philippe Egalon offered several outrageous, opulent creations such as a stiff "paper bag" made of orange-flavoured dark chocolate filled with pineapple milkshake, to be sucked through a chocolate straw.

My godfather, who always left room for pudding, would have enjoyed it. To him, hotel restaurants carried no curse. He approached every dining room, regardless of its grandeur or location, with an open mind, a free spirit, and a healthy appetite. Years after our first trip to this city, he came back here for a weekend to film a commercial for British Airways and stayed at the Windsor Arms. We had tea together in that cosy front parlour and talked about the play we had brought to the Royal Alexandra in 1977, how he never had found the answer to the problem of the third act, how the tour had returned to England, dwindled in Bath, and finally disappeared into the sand during a two-week eternity in Brighton. As usual, the conversation drifted into a discussion about restaurants. Of all the meals he had ever eaten in Toronto, I asked him, which had he most enjoyed? "Breakfast this morning," he answered. "I walked up to the corner of Bloor Street and had a beer and a sandwich at the Danish Food Centre. Delicious!"

☙ THE LAST PICTURE SHOW ❧

H E S H O W S M E to my table, makes sure I'm sitting comfortably, promises to be back in a little while. A big, friendly man who looks much younger than his seventy years, he even moves like a maître d', covering a lot of ground quickly but without appearing to hurry. He greets a couple who are standing by the bar, waiting to be seated. A piano player conjures mellow standards from a baby grand, quietly crooning a lyric: "I'm gonna be a part of it, in old New York …"

It's a summer evening in 1997, but the season and the year are of little importance in Louis Jannetta's Place. There are no windows, and the mood is timelessly elegant. Deep, horseshoe-shaped banquettes are upholstered in dark, emerald green velvet, the same colour as the ceiling. Mirrors reflect displays of fresh flowers and tablecloths of heavy white linen. Knives and forks have the weight of cutlery from a more generous age. The candles and the dim bulbs in their ornate little wall sconces cast exactly the sort of golden glow that most flatters a complexion.

Around the walls of the restaurant are innumerable photographs, framed in gold. Most of them show two people in evening dress, one of whom is always Louis Jannetta. The other is a star, of greater or lesser magnitude: Tony Bennett, Raquel Welch, Count Basie, Joey Heatherton, Don Rickles, Sonny, Cher ... The smiles and the signatures span the show-business generations from C. Aubrey Smith to Jim Carrey. They are the mementoes of a life, the souvenirs of Louis Jannetta's other place, the Imperial Room of the Royal York Hotel.

This restaurant is also in a hotel, though the Comfort Hotel on Charles Street, a few steps east of Yonge, will never be confused with the Royal York. The family of six at a distant table are staying upstairs. They are tourists from North Carolina and they came down for an early dinner, expecting no more than a meal. Jannetta has charmed them as he charms every customer, noticing their interest in his gallery, sharing the anecdotes that accompany each photograph, a host of memories triggered by a name. Starstruck, the Americans pose for their own snapshot with Louis Jannetta, vowing to have it framed, to hang in their dining room at home.

Now the pianist segues into a contemplative version of "My Funny Valentine." A graceful young maître d' takes my order. Jannetta comes over again to my table. He doesn't look all that different from the guy in the photographs: a large man with strong hands, a curl of hair brushed onto his forehead. I ask him about the photographs, and over the course of the evening, the story unfolds.

LOUIS JANNETTA was born in Molise, that mountainous and impoverished corner of southeast Italy between Abruzzo and Puglia. He came to Toronto when he was seven years old and fell in love with the game of hockey, but his family were too poor to buy him a pair of skates. He spent much of his youth sitting on the pines at the local arena, wishing that he too could play.

When he turned fourteen, in 1942, he got a job as a busboy in one of the Royal York Hotel's secondary restaurants. He soon got fired for dropping a tray full of glasses, but he must have had charm even then. He went down the hall to the office of David Chiascu, maître d' of the Imperial Room, and asked if he needed a busboy. Chiascu laughed and hired him back.

"Can you imagine?" asks Louis Jannetta, still chuckling at his nerve and his good fortune. "You must understand, the Imperial Room was one of the greatest rooms in the world. We looked after the Eatons, the Bassetts, the Bronfmans – that's the original Bronfmans – the Rothschilds, the Dunhills, so many lords and ladies from England, so many stars ... The society of the world. For many people in the city it was a weekly thing. There was dining and dancing then, with Horace Lapp and his orchestra – great musicians, many of whom went on to join the Happy Gang on the radio. Then later, Moxie Whitney. Wonderful food – steak Diane, frozen log with cherries flambé, crêpes Suzette ... I grew up in that room, became a waiter, a captain.

"Then one day in 1962, after I'd been there twenty years, the great Angus McKinnon, general manager of the hotel, promoted me to maître d' and manager of the Black Knight Room. I was there one year, organizing the entertainment, local acts. It was my brainchild, my baby. We filled the place every single night. That's when I started collecting my photographs. A year later, the great Mr. David Chiascu retired. When I was a busboy I used to pick up his dirty socks and take them down to the laundry in the basement. Now I was promoted to take his place. Maître d' and manager of the Imperial Room. I had a staff of eighty-two under me: forty-five waiters, sixteen captains, sixteen busboys, two linen men, a glass boy to pick up the glasses, two porters. The greatest team in the world. Excuse me, I'll be back ..."

He gets up from the table to greet some more customers. A waiter brings me a plate of bruschetta – warm crusty bread spread with tomato, onion, a little basil, a little oil. I ask to see the wine list. No one is offered the wine list at Louis Jannetta's Place; you have to request it. The custom goes back to the Imperial Room. Sometimes a young man might have saved for weeks to take his girl on a special date. Perhaps he couldn't afford the extra expense of a bottle of wine, and Jannetta always felt that presenting him with the wine list put him in an embarrassing position. The courtesy of a more gentle time.

Two tables away from mine, Jannetta is teasing the new arrivals: banter and insults, laughter. He comes back to explain. "I first met that gentleman when we were both nine years old. We played on the same baseball team. Most nights I know 95 percent of my customers here. I have youngsters come in: I remember serving their great-grandfathers. Others of them are older than me. I used to be a busboy round their table; I'm still a busboy round their table, pouring their water.

"Where were we? In 1963. That's right. Toronto was changing. It was no longer just the Royal York and the King Edward. And dining and dancing was becoming old-fashioned. For a year I kept imposing on the great Angus McKinnon, telling him we had to have entertainment in the Imperial Room, and finally he agreed."

With Jannetta to oversee everything, the transition was a smooth one, but the stars who came for their week's engagement were not always so trouble free. Joey Heatherton made such a fuss during rehearsals that by the time she opened on Thursday night all but four of her twenty-eight-piece orchestra had walked out. And one of the four was her manager. Ella Fitzgerald never went on or off stage unless Jannetta was there to accompany her. Pearl Bailey insisted he join her in a duet. He had enough sense not to sing with Nelson Eddy.

The stories go on. Jannetta and two writers once wrote a book about it all, but the manuscript was never published. Its title would have been *The King of the Maître D's*, a reflection of status and also of isolation. The Imperial Room was his kingdom, set apart from the city, with its own standing army of staff. On any given night, Jannetta would know 70 percent of the guests by name. Sometimes a party of eight or twelve would telephone in advance and ask him to order the meal for them; the appetizers would appear on the table as they walked into the room. Those who came for the show arrived at seven-thirty – four hundred people all needing to be served at the same time, and so much of the cooking done tableside from flambé carts.

Happily focused on his particular world, Jannetta paid little attention to the way the city was changing outside the walls of the hotel. In the end, however, the revolution came from within.

"We got a new general manager who decided to change the kind of acts the room booked. They brought in a revue from Montreal. The Folies Royales. Topless dancers. I remember the producer's words to this day and it still makes me so angry: 'We're gonna get rid of all these snobs!' People, families, who had been coming for generations. It was their room! Toronto's room. I protested, but they were adamant.

It was a disaster. From eight hundred guests a night down to forty guests a night. Then they decided to go back to dining and dancing. I told them, 'We had dancing thirty-five years ago, and if Guy Lombardo couldn't fill the room the last couple of times he was in, who else is going to?' Another total disaster."

For Louis Jannetta, 1988 and 1989 were unhappy years. His health suffered; the emotional stress was intolerable. And there was new pressure from the Bitove family, offering him a fortune to leave the Royal York and join their catering operation at SkyDome as director of the luxurious, private Skyboxes. It wasn't the six-figure salary that persuaded him so much as the thought that he could spend Christmas and New Year's Eve at home for the first time in forty-eight years.

Jannetta stares through me into the past. "I should never have left. It's still one of the great hotels in the world. Once you leave the Royal York, you know you should never have left. SkyDome didn't work out. Then one of my daughters suffered an accident. She was in a coma. We nursed her for eighteen months, down at the hospital in Pennsylvania."

MANY TIMES over the years, friends and customers had told Louis Jannetta he should open a restaurant of his own. He always answered that the Imperial Room was the greatest place in the world, more exciting than any restaurant. In 1993 he took stock of his life and decided that maybe the time had finally come. He had his strength, his vigour, and the nights at home were long. Someone called him about the property under the Comfort Hotel. It sounded right. He could keep a room upstairs for afternoon naps. A restaurant would give him somewhere to hang his photographs.

The first few years were not an unqualified success. For all his experience, he knew little of bookkeeping and taxes. He gave too much away to his customers. But he survived, supported by the loyalty of his clientele and a talented team. His maître d', twenty-seven-year-old Zoltan Szabo, for example. Every gesture is correct, executed with a dancer's precision; he glides effortlessly into French to chat with a quartet of tourists from Montreal. Anyone who works as a waiter at Louis Jannetta's Place has a chance to train under a master. The chef, Adam Rogala, is young and ambitious: another good move. He interprets the old-style Italian menu with a modern freshness, pairing moist carpaccio with bitter radicchio and sharp little capers, smothering a perfectly timed veal chop with a red wine and Portobello sauce that is neither too heavy nor too sweet.

These days, more people are finding their way to Louis Jannetta's Place, and old friends still drop by. "A month ago, Tony Bennett was here," he beams. "He was only in town the one night, performing at Ontario Place, but he made sure he came here for dinner after the show. We sat and talked for five or six hours about old times. Last week, Bobby Herriot and Howard Cable were in, with his granddaughter Amy, who's married to Dougie Gilmour. Yes, Dougie was here as well."

The boyhood enthusiasm for hockey shines in Louis Jannetta's eyes. He never did get to play, but he created and supervised an organization of teams, the Canadian Italian Amateur Hockey League, that flourished for decades. There are scholarships in his name at several Toronto schools. For his discreet services to charity, he was made a Knight of Malta, and he met Pope Paul VI, a moment commemorated, naturally, by a photograph.

Ginger Rogers, Lena Horne, Charo, Sir Laurence Olivier; from the SkyDome days, President George Bush. Louis Jannetta takes my arm. "And that is my daughter, Patti Jannetta. She played the Imperial Room twice. That picture's from her Christmas special on television, with Barbara Hamilton and John McDermott." It may be the photograph that gives him most pleasure of all.

Louis Jannetta is proud of his place. He wants me to remember that. It's more than a shrine to an extraordinary career and to the room where he worked for forty-eight years. He is here every day from noon until two or three in the morning, meeting and greeting, talking and teasing, keeping the memories alive. As I leave the restaurant, the four tourists from Montreal are standing in the little corridor that leads to the door, gazing at the images in the frames, at the Pope with the King of the Maître D's. The old, old joke springs irresistibly to mind. Easter Sunday, St. Peter's, Rome. A man in the crowd turns to the stranger beside him. "So tell me," he says, "who's the guy in the white beanie cap standing next to Louis Jannetta?"

ᴢᴏ SEPARATE TABLES ᴏᴢ

MY FATHER was an actor who specialized
in long runs. For years he played Colonel
Pickering in *My Fair Lady*, first in the West End
and then on the road. At some point during
the sixties, the musical came to Toronto and he
returned with tales of the Skylon Tower at
Niagara Falls and of the O'Keefe, a new theatre
he found ugly and ill-conceived from the actors'
side of the curtain. For my brother and me he
brought souvenirs of maple candy and mineral

samples stuck to thick white card. He never said a word about Toronto's restaurants, but they were probably at odds with his taste in food. Like every English actor I've ever met, he loved a good curry (not available then in Hogtown), and he could cook one better than most, having spent most of the Second World War in the Indian army. Otherwise, his regime when on tour consisted of cornflakes and scrambled eggs on toast. There was, however, one establishment in this city that he remembered most fondly. An oasis of civilization, the Toronto Press Club was the only place he ever found that stayed open late enough to serve him whisky after the show.

He never discovered Winston's Theatre Grill. Which was probably just as well. My dad couldn't bear a snob.

WINSTON'S WAS THE FIRST in a series of highly influential, independent restaurants that spanned the sixties, seventies, and early eighties, strung like a rope of pearls across the city. Its story, however, began decades earlier, a story that has been elegantly told in a book by Herbert Whittaker and Arnold Edinborough. They describe the arrival in Canada of a sophisticated couple from Budapest, Oscar and Cornelia Berceller, and their small son, Tommy, escaping the gathering doom of Europe at the end of the thirties. The Bercellers fulfilled the obligation imposed by Canadian Immigration and worked for a year on a farm. Then, in 1938, they made their way to Toronto and spent much of their last $10,000 on a hamburger joint in the shadow of the old Globe and Mail Building at King and York Streets. With the Globe's publisher, George McCullagh, as patron, they christened the enterprise Winston's and started the long process of changing a greasy spoon into a restaurant to match their ambitions. Their first customers were the journalists from next door, but soon they attracted a second clientele of Allied airmen, stationed for training in Ontario. By the time the war ended, the Bercellers were established.

It was Winston's proximity to the Royal Alexandra Theatre and Oscar Berceller's realization that actors and actresses like to go out for dinner after work that brought the restaurant stardom. The great and the glamorous stepped off the stage and walked down the street to Winston's Theatre Grill, as it came to be called, where they were greeted by bows and applause and generally treated like royalty. Toronto's social aristocracy was also welcomed, but people without wealth or title might be turned away at the door, especially after Berceller introduced the notion of Winston's keys. These pretentious little talismans were handed out to favoured customers, playing shamelessly to the deep-rooted, clubby snobbism of the city's élite.

The years passed. The Bercellers had divorced by the time my father's company visited the O'Keefe. Winston's menu no longer intrigued Toronto, the room seemed shabby, the white gloves worn by the waiters were threadbare and stained. But some of the old clientele still cared enough to try to ensure its survival. In 1962 an influential customer called William Gilbride had bought a partnership in the business and created a company to keep the restaurant clear of bankruptcy. But Berceller refused to make desperately needed changes, and in 1966 Gilbride forced him out and sold the restaurant to someone he felt could turn the red into black. He was the forty-two-year-old clubhouse manager at the Rosedale Golf Club, a short, solidly built Italian with dark, heavy eyebrows and a ready smile. His name was John Arena.

A marvel of the twentieth century is the memory of John Arena, a life story in many volumes, fully annotated and written with fluency and panache. The narrative can be entered at any point, with full dialogue and no name forgotten, spelling and addresses provided. I had only to mention a certain morning in 1966 and rewind was instantaneous.

"Brigadier General William Preston Gilbride was a member of the board at the golf club and one day he said to me, 'You know, you're making money for the club, why don't you work for yourself?' And I said to him that I was in no position to buy a restaurant but that it would ultimately be my dream. He said no more, but the next day he came back to me and he said, 'Look, I have a restaurant. Can you afford two dollars?' I wondered what sort of a restaurant it could be, but I said, 'Yes I can, of course.' He said, 'Give me two dollars. One dollar is for a debenture that is redeemable in 1972.' Which I did later redeem – $350,000, I think it was. The other dollar was for the shares.

"Well, I was quite moved. Here I am in Canada since 1958, almost six and a half years, and someone is gracious enough to offer me a restaurant that has an incredible reputation. It all happened within four days."

Before those days were up, Arena had learned a new word: liabilities. Winston's owed $45,000 to unpaid suppliers, and the city had twenty-six work orders outstanding against the restaurant, all of which would have to be acted upon before the liquor licence could be transferred. Fortunately, Gilbride was also a director of the Canadian Imperial Bank of Commerce, and a $30,000 line of credit materialized. Arena mortgaged his home to raise the remaining $15,000. In the end, the money was spent on repairs and renovations; the suppliers, with the exception of St. Lawrence Fish Market, agreed to settle for 30 cents on the dollar.

So John Arena had a restaurant of his own. Its carpets were soiled, its curtains filthy, and its china chipped. There weren't enough glasses to serve a party of seven, but the new owner knew what he wanted to do with it. His childhood had been spent in an impoverished Calabrian village, but in 1939, at the age of fifteen, he had set off for Australia to join his emigrant father. He arrived to find that Gregorio Arena had been interned because of the war, but an Italian-speaking family, the Azzolinis, took him under their wing and found him a job as a kitchen boy at Mario's, Melbourne's most prominent restaurant. By the time he was twenty-one, he had become maître d', already a master at anticipating the needs of a well-heeled business clientele; now he returned to Italy, to receive formal training at the famous hospitality school in Stresa. The next ten years completed his education: in Italy, Sweden, then back in Melbourne at Mario's. North America, however, was the land of opportunity.

"I already had Canada in mind," he said, "but it was a long journey by boat from Sydney to London to New York to Toronto. The last stage I travelled by cattle train, arriving at Union Station on November 27, 1957, with my clothes in a cardboard box and $60 in my pocket. I came out of the station and saw this enormous hotel, the Royal York, and I went up to the mezzanine, found an armchair, and started to snooze. When the houseman moved me on, I went down to the washrooms in the basement, washed and shaved, changed my clothes, put on my lucky bow tie, a blue one with white polka dots, and went out to look for work. One of the places I tried was Winston's, but Mr. Berceller was not interested." Arena assumed a heavily accented basso profondo: "'I do not engage waiters with no Canadian ex-pe-ri-ence.'"

But other employers did. Arena was offered jobs at the Royal York, the Lord Simcoe, the Westbury, and the King Edward. He chose the King Edward. To say John Arena had energy and ambition would be a wild understatement. Within fourteen weeks, he had risen to the position of maître d' of both the Oak Room and the Victoria Room, had met and married his wife, Reingard, had moved to a home in Don Mills, and had started to establish a personal clientele among the city's richest and most powerful men.

It was to them that he now dedicated Winston's when it reopened in April 1965, after considerable renovation. The famous Robert Shaw sketches of theatre stars that Berceller had commissioned were no longer on the walls (Arena has them still, and would like to see them hanging in a restaurant again). Instead, the room sparkled with a dazzling Art Nouveau décor, created by stage designer Louis Kerenyi. Arena had delivered invitations to visit the new Winston's to every important office within walking distance and had mailed hundreds more to his King Edward clientele. The old theatrical ties were being consciously unravelled. Arena wanted his customers from the Oak Room and the Rosedale Golf Club. Experience had taught him that prosperity and stability lay in cultivating exactly that sort of business.

"I aimed to be a corporate restaurant – *the* corporate restaurant – and I did it. It was a challenge. I was not one of the establishment, but people in this country are wonderful. You show them courtesy, show them you are not there to please yourself but to please them, and never hesitate to feel subservient to the hand that feeds you. Never hesitate. Today, mediocre restaurateurs think they're gods and they treat the client with disdain. There is no great corporate restaurant today. No one has the foresight or guts to do that."

The new Winston's was an instant success. When it moved north to Adelaide Street West, six years later, success moved with it. Again, Kerenyi designed the Art Nouveau room, all dark carved wood (shades of Maxim in Paris), deep red velvet sofas and chairs, gilded canvases stretched tightly on the walls. Downstairs was the Grill Room, intended for junior executives, according to Arena, who liked to cook their own pheasants and quail on the four open barbecues. The game came from Arena's own four-hundred-acre game farm near Shelburne. Upstairs, the chef was Peter Colberg, a man who had trained at Three Small Rooms under Herbert Sonzogni and who stayed with Arena for eleven years. In 1978, when Colberg bought the Corner House, a veteran restaurant in the shadow of Casa Loma, his sous-chef, Rolf Romberg, took over at Winston's, where he remained for the next seventeen years.

Old menus, like old theatre programs, are excellent aide-mémoires. Winston's dinner cards read like timeless documents of classic French-International cooking: each main course presenting its butch slab of expensive protein, its rich, suave sauce, its afterthought of vegetables. There was tableside filleting to be done, and dishes that needed to be finished on the flambé cart – the cuisine in which Arena had been trained in the 1940s. But lunch was Winston's true power base. The midday menu was considerably less elaborate – consommé, lobster, Dover sole, salads, lamb chops – all conservative and relatively lightweight, with nothing to intrude too dramatically upon the conversation of the day: the comfort food of the rich. Thirteen of its twenty-three tables were permanently booked by major corporations and political heavyweights – Conrad Black, Douglas Bassett, Premiers Bill Davis and David Peterson, John Turner ... The room was their club, and Arena ran it as such. All drinks were doubles, and more often than not, no bill appeared. Arena or maître d' Larry Lovely signed the tabs, and accounts were sent out at the end of the month. At Christmas time, a side of Norwegian smoked salmon was delivered to valued regulars. A small extravagance. In its heyday during the seventies, Winston's served three hundred meals a day and pulled in over $3 million annually.

Catering to the establishment led to catering to establishments. Arena's meticulous professionalism earned the trust of power brokers when important events were planned: the Royal Ontario Museum Ball under the auspices of John Robarts, the opening of Roy Thomson Hall, the Pope's visit at Pearson Airport, fourteen launching parties for vessels of the Canada Steamships Line at Collingwood. For sixteen years, Winston's catered lunch and dinner at the O'Keefe Centre. It surprised no one when Arena got the contract for the Trillium Restaurant at Ontario Place.

His most lasting legacy, however, is the Ontario Hostelry Institute at George Brown College. In the late seventies, it became apparent that there was a dangerous dearth of trained cooks and service staff at the entry level of the industry. The stream of professionals from Europe had been narrowed by immigration legislation, and the province's educational resources had not taken up the slack. In 1977 Arena put together a team, did some research (nine thousand vacancies for cooks, provincewide) and presented the figures to Bette Stephenson, Ontario's minister of education. "Eventually the provincial government was persuaded to give us $5 million," he told me with considerable satisfaction, "which was matched by the federal minister, John Roberts. We raised another $2 million from the industry.

Ten years after we began the project, the new OHI building opened on Adelaide Street East."

Arena was the first chairman of the enterprise, a role later held by restaurateur Charles Grieco. In the late nineties, the facility was training two thousand cooks a year, plus four thousand part-time students. Ninety-five percent of graduates found full-time employment in the hospitality industry.

John Arena's connections with the ruling classes gave credibility to the project in its early stages and oiled its progress along the way. Not every venture, however, was so successful. The game farm eventually went the way of all flesh. He bought the Terra Cotta Inn, on the banks of the Credit River, but it burned down in 1974. Nine years later, two attempts at creating restaurants at Front and University, Giannino and Panarello, turned out to be expensive flops. Failure did not match the Arena image, but he was able to extricate himself from the mess relatively easily, disposing of the properties for a surprisingly good price.

He was a boss of the old school. The core front-of-house staff of Winston's stayed with him for most of their careers, showing their fingernails for inspection every day before starting work, respecting his dictatorial insistence that every detail must be attended to. Even those who stayed only a few years – men such as Franco Prevedello, Michael Carlevale, and James Morris, all of whom worked for Arena during the late seventies – acknowledge that he was the consummate professional, a public relations master, a man who loved the grandeur of his calling. Ten years later, those men had their own restaurants, and it was the cooking at Centro, Prego della Piazza, and Rundles that excited the critics. The city's gastronomic tastes had moved on.

Sooner or later, the issue faces every successful restaurateur: stick with the food you know, the food that pleases your most conservative clientele, or evolve with the times and hope that your star is hitched to a wagon that is trundling down Main Street, not up some culinary cul-de-sac. In the early sixties, when the menu at Winston's Theatre Grill came under attack, Oscar Berceller had roundly declared that French food was a fad that would pass. In the late eighties, a dinner at Winston's once again seemed a blast from the past. A few nouvelle squiggles had appeared on the menu, in such shapes as grapes and bananas with the veal medallions, a lime sauce for the trout, but they merely seemed contrived.

My first visit to Winston's took place in 1991. John Arena was there, a stout, charismatic figure, exercising his charm on the half-dozen nervous young suburban couples who had come for a Big Night Out. In deference, perhaps, to Wendy's beauty, he gave us a prominent table. I remember an astonishing wine list, laden with Bordeaux and Burgundies I couldn't afford and more fine German wines than I have ever seen on this continent. I recall a meal of weight and richness that began with a complimentary ramekin of chicken liver pâté, smooth as butter, moved through sautéed duck foie gras with a crudely tart citrus garnish onto venison with wild mushrooms, and finished with a very good Grand Marnier soufflé and a tableside flambé of cherries jubilee in all their brandied magnificence. The décor, with those golden, Klimt-like canvases of a jeunesse dorée dressed in sixties fashions, seemed extravagant and heavy. We might have been dining in Julio-Claudian Rome.

When I returned a year or so later, a great many things had changed. Most obviously, Arena had gone. His last night in the restaurant was May 1, 1992, a magnificent farewell party thrown in his honour by John Turner and Doug Creighton and attended by Emmett Cardinal Carter, Lieutenant-Governor Hal Jackman, and many more of the Great and the Good. The *Toronto Sun* printed a mock obituary the following day, marking the end of an era. In fact, Arena had sold Winston's eighteen months earlier but had stayed on as manager at a generous salary. Considering the imminent advent of the recession, the deal looked very like another masterly extrication.

The buyer, who paid a seven-figure sum, was an aristocratic German adventurer and real estate wizard called Karsten von Wersebe, whose company, York-Hannover Developments Ltd., seemed at the time to have the golden touch. The purchase incentive was a plan to franchise the Winston's style and Arena's proven expertise into the Skyline Hotel, out by the airport, and the six other hotels owned by York-Hannover. The restaurants would be called Winnie's and Lady Sarah and other names associated with Winston Churchill. In the end, all the dreams came to nought.

The recession was not kind to Winston's. The three-Martini lunch suddenly became extinct and captains of industry had more important things to worry about than making sure their favourite table was secure. Queen's Park had put bums on Arena's seats for decades, but the NDP ministers were not really Winston's material. Bob Rae preferred to eat at Centro. "I had begged Mr. von Wersebe not to announce the sale," said Arena, "but at a Christmas party he did. When a restaurant is sold, a lot of your clients wonder why. They don't think of it as your place, they think of it as theirs, and they are right to do so. Perhaps, also, it was me. Without my knowing it, the feeling, the passion just wasn't there any more."

His eighteen-month tenure passed. Arena had his farewell party and left, bound by a promise that he would not open another restaurant in Toronto. A year earlier, Karsten von Wersebe had asked restaurateur John Maxwell to create a new project in Winston's basement, where the Grill Room had been. Its name would be called Oscar's, and it was to be a bar and grill of unashamed opulence and exotic sophistication, a glittering jewel cut by the top design company Yabu Pushelberg as an oval within an ellipse. As proprietor of the excellent Orso, on John Street, and of the enduringly delightful Allen's, a New York–Irish saloon on the Danforth, Maxwell had the restaurant savvy to get the job done. Plans for the place were well under way when von Wersebe decided that he was also the perfect candidate to replace Arena and take Winston's into the new decade. Promised the Earth and all that is in it by way of a budget, Maxwell accepted the job. He was in John Arena's old upstairs office at Winston's when I called by to find out how things were going.

John Maxwell has the gift of the gab. When he cares to comment on the dining industry, he is the most urbane, perceptive, opinionated, and amusing critic in the city. The writer Alison Gordon once described him as looking like "a decadent little owl" on his bar stool at Allen's, and the phrase cannot be bettered. His round, professorial spectacles lend an academic air; the silver star set in his tooth hints at another, more debonair philosophy. On that evening in Winston's, enthusiasm for the beast in the basement added a righteous energy to his eloquence. He easily convinced me that Oscar's was all set to deliver the knockout blow to the recession.

"It will be irresistible!" he exclaimed, unrolling the architect's drawings for me to see. "A riveting design! And genuinely smart.

Smart is not something that this city with its mean-spirited and fearful egalitarianism really countenances. That's not what they're into here. What they are into are places of conventional substance à la Scaramouche, or else ersatz ethnic joints that remind them of their vacation. There are only about three truly smart places in Toronto – and they are all doing fine, incidentally. There is room for another. Not everyone follows trends. There are enough eccentrics out there for Oscar's to thrive."

Where Winston's itself was concerned, he was not quite so bullish. Oscar's, the prodigy, had the dazzling gloss of novelty; Winston's was encumbered by its reputation, dragging its past behind it like a sea anchor choked with weed.

"Here you have a place," said Maxwell, "that was once tremendously popular, tremendously powerful. In some North American cities, and certainly in most of Europe, that would appeal to the new generation. In Paris, for example, the great sign of coming of age would be to assume the table your father had had for thirty years. Here in Toronto, growing up means rejecting the cultural behaviour of your forebears. Our market is very immature and fickle, making places that have a long and honourable tradition very difficult to maintain. Nevertheless, I think something can be done."

Was Winston's doomed to dance the mortal coil shuffle? Or would Maxwell's energy and von Wersebe's cash pull it safely through the recession? A few weeks later, I slipped into the restaurant for dinner. I did not recognize the waiters. Maître d' Larry Lovely had gone on to John Arena's new acquisition, Prego, in Aurora. There was no one playing the piano, and very few customers. The wine list had been trimmed, its French nobility usurped by more affordable New

World labels, and the menu bore the signs of a modern sensibility grafted onto its classical roots. Looking for the young idea, Maxwell had hired Ellen Greaves, a recent graduate of the Stratford Chefs School, as chef. There was still foie gras among the appetizers, perfectly sautéed, molten within, but now it arrived refreshed by a salad of baby wild greens in a sharp balsamic vinaigrette. There were still sweetbreads, perfectly prepped, lightly crisped in the pan, but they came with a very contemporary glaze of sesame and soy. The vegetables were dull and depressing, but desserts were sublime: three miniature pots de crème of Elysian texture flavoured with vanilla, orange, and chocolate, and a tart of spiced quince and orange served with a lightweight mascarpone cream on a ginger buttersnap crust.

It was a start. It was given no chance to proceed. Von Wersebe's promised funding failed to materialize, and Maxwell's plans were abandoned. Oscar's never opened. I'm not sure how much of it was even built, but for years I imagined its virgin furbishings gathering dust in the basement, a would-be femme fatale leading apes into hell.

I went back to Winston's in 1994. Maxwell had extricated himself at the beginning of the year, and chef Christopher Klugman was now in charge, valiantly administering culinary CPR to a dying patient. This time, the foie gras was partnered by sautéed mango, tart lingonberries, a pear and ginger purée, and buttered sourdough bread. There were also grilled squid, the tender pouches stuffed with breadcrumbs, garlic and herbs, sharing the plate with pseudo-Japanese rolls of gravadlax and rice in a nori wrapper, with a squiggle of ketchupy cocktail sauce. The food was inventive, but a long way from Klugman's best work.

For old times' sake, I ordered a good German wine. It was

corked, and there were no other bottles left in the bin. The waiter was apologetic: much of the shrunken cellar had passed its prime. He came back with something young and Alsatian by way of a substitute and left me alone with it. I was the only customer in the restaurant that night. There was no music, no sounds from the kitchen; the silence was so heavy and so profound I could hear the blood in my ears. Figures in flared trousers posed on the gilded walls, gazing into the past. The place had the feel of a tomb.

Not long afterwards, Klugman threw in the toque, tired of waiting for his salary to be paid. He wasn't the only one. Von Wersebe's empire turned out to have been a cobweb of fraud and embezzlement. Its collapse cost banks and investors on four continents more than $3 billion, and by March 1995 the man himself was fretting inside a Swiss jail. Winston's, one victim among countless others, had closed the previous August, fifty-six years old and once the most important restaurant in Canada. Few people mourned its demise. For those who remembered, it had died years before, when John Arena departed.

HARRY BARBERIAN tells a story. It must have been in 1962, just after the Lord Simcoe Hotel, on University Avenue, had gone under, and the receivers were auctioning off the tangible assets from the hotel's sumptuous but pretentious restaurant, the Pump Room. Barberian was there for the show, with three of his friends, all of them leading restaurateurs: Oscar Berceller of Winston's, Tony Amodeo of Mr. Tony's, on Cumberland Street, and Julie Fine of the Gaslight on Yorkville, who was already eyeing the beautiful Massey family home on Jarvis Street with a view to opening a new restaurant. He planned to call it Big Julie's, in reference to the Chicago gangster from Damon Runyon's stories, but the Liquor Licensing Board would not hear of such dangerous decadence and Fine later settled for Julie's Mansion. The mood of the high-powered quartet was something less than reverent, especially when they realized that a man on the other side of the room was buying up all the silverware – cutlery, ice buckets, flambé pans, roast beef carts, everything – at 10 cents on the dollar. "Maybe he doesn't know it's all monogrammed LS," they whispered, chuckling.

The man was John Grieco, a well-respected executive in the wine and spirits business who had decided, quite late in life, to become a restaurateur. He had found a property at the corner of Bay and Charles and persuaded his son Charles to leave the advertising industry and join him as manager. On July 20, they opened their restaurant. It was called La Scala, and it boasted the most glorious silver, engraved with an elegant LS.

"And we used it all," Charles Grieco assured me, years later. "We had maître d's who had come out of the Westbury and the Lord Simcoe's Pump Room who knew how to flambé a steak and flame a café brulôt in the proper way. We were a success from the first day we opened, and those other restaurateurs soon became friends. There was room for everyone in those days, in a city that was just discovering you didn't have to go to a private club or a hotel to dine well. We each filled a different niche."

La Scala was unique in the way it surrounded the statutory steak and lobster with a sophisticated northern Italian menu that consciously avoided spaghetti and meatballs. A woman known as Suzanne played the harp, and tables were spaced far enough apart to allow discreet conversation, a fact that was not lost on the dominions and powers of the Tory party, who quickly made it their unofficial headquarters. It was there that Bill Davis and René Lévesque first met, and there may have been some truth in the rumour that more cabinet meetings took place in La Scala's private dining rooms than in Queen's Park in those years.

Strange as it seems today, an upscale Italianate menu was a bold innovation in the mid-sixties, for this was still an era when serious cooking was synonymous with French cuisine. French restaurants carried an automatic cachet, the unshakeable presumption of sophistication. Burned into the universal consciousness was the knowledge that French food was cultured and sensual and exotic – every Canadian child knew that people in Paris ate snails and frogs – and if sometimes a waiter or maître d' seemed a tad supercilious, or even downright rude, customers tended to blame their own ignorance for his attitude.

Bad manners would one day come back to haunt the city's French restaurateurs, but in 1965, they were riding high. Gaston Schwalb of Chez Gaston on Markham Street took a leaf out of Harry Barberian's book by providing a Rolls-Royce to ferry his favourite customers home. On the same street, but in a humbler setting, stood L'Escargot, where owners Jacques Abbécassis and Christian Vinassac cooked and Elizabeth, Christian's wife, ran the front of house. Vinassac came to Toronto in 1963, from France via Montreal, but he had spent much of his childhood in Tunis and the couscous at L'Escargot was exceptional. So was the onion soup (a bistro had to have onion soup), and the snails, of course, prepared in so many ways, with butter and garlic certainly, but sometimes in a salad with herbs and a light mayonnaise.

That the Vinassacs had more elaborate ambitions became clear in 1969, when they sold their share of L'Escargot to their partner and opened Napoléon. Boosting their savings with loans from Christian's father in the south of France and from Elizabeth's family in Ontario, they bought an attractive old house on Grenville Street, close to Queen's Park. They furnished it with beautiful antiques, set two swans made of white Carrara marble outside the front door, and filled the house with flowers, in the dining room, the foyer, the washrooms. The decorative conceit was that of a French Imperial salon, and no detail was overlooked. Butter was pressed into the form of a rose, the Empress Josephine's favourite flower. Each antique plate, each glass decanter was perfect.

"What we brought to Toronto at that time was a form of elegance," mused Christian Vinassac, his accented voice falling to a whisper, his tone reverent and dreamy. We were standing in the immaculate kitchen of his apartment, surrounded by photographs and menus from Napoléon's years of glory. With his precise gestures and air of quiet authority, Vinassac had something of the look of Bonaparte the First Consul. "*Très élégant*, but we also made sure it was comfortable and friendly. We paid especial attention to the young people, who could have been a little bit timid, and made sure to give the better tables to ladies, whether or not they came with their men.

"Most of the time, we didn't work with a menu. I would come out and stop by every table, ask the guests what they felt like eating, some meat or fish or poultry, did they want more cream, less cream, whatever. It was quite new for a chef to come out and people found it very personal and sophisticated. Ninety percent of the customers left it up to me."

Vinassac insisted that Napoléon was a restaurant without pretension, although some of those who ate there found the room too ornate and resented what seemed like pressure when the chef appeared at their table, inviting decisions. Most entered into the spirit of the place, charmed to have Vinassac create a sauce especially for them, a jus de veau, perhaps, thickened with a knob of butter or enriched by a scattering of truffles for those who wanted less fat. Hors d'oeuvres were a succession of little plates: a slice of pheasant or two impeccably timed scallops, some moules marinières or a single lamb cutlet with a coulis of watercress and another of tomato, everything arranged to delight the eye, everything *très posé*.

Each summer the Vinassacs closed their restaurant for the month of August and went travelling. A trip to France was mandatory, with visits to vineyards and to dining rooms ablaze with Michelin stars. They would talk to chefs and maître d's, winemakers and restaurateurs, and discover new dishes to introduce to the customers back in Toronto.

"I was a kind of ambassador," said Vinassac. "In a hotel in Aigues-Mortes, I first tasted magret du canard and brought it home that year. People accustomed to well-cooked roast duck found it hard to accept at first, but they trusted me. On holiday, if we heard of a small local museum connected with Napoleon, we would always visit it, and we looked for antiques and objets d'art to add to our restaurant's décor. I would study cookbooks from Napoleon's own time, adapting recipes such as veau Marengo *à ma façon*, not as a stew but as a paillard of veal with beautiful little vegetables. Because of the time Empress Josephine spent on Martinique, I felt able to use the tropical squash called christophene or fruits and vegetables from the island, just a little, for originality. People appreciated it. The excitement of creating those new dishes kept me fresh. Every day was a new challenge, with nothing taken for granted, and a little bit of useful stress."

All through the seventies, Napoléon marched on, a restaurant immune to fashion. The wine list grew ever richer in rare old French bottles, Vinassac's cooking became more complex, his presentations more elaborate; the cost of dining *à sa façon* crept inexorably higher.

The end came unexpectedly in 1984. One night an explosion brought down a wall of the property – a bomb, perhaps. There were rumours of some kind of vendetta, of a powerful man's wife who felt she had been insulted in the dining room and took her revenge ... Christian Vinassac has never discussed the matter, politely suggesting that some memories are better left undisturbed. The house was sold to the Ontario Nurses' Association for a good price; the antiques were sold off separately. Not long afterwards, the Vinassacs' marriage ended. Christian never opened another restaurant, though he often talked about the possibility, a Napoleon on Elba, dreaming of new campaigns. The old guard would have welcomed him back from exile. A return would have lasted more than a hundred days. Instead, he cooked occasional dinner parties in the houses of friends and offered advice to those who sought it. Deploring the uniformity of modern restaurants – "The décor! Nothing but colour! So dated, so soon!" – he reserved his warmest praise for those who had broken the established mould, people whose work was imbued with passion.

High on this list were two men who came regularly to Napoléon for inspiration and became good friends of the Vinassacs. Cecil Troy had started out as a banker, became a painter, and then, in 1971, turned his beautifully restored old house on Marlborough Avenue, close by the Summerhill railway tracks, into a restaurant. An entirely self-educated cook, he took on the duties of chef, while his friend and partner, Lazlo Stibinger, was maître d'.

"Cecil and Lazlo came to Napoléon once a week in the early days," recalled Vinassac, "and we also went to Troy's. It was a delightful little place, cosy but elegant, like a bourgeois dining room in Normandy or Brittany, with Cecil's collection of French-Canadian art and antiques everywhere. And he was a true artist, a creator. It was difficult to believe he had never cooked professionally, never taken a lesson. It was all done with love."

Toronto discovered Troy's quickly. The dining room could accommodate about twenty-six customers, though Stibinger usually fitted two sittings into an evening. It was pleasingly informal in a city where jacket and tie were required at most smart establishments, and the menu changed constantly as Troy experimented with new recipes. Prices were low, around $20 for dinner for two, and remained that way even after the restaurant received its long-awaited wine and beer licence, for Troy and Stibinger owned the house and paid for everything as they bought it.

They did have help, however. Soon after they opened, an eighteen-year-old kid just arrived from Winnipeg showed up at their door, sent there by Canada Manpower. His name was Greg Couillard, and he had had some experience waiting tables at a restaurant near the Winnipeg racetrack where his mother and sister worked.

"I stayed at Troy's two years," Couillard remembered. "A long time for me. It was a good place for a hungry mind to arrive: beautiful and crazy. Fifty-two dinners a night, six days a week! They paid me $1.80 an hour and my days were spent gutting things and rolling things until my arms ached, peeling vegetables in the backyard, whisking cream and sauces, cleaning up the kitchen. Lazlo looked like Peter Lorre and was just as scary, but it was the whole environment that was so attractive. They lived, gardened, cooked, entertained, got drunk, fell into bed, all in the same house.

"It was more than an apprenticeship, seeing the way Cecil worked, how he cared for the restaurant. I had no thought of becoming a chef in those days, I didn't have any of that formal sort of vision. I was just having a good time, which is always somewhere up there in my top two priorities. It's Cecil's philosophy that remains with me, his outlook and his spirit for life: the way he would change the décor of the dining room, tinting little marzipan shapes for Christmas, making after-dinner mints and truffles and petits fours and setting them all out in an antique armoire. The food was all very classically French, Escoffier and Carême sort of stuff, cooked in copper pans because that was the way Cecil had read it should be done, but all executed with so much passion. Torontonians didn't know what hit them."

Couillard left at the end of 1973, to work in a postal sorting office. Two years later, Cecil Troy died suddenly, far too young and sorely missed by his clientele. Lazlo Stibinger decided to carry on. He went looking for a chef to take over the kitchen, and found one of the best in the city: Claude Bouillet from Auberge Gavroche.

WHEN GEORGES GURNON came to the Windsor Arms in 1972, David Barette had been particularly helpful and welcoming. Gurnon wished to express his gratitude and decided to take him out to dinner, asking Barette to choose the restaurant. Barette booked a table at Auberge Gavroche.

Gurnon found it very French, "*genuinely* French – and utterly charming. I don't think it had been open much more than a year. Claude, of course, was the chef. We had some of his marvellous terrine. A watercress salad. Rack of lamb. I had not met him yet. I came to know him first through his cooking."

Auberge Gavroche was the creation of Jean Michel Centeno, a Frenchman who owned a men's clothing store and a successful bakery in Hazelton Lanes. Like Christian Vinassac, he wanted to show Toronto that there was more to French restaurants than steak au poivre, escargots, and onion soup – the new decade demanded a new understanding – and he decided the best way to do it was to open a restaurant of his own. So he sent word to France, inviting a young chef called Claude Bouillet to fly out to Canada, land of opportunity, and assume command of the kitchen in a property he had found, a small, rather elegant house on Avenue Road.

The days before his departure were anxious ones for Bouillet. It could all be a great mistake. With his boyhood friend Marcel Réthoré (the two had apprenticed together in Brittany at the age of fourteen, Claude in the kitchen, Marcel front of house), he went shopping for a heavy anorak, convinced he would freeze in Toronto. They said their tearful goodbyes in Paris, then Bouillet boarded the plane.

His initial reaction to the city was not uncommon among new chefs arriving from Europe, circa 1971: a feeling of adventure balanced by a sense of restriction, and horrified incredulity at the tools available. Without the resources of a grand hotel, it was hard to find produce in those days. No leeks, only iceberg lettuce. Few fresh herbs beyond parsley and mint. The biggest shock, however, was the discovery that his new restaurant would have to wait at least six months before customers could legally drink a glass of wine with their meal. Standards of service were also a tad Jurassic. Before too long, Centeno and Bouillet brought Marcel Réthoré to Canada to add a little Gallic authenticity and tone to the dining room. His arrival coincided with that of Auberge Gavroche's liquor licence, and the party began.

Fresh Dover sole in tarragon butter, deftly filleted tableside by Marcel. Leg of lamb for two, carved by Marcel in full view of the customer. Bouillet's classic pâté, a change from chopped liver. Saddle of rabbit, once standard pioneer fare but now seeming so new, so exotic. Auberge Gavroche swiftly acquired a discerning clientele, while the bar upstairs became a rendezvous for expatriate French in the industry.

"Up there had the feel of a coffeehouse," remembered Gurnon. "It was cosy, simple, without chichi. There was the bar and a guitarist, light fare or the menu from downstairs, if you preferred. It became a habit to gather there and sample Claude's cooking. His wife-to-be, Martine, was working there too. It was almost a club."

Once a month or so, around one in the morning when the last Saturday-night customers had finally left, Réthoré and his girlfriend would load up the car with friends and drive through the night to Montreal, doing without sleep to live the life of boulevardiers for twenty-four hours, crawling back to sober Toronto by Monday's dawn.

"There was no choice," Réthoré explained with a shrug. "The only place to eat on a Sunday in this city was the Colonnade."

"And if there was a bottle of wine on your table at ten o'clock," added Gurnon, "the waiter would simply walk over and remove it. Without warning. Even if it was only half full! We all found it barbaric."

Ah, but he should have been in Toronto five years earlier. It was in 1967 that Premier John Robarts, virtually acting alone, forced a revolutionary change in the law, allowing restaurants to serve alcohol on a Sunday. Judge Walter Robb, chairman of the LLBO, warned the province that no good could come of it, that jails would be filled on Monday morning by hung-over revellers, in no state at all for work. He was wrong, of course. The jails were no fuller than usual. A few months passed, the fuss died down, and it became clear that very few of the newly empowered restaurateurs intended to open on Sunday in any case.

Nevertheless, Gurnon's displeasure at the state of wine appreciation during the early seventies was entirely understandable. The acquisition of a liquor licence still necessitated months of patience, followed by endless computations proving that the ratio of food sales to those of beverage alcohol fell within the killjoy guidelines of the LLBO. Restaurants sold more beer and spirits than wine, and most wine lists showed a yawning gulf between Mateus Rosé and high-priced Bordeaux and Burgundy. Italian wines, it was generally understood, just didn't travel.

But Torontonians did, and they returned from vacations in Europe with new ideas about food and wine. Foreign adventure helped educate the city's broadening palate for more than just good French cuisine, inciting curiosity about all kinds of cooking and slowly building confidence in those who enjoyed dining out. While the exciting new restaurants of the early seventies had drawn directly on European traditions for their inspiration, the next major arrival seemed more Toronto's own, and it was welcomed with greater fervour than any of its predecessors.

For much of his distinguished career with the Four Seasons Group and at the Windsor Arms, David Barette had resisted the idea that he liked the food and beverage side of the hotel industry better than anything else. But by 1974, after years of turning George Minden's ideas into realities, the notion that he and his partner Nicholas Pearce, a high-ranking manager with the Four Seasons Group, might create their own consulting company had begun to seem irresistibly exciting. The first project the two Englishmen undertook was the rejuvenation of the dining room at the Prince of Wales Hotel in Niagara-on-the-Lake, and it occupied them for all of 1975. Georges Gurnon drove down with his mother, who was visiting from Marseilles, and found the restaurant enchanting, full of sunlight and fresh flowers, and blessed with the cooking of an eighteen-year-old prodigy from Germany called Werner Bassen.

To Barette and Pearce, the year in Niagara was a dry run for their Toronto début. By the summer of 1976, they had found a location they liked and could afford, in the basement of a rambling nineteenth-century building on Gloucester Street, just steps from Yonge. The space had already been used as a French-Canadian restaurant called L'Habitant, but Pearce and Barette had their own ideas for the way their brainchild should look. Bare brick walls and masses of flowers recalled a garden, grey napkins lay upon dark brown tablecloths, there were Hockney prints on the walls and the finest china and stemware from Rosenthal. Strategic mirrors and intricately created dynamics of light and shade brought the elements together. Now all they needed was a name. One of their partners, Robin Carlson, the restaurant's controller, had an aunt whose last name was Fenton. It sounded suitably English, not pompous exactly, but proper. Within a month of its opening that July, Fenton's was the most discussed and admired restaurant in the city.

"Yes, it took off quite quickly," recalled Barette modestly. "We had very little money, but we were bursting with ideas and, for the first time, in a position where we did not have to compromise. Our driving aim was not to make money, though of course we wanted a healthy bottom line, so we chose to plow most of the profits back into the operation. The budget for flowers and plants, for example, was astronomical, but we found that if you dared to take chances and do things properly, the city was very generous."

Critics raved about Werner Bassen's meticulous, sophisticated cooking: lamb chops stuffed with lamb purée scented with basil and rosemary; chicken stuffed with veal, ginger, and nuts; that immortal leek and Stilton soup; customers delighted in the ministrations of maître d's Jesus Navazo and Roberto Tiso, who had left Noodles' mezzanine. Above all, it was the impeccable taste of Pearce and Barette, expressed in every detail of the experience, that impressed. Even the washrooms were little works of art. In the ladies' room, the flowers were always fresh, the soap lemon-scented, and the gleaming brass fixtures so attractive that they were frequently unscrewed and stolen by customers. At one time, Barette was replacing them every week.

A young Portuguese waiter called Tony Vieira joined Fenton's in 1978. It was his first job and he stayed for eleven years. "Everything was perfect but at the same time so simple. The English way: a touch here, a touch there, and suddenly something looks grand. David and Nicholas were perfectionists about details, and watching them taught me a really good, thorough way of looking at this business. Never cheat with a recipe or a situation because it'll catch up to you, and that's embarrassing."

A couple of weeks before Vieira joined, Fenton's had expanded. Years earlier, the building above their basement, Gloucester Mews, had been turned into a kind of alternative shopping arcade, with several small stores built around an open courtyard. The idea had fizzled by 1978 and Victor Biasi, the landlord, was considering his options. Pearce and Barette took the lease and set about creating another triumph. A roof was put on the courtyard, with plants up the fire escape and flowers everywhere, transforming it into the Garden. The rooms looking out on the street became the Shop, where the products of the kitchen were retailed, and the Front Room, with a magnificent fireplace and bar and an ambience like a miniature London club. Expansion is always risky, success in the restaurant business so often relies on fragile intangibles, but Barette and Pearce had done it again and Fenton's merely became more significant, achieving the rare double of being a major establishment rendezvous and at the culinary cutting edge.

There wasn't a gram of stuffiness about the place. The same welcome, the same discreet but impeccable service was extended to everyone. Politicians discovered it (the ubiquitous John Turner was a regular) and visiting stars such as Richard Burton, Lee Remick, and Christopher Plummer made it their new Toronto base. One hot Saturday afternoon, Plummer dropped by on his way to a game of tennis, dressed in whites, with twenty minutes to kill. He was having a glass of wine in the Front Room when Nicholas Pearce looked in. Lunch was over, the restaurant empty: he joined the actor for a drink. Then another. Then another. It became apparent to the two young barmen, Tony Vieira and Andrew Laliberte, that their boss, usually so proper, was intimating to Plummer that he could drink him under the table. By five o'clock, when the staff began to arrive for the evening's work, the two men had worked their way through seven bottles of wine. The bartenders were in awe. "It finally ended when Nicholas fell off his bar stool," reported Laliberte. "Plummer managed to walk out of the restaurant on his own."

Legends of the largesse that Barette and Pearce showed their staff are still retold when old Fenton's hands get together: staff picnics at their gracious home in Alliston, marvellous meals and wines in the restaurant kitchen. The first six or seven years were blessed with a kind of magic, a glamour that made the hard work seem more like an endless party. Eventually, the dazzle faded. The party moved on to new locations; Fenton's began to seem passé to a generation obsessed with novelty. Overheads could no longer be met, stress levels rose ... But, for a while, it was Camelot.

In May 1989, exhausted by the efforts of keeping their restaurant's head above water, Barette and Pearce sold the business to Tony Sabato, a construction company tycoon, and lawyer Michael Markoff. Neither had any restaurant experience, but they knew enough to see that expenses would have to be seriously trimmed and customers wooed all over again if Fenton's was going to survive. However, cutting costs and changing personnel proved to be the wrong solution. By May 1990, they were forced to face the inevitable. Unannounced, and with the suddenness that attends such suicides, Fenton's disappeared.

David Barette and Nicholas Pearce were not around to hear the obsequies. They had pulled up their roots and moved to an elegant farmhouse in Nova Scotia's rural Annapolis Valley, there to enjoy the life of retired country gentlemen. Then their old friend and partner, chef Werner Bassen, showed up at the door. Gradually the conversation shifted from bygone glories to future possibilities. The frisson of a new adventure ... Within a year, they had opened Acton's Grill on the main street of Wolfville, a quietly sophisticated university town in the valley. Those who have eaten there speak admiringly of the cooking, the ineffable charm of the room where every detail is perfect, right down to the extravagant displays of fresh flowers.

There is one other Barette and Pearce creation that looms large in my personal list of favourites. Soon after Fenton's opened, the two men were hired as consultants at Hazelton Lanes, to develop the Café and Terrace in the open courtyard at the heart of the ritzy shopping arcade. "We had this concept of making it into a series of medieval jousting tents with tables underneath," recalled Barette. "Just good food and reasonable prices. It was slightly ridiculous, but absolutely fun."

Indeed it was, and for me it will always retain a position of honour as the place where Wendy and I had lunch on our very first date, in June 1977. A week later, I went home to England, where I found work as an actor in the West End production of *Jesus Christ Superstar*. Like my father before me, I liked the idea of settling in for a good long run. A year passed by. My month in Toronto seemed a distant though still vivid memory. Then one night, during the interval, when I was deep in the endless poker game that flourished in Judas Iscariot's dressing-room, the stage door keeper called me over the Tannoy. It was a bad moment for an interruption. Jesus was bluffing on a busted straight, Judas had raised ten pieces of silver on a miserable pair; my three kings were about to scoop the pot. Luck was with me that evening. When I got down to the stage door keeper's cubicle, he handed me a note.

"A young woman brought it. Very pretty ... She said she knew you," he added, squinting with suspicion and disbelief.

After the show, Wendy was standing by the stage door. She had left Toronto to see the world, starting with England. We walked up Greek Street to a Cypriot restaurant called the Greek Prince and drank much too much red wine. A few weeks later, she moved into my flat in the shabby South London borough of Tooting Graveney, but that is another story.

⚡ SALAD DAYS ⚡

MY MOTHER is a terrifically good cook. Most of what I know about cooking I learned from her, standing on the kitchen chair to reach the stove while she showed me how to stir the lumps out of a roux or make gravy from stock and pan juices or season a kedgeree to feed twenty. Through innumerable repetitions, those basic principles of culinary cause and effect worked their way into my subconscious like the rudiments of a second language. In the end, they left me with a tendency to rely on instinct rather than written recipes, and a degree of confidence in the kitchen that remains far in excess of my abilities.

For a little while in her youth my mother had cooked professionally – kind of. The Second World War was over, and she was working as assistant stage manager in the West End production of Daphne du Maurier's *September Tide*.

In one scene, the play's temperamental star, Gertrude Lawrence, had to fry an omelette on stage and then eat it as part of a romantic dinner à deux with the actor Michael Gough. Each night my mother cooked the omelette in the wings and slipped it into Miss Lawrence's frying pan through a hole in the back of the fireplace in the set. On matinées, for the sake of variety, she made them a crêpe with a squeeze of lemon and sugar.

By the time I was growing up, my mother had become a successful theatrical agent, while her culinary skills had assumed the status of legend. Young actors lucky enough to be on her books often showed up at the front door of our cosy old house in Chelsea on a Saturday afternoon. They said they had come to drop off a script, but there was teatime in their eyes. The favoured few were invited to dinner parties, and on those evenings the kitchen became as busy as Christmas as we all helped unpack the shopping she had bought on her way home from the office. The gas jets were turned up high, small jobs assigned, and in less than two hours another lavish feast was ready.

The one thing my mother never made was pastry, for that was her own mother's matchless specialty. Gran moved into our house the week I was born, and looked after us all from that day on. Born in 1887, she had grown up on a farm in Devonshire, an upbringing that was reflected in her own repertoire of dishes, all cooked from memory. Her casseroles and hotpots and braised lamb chops spent all day in a slow oven, quintessential comfort food. For my father she simmered tripe with onions and white pepper to pale perfection; for herself she poached fillets of plaice in milk. For the world in general, she made cheese straws that turned to air in your mouth, and sugared piecrusts that were nothing less than ethereal. Well into her nineties, she still liked to be up and about before anyone else, creeping down to the cold, dark kitchen at six o'clock every morning to make the first of innumerable cups of tea. Throughout my childhood, there was always a kettle of water simmering on the stove.

Born in the same year, and every bit as eccentric in her own, very different way, my father's mother lived alone in a large house in the country. Every other Sunday, we drove out to see her, arriving in time for cocktails and leaving soon after tea. Her huge garden was a source of endless delights for my brother and me, with its strawberry beds and raspberry canes, gooseberry bushes and tiny orchard of apple trees. There were broad beans and peas to pick, pussy willows and conkers to collect as ammunition, and hazel wands to turn into bows and arrows. Down at the end of the garden, an underground air raid shelter rose from the vegetable beds like some grass-covered Iron Age tumulus. The Luftwaffe had been defeated twenty-five years earlier, but my grandmother was taking no chances. She threw nothing away. The portraits she had painted during her art college days, circa 1905, were still stacked in the garage, some of them punctured by airgun pellets when my father was a boy. In the gardening shed, among the smooth-handled tools, flagons of pungent paraffin, and bundles of recycled brown string, we found German and British helmets that my grandfather had brought home from the First World War. Stacked in the cupboard at the top of the stairs were tins of fatty stewing beef sent by Australian relatives in 1942 as part of the war effort. I was always intrigued by the way they bulged. It was only when one of them exploded, blowing the cupboard door off its hinges, that my grandmother was finally persuaded to bid them farewell.

In that time-tethered house, every meal, every hour, every minute was prescribed by habit and ritual. For tea, there was always cherry Madeira cake, Cadbury's Chocolate Fingers, and bridge rolls spread with Gentleman's Relish. On special occasions there were vinegared winkles to dig out of their shells with a pin, or perhaps winkle spiffins, which had nothing to do with shellfish but had been my father's favourite when he was a boy – bread fried in butter and spread with raspberry jam. Rumour had it that my grandmother was rather a good cook, but we never found out, for after her last housekeeper retired, the task of providing Sunday lunch fell to my mother. She would spend the morning in Chelsea making some imaginative and delicious banquet, and then the whole family carried the long parade of casseroles, pots, and pans out into the street and carefully loaded them into the car before setting off for the country.

This moveable feast was one of many bizarre family rituals into which Wendy was inducted soon after our London reunion. As culture shock is measured, her first Sunday at my grandmother's was the equivalent of the electric chair, but she sailed through it all with her usual grace, charming my uncle and aunt and cousins and even winning a word of approval from my grandmother. She later confessed that some of our ways seemed a tad mystifying. Why had somebody gone out into the hall and rung a bell to announce the beginning of lunch when everyone was already together in the sitting room? Why were some of the ancient blankets from the camphor chest by the back door meant to be spread on the lawn when other, identical blankets were not? Why were the tea things wheeled laboriously out of the kitchen on a rickety old trolley when it would have been so much easier just to carry them? These were questions that had never occurred to me. The English never see the need to justify or explain their eccentricities. Strangers are somehow supposed to know.

For lunch that day, my mother had excelled herself, roasting two legs of lamb with garlic and rosemary, finding tender young sea kale, which my father loved, and baking a Queen of Puddings, which was everyone's favourite. She asked Wendy to bring the roast potatoes out to the car, but when the banquet was unpacked in my grandmother's large but Dickensian kitchen, there were only two very small potatoes to be found. The other twenty-five were still in London, waiting patiently in their pan in the warming oven.

"Did you really think two would be enough?" my mother asked Wendy in genuine awe.

It had already become apparent that cooking was not one of Wendy's overriding interests. Indeed, she detested the very thought of it. Handling raw meat or fish made her shudder; egg beaters, whisks, and sieves were the tools of an alien trade. Assuming she knew enough to make herself dinner, I used to wonder why she seemed so hungry every night when I came home from the theatre. She had found a job as a security guard at the Tate Gallery, and there, in the staff canteen, she discovered the glory of the pork pie, that peculiarly English source of nourishment. She would buy two at lunchtime and bring the second one home for supper rather than face the mysteries of the kitchen.

It took some time to persuade her that cooking could actually be enjoyable. The process began at Shree Krishna, a brilliant little Keralan–South Indian restaurant close to the end of our road. It quickly became our local, and on some Sunday nights we ate so much that we literally found it difficult to walk home. Wendy had never tasted real Indian cooking before, and somehow its very strangeness made it seem more accessible to her. All the ingredients used in the dishes we loved could be bought at the covered market on Tooting High Street and we spent many mornings there, learning the names of strange leaves and vegetables, our heads filled with the aromas of turmeric, cumin, and cloves. As they got to know us, the stallholders talked about methods of preparation and eventually recipes, at first shyly, then with pride and contagious enthusiasm. Back at the flat with our purchases, both of us equally at sea, we started to cook.

LOOKING BACK NOW on our first months together, I can only marvel at Wendy's resilience. Eager to weave her life into mine, I had embarked, without realizing it, on a vigorous program of show and tell, reliving in her company every formative experience of my youth. I wanted to share my past with her, to create common points of reference, and also to show her a little more of England in the process. The day trip to Oxford established the pattern. Wendy had been in the country only a week and was still living in a rented room in Earl's Court when I picked her up one bright June morning and set off up the motorway towards the alma mater. Halfway there, we ran out of gas. There was nothing much we could do once I had called an RAC rescue van but sit on the grassy hillside in the warm sunshine, looking down at the plain of Oxfordshire stretching away to the distant horizon.

It might have been a peaceful moment, but I couldn't help glancing at my watch. We were supposed to be meeting a dozen of my oldest friends at the gates of New College in about half an hour. There I had planned to change into gown and mortarboard and walk with them to the Sheldonian Theatre, where we would receive our degrees from the vice-chancellor of the university. We had all graduated years ago, but it was the custom at Oxford to wait for a while before matriculating. It now seemed I might have to wait a year or two longer, but the god of fools was merciful. The RAC man arrived, gas glugged from can to car, and we arrived at our rendezvous with a number of seconds to spare.

The seeds that Oxford plants in its alumni sometimes take decades to germinate. I can see now that my time there provided me with an excellent primary education in the fields I would later follow. Not as a writer, perhaps – it took years to exorcize the precious, rococo prose style so carefully cultivated – but as an eater and drinker. Undergraduates were allowed to buy wines from the college cellars on credit, and though we could not get our greedy little hands on the older vintages, we had access to good hock, claret, Burgundy, and Quinta do Noval port at prices that must have been laid down decades earlier. A nightly alcoholic stupor lay within everyone's grasp, but en route to that brief satori, we somehow absorbed the basics of wine appreciation.

Many dining societies flourished in the older colleges. Seated at a candlelit table in some ancient dining hall, watched from the shadows by the sternly critical portraits of gourmets from earlier centuries, members were treated to the finest meals the college chefs could provide. No whiff of Nouvelle Cuisine yet disturbed the complacent air of their kitchens. The cooking we were exposed to harked back to the dignified, clever, highly accomplished lexicon of Escoffier, and though execution varied wildly from college to college, the harmonic structures of that old-fashioned way of eating still resonated for any who cared to listen.

And there were restaurants. Quite early on in the first, rather confusing term, it occurred to me that there was nothing to stop me exercising my new-found freedom by eating outside college. If I judiciously saved the reimbursed funds from my scholarship, chose places famous for value, and avoided the temptation of any dish that approached extravagance, I could while away an occasional evening in some welcoming, warmly lit den. Once a week, therefore, as twilight came curling like mist about the belltower, deepening the shadows in the quadrangle under my window, suggesting all manner of possibilities, I would grab a book and a jacket and clatter down the stairs in search of gastronomic derring-do. It was often a curry – unless it was Chinese. Or it might have been French, or Italian, or sometimes the fresh, new style of English cooking that was coming into vogue. But in those days, the food was secondary. I wanted the company, the feeling of quiet anticipation as I sat down at the table, straightened the cutlery on a pristine tablecloth, unfolded my napkin. I wanted to take my time with the menu, to share short, formal moments of conversation with waiters, to look around at my fellow customers and eavesdrop on their night out. There were plenty of other evenings spent at the pub, attending concerts and plays, establishing a floating poker game, but going to restaurants was my private recreation and particular pleasure.

Perhaps Wendy had envisioned a long and leisurely lunch among the dreaming spires that day, but I had to squeeze three years of memories into one afternoon. We began with a lightning tour of New College in all its medieval splendour, then a leisurely punt on the river Cherwell, croquet and Pimm's in the garden of friends in Summertown, and, just before dinner, a side trip into Jericho, that labyrinthine quarter of narrow Victorian streets beside the Oxford Canal, famous for having more pubs per square yard than anywhere else in the world.

In our last year at the university, my best friend, David, and I had rented a house there, an unprepossessing, two-up-two-down, terraced townhouse with paper-thin walls and a small backyard full of rubble. At first we had treated the place as nothing more than an academic base camp from which to make the assault on our finals, but we soon fell victim to short, sharp bouts of domesticity. We bought curtains to foil the web of icy drafts that moaned through the downstairs rooms all winter long. We found ourselves constantly rearranging the furniture – the threadbare, greasy sofa, the bottomless armchair, the dining table that sloped slightly to the north. We even began to throw dinner parties.

It is true that alterior motives lay behind these ambitious social diversions. Our first soirée was a crudely transparent attempt to impress two attractive female undergraduates, and we spent hours planning the menu. To break the ice: Bullshot Soup, an invention of David's consisting of equal parts canned beef consommé and vodka, served with toast points. To finish: my own version of crème brûlée, a brilliant gastronomic sleight-of-hand made by folding whipped cream into vanilla blancmange pudding and sprinkling it with brown sugar that caught fire when we melted it under the grill. The main course was our combined tour de force, a blanquette de veau for which we grudgingly used a recipe from a cookbook. It took us all day to make, in an electric crockpot, but the results exceeded our wildest hopes. By some miracle, it turned out perfectly – rich, subtle, layered, wholesome and yet sophisticated. Amid much ceremonious fanfare, David carried it in from the kitchen, but in all the excitement he forgot to unplug the crockpot's electric cord. With one smooth, slow motion, the casserole turned itself upside down in his hands, neatly blanquetting his shoes and a large area of the carpet. Four mouths fell open.

"It's a new, Dadaist dinner party art form," said David quickly. "What do you think?"

Driving back up Memory Lane, Wendy seemed strangely silent. Had she been moved beyond words by my light-hearted anecdotes? Or did the final ordeal of the day loom larger for her than for me? A dinner had been arranged, a grand reunion of assorted old friends and cronies, including my previous girlfriend of many years, all of whom were eager to meet Toronto's child. We had chosen a restaurant called La Sorbonne, an elegant room in which chef-patron André Chavagnon had introduced many of us to the glories of Alsatian onion tart, unctuous duck terrine, and bavaroise au cassis. But even as I prattled away about the treats that lay in store, I felt a sudden disturbing qualm. We parked and went upstairs to the restaurant, but as I made the introductions the qualm grew more insistent. That afternoon, on our punting expedition, we had reached the Victoria Arms, a delightful old pub on the bank of the river. Out of bravado as much as greed, I had purchased a jar of cockles, molluscs that almost always gave me a violent allergic reaction. Perhaps having Wendy beside me made me feel superhumanly lucky, for I had eaten more than my share ... Now purple spots were dancing across the menu. The qualm became a tremor, presaging an eruption. By the time I returned to the table, coffee was being served and Wendy was surrounded by ardent admirers.

Our relationship survived the débâcle. As the seasons passed, we gave many dinner parties in our flat in Tooting, taking the bedroom door off its hinges to use as a tabletop when the numbers demanded it, learning to cook together. One night, a publisher friend who had thrilled to my kipper pâté but was less enthusiastic when faced with the manuscripts of my novels suggested that humorous books about food had a loyal, if limited, following. Not everyone saw the joke when *The Seducer's Cookbook* appeared in 1981. One outraged feminist organization chose to read it as a serious guide to sexual predation, which helped sales considerably. It was a very slim volume in every sense of the word, but holding it in my hand made me realize once and for all that I wanted to be a writer more than I wanted to act. I envisioned short stories, plays, libretti, novels picaresque and novels epistolary, debonair travel books, tales of romance and adventure. On one point, however, I had already made up my mind. The rigours of drumming up sixty recipes for the cookbook, testing and tasting them all ad nauseam, had been much too much like hard work. There would be no more writing about food.

4

⚥ ETHNICITIES ⚥

WALKING HOME from the Sherbourne subway on late October afternoons, it seemed to me that Howard Street must always be cold. The sun stayed low in the pale southern sky, hidden by the soaring apartment towers of St. James Town. The sidewalk and the old brick houses on the other side of the street were always in shadow. Black squirrels scuttled about in the drifts of dirty leaves; the noise of the traffic on Bloor was a perpetual murmur.

In 1981 Wendy and I moved back from England and into a tiny rented apartment on the sixteenth floor of a building on Howard Street. From our balcony, we could see most of the rest of St. James Town, looming canyons of stained concrete pierced by thousands of distant windows that flickered after dark with the cosmic aurora of countless television sets. By some architectural oversight, a space had been left between two of the towers, and through that narrow chink, on clear autumn days, our view stretched as far as the glittering lake, many miles to the south. At other times, the mist came in and everything beyond the canyon walls was as dim and opaque as a blind man's eye. The heat in the building was always too high, which suited the cockroaches just fine. Once a week, just before dawn, the fire alarm would pluck us untimely from the womb of sleep – a regular act of vengeance perpetrated by an angry shiftworker. You could set your watch by it.

Life was necessarily simple. Wendy worked all day in the curatorial department of the Art Gallery of Ontario while I stayed home and wrote second-rate occult fiction. In the evenings we watched *Laverne and Shirley*, played board games, and went to bed. We were flat broke, utterly self-involved, and entirely happy. Finding the monthly rent of $236 was our principal preoccupation. It is safe to say that the great revolution in restaurant dining that was then taking place in the city was no concern of ours. Instead we had Howard Street, the J.C. Char-pit, and Michelino's Pizza.

From the outside, Michelino's did not look fantastically prepossessing: the blue paint was grubby, the signs in the window had mostly been picked away by children when Mike's back was turned. Inside, it was brightly lit and the warm air smelt of dough and garlic salt. Aliens bleeped and growled as they marched down the screens of two bulky arcade games; there was a table and two rickety wooden chairs close to the door. On the wall above them, a pair of greasy, faded signs written on cardboard that had long since buckled and browned said "No Loitering" and "No Credit Positively."

Mike himself seemed to live behind the counter; he certainly slept there, on a low camp bed close to the ovens. He was a Sicilian, small and thin, maybe forty years old, and he dressed in white trousers and a T-shirt, with a woollen hat on his head for reasons of hygiene and to show that he was a chef. He had seen a lot of the world in his twenties, he told me once, but now he was settled. His pleasure was to watch the people coming home from work after dark, carrying shopping and treats for the kids – a bag of doughnuts, a potted plant – a constant stream of faces caught in the light of his window, then vanishing neatly into their buildings until the street was empty again.

The J.C. Char-pit was on the same parade of shops. Owned and run by angry Greeks, it was a noisy, smoky take-out that served the best banquet burgers I have ever eaten. "It's Toronto's burger!" one of the cooks informed me on several occasions. "Invented right here in Toronto, in the year 1940, by Fran Deck, the guy who created Fran's!"

"Is that right!"

"You call me a liar?"

Fran's, at Yonge and St. Clair, has other claims to fame. It was the city's first air-conditioned restaurant, and for years it was the only place north of Bloor Street where a person could buy a meal on a Sunday. But for me the name is forever linked with the banquet burger: a cheeseburger, all dressed, with crisp Canadian bacon. Vienna has Sacher torte and Wiener schnitzel, Marseilles has bouillabaisse, Orillia has the butter tart; Toronto's status as a culinary capital rests on the banquet burger. Of course, Fran Deck came from a creative family. It was his brother who made the first cheeseburger, in New York, in 1921.

Around the corner on Sherbourne was the Allnite Donut, and sometimes during the winter, long after midnight, I would go there for coffee and inspiration. Stairs led down from the street to a plate-glass window and door that were always foggy with condensation. Eventually I got to recognize some of the good old boys who spent part of their nights there. They never spoke to each other but took turns carrying on a fragmentary monologue, a braid of complaint and braggadocio that was addressed to and inspired by the demure young woman behind the counter. There was a kind of gallantry in their attentions, an implicit respect that put each of them on his best behaviour. She must have heard their stories a hundred times over, their tales of relatives back in the Maritimes who would one day be glad to see them return, their daily problems with cops and shopkeepers and recalcitrant liquor store personnel. If she was bored, she hid it behind an endlessly patient smile that stayed on her face even when she turned away to stack coffee mugs or bag the last few doughnuts left in the basket trays. And when all her small chores were finished, she would lean up against the till and the game of buck poker began.

It was an event that I saw only twice, but it had such an air of ritual that I am convinced it was a familiar ceremony. First, one of the old guys would make his way up to the counter, fish out a dollar bill from some deep recess, and smooth it flat on the orange Formica. He might say, "Well, what have we here?" Or else, "Well now, would you just look at this! Three fives and a pair of sevens." A silence, touched by anxiety, filled the room. The radio high on a shelf, murmuring hits from Q107, seemed suddenly loud. Then the lank-haired girl would pull out a folded bill from her jeans, glance at the serial numbers, and tilt back her head.

"Oh, yeah?" she would ask. The company hung on her every word. "And is that the best you can do? This one has four nines." The challenger had to see her buck for himself and then, with good grace, he would hand her his own, comically cursing his luck while the other men fairly glowed with wordless glee.

When the contest was over, a quieter, more casual mood descended upon the room as the insomniacs retreated into their own thoughts, each nursing the mug of coffee that gave him the right to come in from the cold. Soon after that I would leave, walking home along Howard Street, my footsteps ringing on the frozen sidewalk as the first snowflakes spiralled down out of the darkness.

Sometimes, during the day, I left Howard Street and ventured more deeply into the city. I steered well clear of my old stamping-ground around the Royal York and the Royal Alexandra. I felt no companionship with the rich. Instead I went looking for Bohemian cafés that mirrored my old haunts in London's West End – anywhere that wasn't too phoney and had staff who were easygoing about one-cup squatters.

My favourite place was the Ritz, a cramped, low-ceilinged basement on Charles Street West that served slices of carrot cake heavy and moist enough to pass muster as lunch. No one could have mistaken the place for equivalent dives in New York or Paris or Berlin, but at the time it seemed as close to la vie de Bohème as Toronto was likely to get. Student poets met there to talk and occasionally write; young couples

spent hours sitting elbow to elbow, earnestly defining their relation-
ships. And when their conversation became too smug and too self-
referential, or when my small urban beat seemed too stiflingly insular,
there was always the shrine, Toronto's cathedral to the gypsy spirit: the
restaurant at the Gray Coach Bus Terminal. It had generous hours –
6:30 A.M. until half past midnight – and a priesthood of sad-sack old
waiters in tight red jackets who never met the customer's eye:
guardians of the flame. Characters from an Edward Hopper painting
sat slouched over the scratched yellow counter; travelling people
stomped in from the slush, smelling of wet coats, to be followed long
after dark by a select posse of elderly vagabonds.

The restaurant has been bulldozed now, but I remember it as a
room that possessed a classical grace, the indifferent dignity of all
waiting rooms. Slices of pie grew old in the glass-fronted display,
franks turned slowly in their warming box, steam drifted out of the
huge stainless steel coffee machine. A silent, mournful little couple put
a quarter in the Seeburg Consolette above their booth: "Tear in My
Beer," by Hank Williams Jr. You could buy a Mountie doll or a gold-
painted model of the CN Tower as souvenirs, but the muse of the terminal conjured images from far beyond this fussy town, Toronto's last
true source of transcontinental melancholy.

"WE ARE A CITY of proud and well-defined ethnic neighbourhoods. Not a melting pot, but a multicultural mosaic." So I was told,
a hundred thousand times, by new friends and old acquaintances,
by print journalists, radio pundits, and television announcers, by
waiters and shopkeepers and once by a cop. It was a universal anthem,
except where I lived. I guess St. James Town was some kind of weird

demographic aberration, for our cluster of apartment buildings seemed a vertical Olympic village. It was only when I walked out of the town and into the city that I realized we were the exception.

When a new group of immigrants reaches Toronto, the first signs of their arrival are the small, inexpensive restaurants that spring up in their particular neighbourhood. They are as much social clubs as places to eat, cultural lifelines for the homesick. The entrepreneurs who set them up, serving their displaced countrymen and finding employment for relatives, are often amateurs with no restaurant experience. Survival is their motivation and costs are held to a minimum. Kitchen equipment tends to be third- or fourth-hand; customer comfort is a low priority. The ingredients of their culinary birthright, assuming they are available at all, are the cheapest versions money can buy, which often means frozen or canned.

Time passes. In a perfect world, these small ethnic places would grow more secure, more professional, and eventually they would attract the attention and admiration of the host community. Then their future would be assured – in a perfect world. In Toronto during the 1950s and '60s, however, the conditions required for such growth were less than ideal. A deep cultural conservatism still gripped the Anglo middle classes (never the most daring restaurant-goers at the best of times) and was just as strong within the immigrant communities themselves. Korean families did not eat at Italian cafés; Hungarians did not patronize the basement dining rooms of Chinatown. More important, the provincial government did its level best to crush the ambitions of small-time restaurateurs. The extraordinary difficulties faced by anyone hoping to acquire a liquor licence crippled free enterprise, limiting innumerable rooms to a lunch-only trade.

Moreover, in 1969, the provincial treasurer, Charles McNaughton, clamped a 10 percent sales tax on meals that cost more than $2.50, placing another obstacle in the path of every greasy spoon that wished to become a knife and fork.

Nevertheless, some non-European ethnic restaurants did make that quantum leap into success outside their community, and the first and most obvious cuisine to find favour was Chinese-Canadian, that curious hybrid better known as Junk Chinese.

Chop suey, egg foo yong, sweet-and-sour pork, egg roll, chicken chow mein ... The litany of dishes is identical across the English-speaking world. In this country, its origins go back to the nineteenth century and the West Coast, when immigrant workers, fleeing famine, arrived en masse from Canton to help build the railways. Leaving their wives behind, lacking any culinary training, they improvised with the strange North American ingredients they found, working without garlic, ginger, chilies, abandoning spice and subtlety, creating their own culinary genre of bland compromise. As this century began and railway work in the west disappeared, they moved east, and many settled on the northern fringes of Toronto, around Bay and Dundas. The city enveloped them, a tide around an island, but by then Chinatown was established, a self-sufficient downtown enclave. Its principal points of contact with the world beyond its frontiers were the restaurants that served the generic Junk menu.

Today, such cooking seems utterly commonplace, without a vestige of grace or energy. To Anglo 1950s Toronto, however, it was the last word in exotic glamour. Mature gourmets still remember the childhood thrill of a meal at Lichee Garden on Elizabeth Street, the extraordinary colours and flavours, the sweetness in everything, the tang of their first taste of soy sauce, the limp, pale, alien bean sprouts. Lichee Garden opened in 1948, sharing its building with a grocery store and a barber shop. The owners were smart enough to open accounts for their regular customers, and to invest in opulent décor, a dance floor, and a swing sextet. On Fridays, high school students would turn the place into a hop; on Saturday nights, CFRB Radio broadcast live from the dining room. The menu included fried chicken and steak as well as such famous dishes as honey garlic spare ribs. Above all, Lichee Garden had a liquor licence. Cocktails were the lure for the evening crowd, and the fuel of many a long business lunch.

Eventually, other Chinese restaurants challenged Lichee Garden's supremacy. By the end of the 1960s, the place had begun to seem formal and old-fashioned beside Kwongchow and Sai Woo. Before the land assembly of 1969-70, when a group of anonymous Swiss investors known as Circuit House bought up most of Chinatown, razed it to the ground, and developed it into office space, there were as many as a hundred Chinese restaurants and cafés in the area. Many moved onto Spadina; others spread further afield. Danny Wu's restaurant, Sea Hi, was demolished, but he moved to Yonge Street and opened Sam the Chinese Food Man in partnership with Sam the Record Man Sniderman. Suzie Wong's opened on Bloor Street West's international strip, offering the city's first Chinese buffet, "with gourmet dishes for the connoisseur by request."

For there were connoisseurs by now. By the early 1970s, curious sophisticates had begun to explore more obscure menus, to boldly go where few Canadians had gone before. They discovered dim sum, though not yet dim sum carts – those, by most accounts, were first introduced at Treasure Restaurant on Dundas West in 1975. They tasted Peking duck at China House, Toronto's first Mandarin restaurant, on the distant reaches of Eglinton West. They learned of the existence of Szechuan cuisine through the decidedly toned-down dishes of Chinese Garden on Dundas near Bay.

Of course, it wasn't only the Chinese who figured out how to tickle Toronto's palate. In the late 1960s, many an ambitious restaurateur realized that ethnicity was a valuable gimmick when it came to selling food. Costumed waitresses, atmospheric décor, dishes with foreign names, gimmicky plate presentation had begun to lure Canadians out to dinner. Often the food was merely good old meat and potatoes in a funny hat – so much the better, from the customers' point of view.

A glance at a copy of *Toronto Life* magazine from 1968 reveals a fairly cosmopolitan list of "ethnic" restaurants (the notion was still strange enough to merit inverted commas). Acropole, on Dundas Street West, was "an authentic Greek restaurant where one selects one's dinner in the kitchen." Further south, on Elm Street, stood the Balkan Restaurant, its cuisine described in different issues of the magazine as Arabian, mid-Eastern, Turkish, or Balkan. Confusing, but perhaps it didn't matter that much to the reader: the place was *foreign*. George's Spaghetti House was obviously the real Italian experience: you could tell by the checkered tablecloths and the candles stuck into Chianti fiascos. The food, if not the mood, was Viennese at the grand Franz Josef Room at the Walker House Hotel, and way out east on Kingston Road, a place called Paprika Tavern drew a crowd with "a flaming wooden platter."

It is strange to look back and see which cuisines were important, which obscure, which notable by their absence. Throughout the sixties, the Hungarians were a powerful force, backed up by German and Austrian establishments. The Japanese were not yet a power in the land, and aside from the Acropole, Greek cooking was still risqué. *Toronto Life* found La Scala a puzzling oddity, with its "elegant Italian cuisine, delicious steaks and veal but not spaghetti ..."

Completely ignored were the great unlicensed, the small, scruffy premises that catered to an un-Canadianized clientele. It was almost a joke, therefore, when in January 1969, the magazine sent two of its thinnest, wittiest, and most urbane writers, Sid Adilman and Marq de Villiers, into the neighbourhoods to see what they could find to eat for under $2 a head. They discovered gold and mined it repeatedly over the next couple of years, until the series was taken over by Zelda Bruchner, a journalist who wove teasing little anecdotes of her private life and long-ago courtship into her copy but proved just as intrepid, worldly, and amusing as her predecessors. This was scarcely surprising, since Zelda was really de Villiers, now contracted to the *Telegram* and therefore writing for *Toronto Life* under a nom de plume.

There were many dishes Adilman and de Villiers felt they had to explain. At the Don Quijote, a Spanish restaurant on College, just west of Spadina, they encountered calamari and tortillas, both of which demanded a translation, as well as "Anglo cutlets," which didn't then but might now. Elsewhere, baklava, latkes, and shrimp tempura were also deemed unfamiliar to *Toronto Life*'s readers. They discovered the city's first satay at the city's first Malaysian eatery, the Singapore, on College Street, and visited both of Metro's only West Indian rooms, the Arawak and Ram's Roti Shop, which had opened in early 1968 on Dupont, west of Bathurst.

I wish I had known about these places during our St. James Town days, for there were times, coincident with the arrival of Wendy's pay-cheque, when the thought of dining out seemed appealing. Above all, we missed Indian cooking, and one afternoon the pangs of nostalgia became too much to bear. We set off on foot, blithely but in completely the wrong direction, heading towards Yonge rather than south to Gerrard Street East, and arrived at last at India House.

Time is a great healer. The details that remain of that meal are mercifully few: a bright, homespun room, a uniformed waitress who may have been Scottish, a much-repeated boast that the paneer cheese was made on the premises, a sense of profound disappointment. I had eaten indifferent Indian cooking before, many times, in England, but India House took the pappadum, the greasy sauces finding a way to be simultaneously insipid and as crudely bitter as stale curry powder.

No matter where in the subcontinent they come from, every single Indian, Pakistani, Sri Lankan, or Bangladeshi person I have ever met who is not involved in the food industry grows disdainful when the subject turns to Indian restaurants. "We simply don't go," they say. "Why should we? The food is so much better at home." Other cultures, most notably the Greeks, make the same irrefutable claim, but the Greeks use their tavernas and psistarias for more than just eating. What sets the Indian places apart from the usual pattern of small immigrant restaurants is the fact that they were never intended to serve their own immigrant community.

To understand why, you have to go back to the very dawn of the generic Indian menu: to England in the early 1950s, and the postwar surge of emigrés from the subcontinent. A hypothetical couple arrives in Birmingham from Bengal. They have no restaurant experience, but they quickly see that opening up a place of their own will employ the whole family. Bengali culinary traditions are profoundly domestic, so they cannot expect to draw a clientele from other new Britons, but as long as they keep the prices at rock bottom, the English will come – students, mostly, and old India hands with nostalgic memories of the food they ate while serving the Empire.

But what will go on the menu? Not Bengali home cooking. Give the customers what they have come to expect. Patch together a list of dishes from here and there: something creamy from Delhi, something hot from Madras, rice from the south, breads from the Punjab, with street food and snacks such as samosas to serve as appetizers. Okay, but the problem is how to cook it. England in the 1950s is no global marketplace. No fresh spices at all. Never mind. One can buy a ready-ground mix called curry powder that seems to please everyone, no matter how stale it tastes. No fresh Indian herbs or mangoes, just a miserable range of odd northern-hemisphere fruit and vegetables. No buffalo yogurt – how can you cook Moghlai dishes without decent yogurt? Use a tomato base. That will also add colour in the absence of saffron or turmeric. No one will know.

And so the generic curry menu was born, out of compromise and ignorance, to be slavishly copied from one restaurant to the next, an awful Westernized parody of the infinite subtlety and regional variety of subcontinental cuisine. To Indian eyes, it was a meaningless hybrid. Naan bread with shrimp vindaloo? That was like eating buttered scones with bouillabaisse. And to make matters worse, the wacky notion arose that this was suitable fare for a lunchtime buffet presentation, as if rice could be appetizing after two or three hours under a heat lamp, or that tandoori chicken would somehow defy the laws of physics and not turn into jerky.

And yet, for those of us who knew no better, the flocked-wallpaper Indian restaurant was a comforting place to eat: the familiar dishes, the bottom-feeder prices, the appalling wine list left behind from the days when Liebfraumilch was a name with which to conjure. Each time we nipped out for a curry, we found, with a sneaking relief, that nothing had changed. For all its regional eclecticism, the generic curry menu is one of the most conservative documents on earth.

India House first brought that menu to Toronto. It opened in 1963, with a customer base that included many British expatriates and a few daring Canadians. Rajput on Bloor West followed in 1967 and, three years later, Indian Rice Factory on Dupont Street. Not exactly a deluge, but in fact there were other places offering customers a taste of first-class Indian cuisine, thanks to a young registered nurse from Bombay.

One afternoon in 1967, Mrs. Amar Patel was having lunch at the Inn on the Park. The hotel's restaurant, Café de l'Auberge, was famous for sophisticated French cuisine, but it was the buffet of the day that aroused her curiosity – a culinary event entitled "From the Chafing Dishes of India." In those dishes were examples of the curious travesty of Moghlai cooking that European chefs were trained to prepare: chicken, shrimp, or beef in a sort of béchamel sauce coloured with curry powder. Mrs. Patel called the manager and gently tried to explain that this was a little less than authentic.

When the conversation moved into the kitchen, executive chef Georges Chaignet listened politely and then invited Mrs. Patel to cook him a meal. She obliged; he was stunned. As Stratford Chefs School instructor Jacques Marie, then Chaignet's sous-chef, recalled: "She showed us what curry is really about. It was a new world to me."

To the kitchen's eternal credit, Mrs. Patel was hired to teach the team all that she knew. After a year, she moved on, first to Julie's Mansion on Jarvis, working her magic in the casual upstairs dining room called the Bombay Bicycle Club, more famous in those days for the lissom beauty of its sari-clad waitresses than its buffet, and then to the Hyatt Regency.

In 1970 she opened her own place, called Indian Rice Factory. Designed by her husband and built on a shoestring by architecture students, the tiny room would be considered avant-garde even today. It seated barely a dozen customers who sat around an open cooking station, choosing from a short and frequently changing list of dishes on a blackboard tied to the back of the fridge. Slender, beautiful and always elegantly dressed, Mrs. Patel radiated a soft-spoken confidence as she worked, preparing many items à la minute, and explaining her recipes to anyone who asked. It was the antithesis of generic cuisine, and it also cost rather more than curry-lovers expected to pay, which bothered a few of the customers.

It seemed as if Toronto had finally taken a liking to "curry." Eleven more Indian restaurants opened in the next three years, some offering the new thrill of tandoor-baked dishes (you can't go wrong in Canada if you serve chicken and shrimp), but none of them daring to follow Mrs. Patel's example by breaking the mould of the old generic menu. There would be exceptions in the decades that lay ahead: Samina's Tiffin Room, near the Art Gallery of Ontario, was by all accounts a place of notable cooking, and more than one nostalgic gourmand has mourned the absence of the partridge in cardamom cream once served at Mindra's on Yorkville.

Only in the mid-1990s, however, did signs of a shift in the status quo begin to appear. Restaurants with regional menus sprang up throughout the city. Rashnaa offered simple Tamil cooking in an ungentrified old house on a Cabbagetown backstreet. On Gerrard Street East, where most eateries compete on price rather than quality, Gujurat Durbar specialized in Gujurat's inventive vegetarian dishes. Most of the surviving pioneers remained nervous of innovation, but not Indian Rice Factory, still on Dupont, though in larger, less impromptu premises.

I ate there in 1995 and found Mrs. Patel was still cooking. Her son, Aman, was the manager, a tall, serious young man who told me he found the popular image of the stereotypical curry house deeply frustrating. They bought their meat from the same suppliers as the most expensive Italian or French restaurants, but customers expected to pay Gerrard Street East bargain prices once it was cooked. He had assembled a fascinating list of wines that worked unexpectedly well with Indian spicing, and was more than happy to spend fifteen minutes at a table explaining such matchmaking, but customers still felt safer with beer. He encouraged the chefs who cooked beside his mother to put experimental Indian-Western Fusion dishes on the menu, but his clientele passed them by.

I asked Aman Patel to choose our meal. The dishes that arrived were the work of three different minds. His mother prepared the delicious fresh fenugreek greens with soft potatoes and chewy fried onions, and also the bowl of fiery little okra tossed with garlic, onion, and chilies. Debebrata Saha, who had worked at leading hotels in Delhi and Qatar before joining the Rice Factory, cooked the traditional Moghlai recipe of chicken chirurchi, a tender breast stuffed with almonds, raisins, and paneer cheese, in a sauce of yogurt, cardamom, and saffron as smooth and rich as cream. The lamb shank in dark, intense bhuna sauce was made by David Eaglesham, a young Canadian chef who had been cooking beside Mrs. Patel for a year. Learning her secrets and combining his new knowledge with past experience, it was he who created the Indian Fusion dishes of which Aman Patel was so proud: grilled sea bass marinated with kari leaf, ginger, and garlic, served with a green curry sauce; grilled salmon on a bed of uppama (like Indian polenta) with deep-fried ginger and a Goan sauce.

Yes, it was the best Indian meal I had ever eaten in Toronto. No, it was neither generic nor traditional. It was a glimpse of one of many possible futures for Indian restaurants, a future in which creative cooking at last finds a place.

ON THE SOUTH SIDE of Bloor Street, just around the corner from St. James Town, was a restaurant called Furusato. As it was priced far beyond our most wayward dreams, we might never have eaten there had it not been for the generosity of an old school friend of Wendy's who took pity on our penury. He was keen to visit the place because he had heard that there were Frapanese dishes on the menu, examples of the experimental union of French and Japanese cooking that was then the vogue in the world's sophisticated gastronomic fora. Wendy and I were delighted to accompany him because we were mightily tired of pizza.

Furusato lacked the intimate serenity I associate with Japanese restaurants – the large, dimly lit back room was actually pretty noisy – but the food was good. We told the waitress we were in no hurry and she took the hint, bringing the dishes in their correct order and giving us time to contemplate the parade of flavours and textures. The organization of Japanese cuisine concentrates the mind on the food in a way that no other cuisine can. Inspired, philosophical, its intricate presentation reminds us how precious is even the simplest ingredient, and how deserving of the utmost artistry of the cook and the due reverence of the consumer. It's easy to gorge like a greedy clod in a carelessly run Japanese restaurant, but the best of them create a subtle ambience that makes such philistinism seem a deliberate act of defiance.

Perhaps that is one of the reasons why Japanese restaurants were not an overnight success in Toronto. The pioneer, I believe, was House of Fuji Matsu on Elm Street, tucked in among the brothels and bootleggers, close to Angelo's and Barberian's. Way ahead of its time, it did not last long. Nikko, the first licensed example, opened in 1960. Ten years later, there were still only three, including Michi Café, out east on Kingston Road, named for the wife of its owner, Masa Hara. Business at Michi was largely a matter of improvisation in those early days. Finding Japanese ingredients proved a major challenge, and Hara kept his menu small. From time to time, Japanese customers calling to make a reservation would ask whether he served this dish or that. He always said yes, adding it to the menu and leaving it there. Canadian customers presented other problems, especially when they tried to pronounce difficult Japanese words. Mrs. Hara, waiting table, spoke no English, but she would smile sweetly and bring what she hoped had been ordered. Perhaps it was her smile, but nobody ever complained.

Michi eventually moved to Queen Street, and in 1977 Hara opened Masa on Church. Japanese food was slowly gathering momentum. There were ten restaurants in the city now, and the city's first sushi bar, created in 1974 at Taste of Japan on Yonge Street, had proved that Canadians had the courage to eat raw fish. No one could have predicted the sudden craving for sushi that swept across Toronto like a gale-force wind in the eighties and that gusts periodically about our appetites to this day. It was an élitist fashion, part of the love affair with new, exotic, and expensive foodstuffs, amplified by the realization that Japanese food was remarkably healthy and low in fat. The rapid expansion of Toronto's Oriental community also boosted the clientele, while the presence of a number of Japanese corporate companies downtown, most of them since driven away by the recession, ensured a certain standard of quality. It quickly became a cliché that our restaurants and sushi bars could not hope to compete with those of Vancouver, that our fish could not possibly be as fresh, but nobody seemed to mind. Sushi was cool.

One problem, however, threatened to contain this tornado of popularity: there just weren't enough properly trained sushi chefs to go round. In Japan, a successful sushi chef enjoys a level of prestige and an income well above that of his peers in Toronto. If he does choose to seek his fortune here, he finds himself with a fight on his hands whenever he tries to extend his working visa. This makes it difficult to pass along his skills, for a sushi chef's training traditionally takes years and the bond between master and apprentice is profound.

But then, this is not Japan, and our attitude to eating out is not Japanese. Hardly any of us share or even understand the lifelong loyalties of the Japanese restaurant-goer; even fewer have the patience and trust required to follow the proper etiquette of the sushi bar. Over there, restaurants are small and specialized. Customers go to one place for sushi, another for tempura, another for noodles, somewhere else for robata or eel or fugu. Japanese tourists arriving in Metro and eating at Masa or Nami are surprised to discover everything under one roof, though many admit to finding the idea convenient. The menu may also astonish them by its disdain for the order of nature. There are countless beloved ingredients in Japan for which gourmets wait all year long, revelling in their two-week season, but no one would dream of ordering them at any other time. Here, they are perpetually available or else not to be found at all.

And yet, hybrid or no, I would as soon eat at a good Toronto Japanese restaurant as anywhere. Getting to know them over the years has been a pleasure, and not only because the screened privacy of a tatami room for two is the most romantic dinner venue I know. Eating out at Edo, Ematei, Nami, Rikishi, Akane-ya, or Hiro Sushi has always proved a foolproof specific against a jaded palate. Especially Hiro Sushi.

Owner Hiro Yoshida is the sushi chef's sushi chef. Before I met and talked with him, I had assumed he was a stern man, as likely to growl as to smile at a foolish journalist. He had a reputation as a guardian of his culture and a strict traditionalist, one reason why corporate demiurges visiting from Japan were said to ask humbly for his personal services when an important dinner was to be prepared. His Church Street restaurant always seemed to me to be a metaphorical hermitage, its austerity emphasized by the purple bars of Boys' Town that bejewel the neighbourhood.

One hot summer afternoon in 1997, I went down to Hiro Sushi. The restaurant was closed, but I was expected. Yoshida, tall, dignified, and courteous, was behind the bar, preparing trays of maki rolls to be sent over to the Four Seasons Hotel. We made small talk while he squeezed rice and pared avocados, discussing his plan to move to a new location at King and Jarvis, comparing fishmongers. Then he came round to my side of the bar. A young woman, the restaurant's kitchen chef, joined us. Given the artificially extended menus of Japanese restaurants in the West, a sushi bar needs a versatile talent in the back room to fry, grill, and basically do the lion's share of the work, with no expectation of fame or recognition. Meiko Kimura, who grew up in her father's restaurant, is one of the best. Her standards are as severe, in their way, as Yoshida's. Her English is slightly better, and she helped him out with the occasional idiom as he explained what it meant to him to be a chef.

The story began when Yoshida was ten years old and a pupil at the local school in his home town just east of Tokyo. The teacher asked the class to write down what they dreamed of being when they grew up, and young Hiro wrote sushi chef. "Everyone thought it was very funny, for a sushi chef in Japan is a glamorous figure. Sushi is very expensive over there. We would eat it only a couple of times a year. My parents ordered it in when we received important guests, and I would taste what was left over. I didn't think much more about it. Then, when I was eighteen, I went off to Takushoku University in Tokyo to read international economics. I had to make money and find somewhere to live, so I got a part-time job in a sushi bar and rented a room upstairs. It suited my boss because he could call me down any time of the day or night to help out. I would cut fish, make rolls, then I graduated and left to work with a company in an office. One year later I came back. That kind of job, with a salary, was not for me. I asked my old boss to teach me properly. Most apprentices start at age sixteen or eighteen and train for ten or fifteen years. I was old, but he said, 'Be patient for five years and I will teach you.'

"So I started again, from the very beginning. I could not touch any fish, any knife, nothing ... I was to learn by watching, standing behind the customers at the bar, pouring their tea, lighting their cigarettes, looking past them at my boss at work. I learned to anticipate their needs, to read their minds. It took longer than five years, but I learned many things."

Meiko Kimura chimed in. "It's amazing! He remembers everything each of our regular customers likes, what they ate last time they were here. He anticipates, makes a tuna sushi for them before they even ask for it."

"If I were to teach my assistant here in Canada in that way," continued Yoshida, "it would seem very old-fashioned. Twice a month, my boss sent me off to the barber's shop. I bought new wooden shoes three times a year. I was unpaid, with two days off every month, but that was the system."

Traditionally, the apprentice reaped his reward when he finally became a chef. His master would set him up in business, giving money and even lending his name to the new restaurant, like a father helping a son. Yoshida, however, came to Toronto. An old university acquaintance, Shigeo Kimura, was a partner at Sasaya on Eglinton Avenue, and he needed another sushi chef. Yoshida arrived in 1983 and has been in the city ever since.

Sasaya, in those early days, was one of Toronto's finest. Yoshida's assistant there was Shigeru Nagashima, who later became Nami's first sushi chef, before moving to Akane-ya, the tiny perfect restaurant in the Beaches that is Hiro Sushi's closest competition in terms of quality. Yoshida made no effort to change his assistant's technique. As one chef among several, his duty was to fall in with Sasaya's own style, and any improvisation would have been inappropriate. A sushi chef who wishes to be creative must first have a place of his own. Yoshida achieved that ambition in 1990, after stints at Takesushi, Tidal Wave, Katsura, and Nami. He had met Meiko at Takesushi, but she had gone back to Japan. He invited her to come back and work for him in Hiro Sushi's kitchen.

"As an owner, I was able to do things my way at last. Caring for the customer is the most important thing. It's a matter of trust. My regulars never order. They come in and sit down. All I ask is whether they're hungry or very hungry. I know their tastes. But I must be broad-minded, think of new ways to please them. In Japan, we have seasons to observe and many more ingredients to work with. So Meiko must also be creative with the small appetizers she sends out to the customers at the bar. She might even prepare sardines in the Portuguese style, grilled with tomatoes and olive oil, to keep them intrigued."

Did it annoy Yoshida when inexperienced Canadian customers sat down and ordered badly, without regard for due form and etiquette? He smiled and shook his head.

"Not at all. Though I don't like it when people leave food uneaten. It shows disrespect for the ingredients, for nature."

The relationship between the chef and his ingredients that lies at the heart of traditional Japanese cooking was exemplified by every detail at Hiro Sushi. No one in Toronto ever balanced the sweet vinegar that flavoured the sushi rice as delicately as Yoshida. No one took such trouble with the soy sauce, preparing it over days with salted sour plums, kombu seaweed, and grated smoked bonito. Most sushi restaurants order their fish by phone, but Yoshida went out every morning to choose his own fish from suppliers across the city. "Each fish is like my child. I have to care. Every single day. Some people think only of business, or they play around with ingredients. They lack the proper spirit. When I see that, I feel sorry for the fish."

We sat and sipped tea as the afternoon wore on, tasting a tangy, milk-white sake from the mountains near Nagoya, talking of eggplants and eels, and why Japanese people won't go to Japanese restaurants owned by Koreans or Cantonese. A matter of attitude on the part of the restaurateurs, he suggested, a question of perceived priorities. A generous-minded man is Hiro Yoshida, but uncompromisingly true to the spirit of his art. I tried to remember exactly what I had eaten at Furusato, fifteen years earlier, and wondered whether I would be so impressed if I tasted that food today. An eternal question, always unanswerable.

THERE IS ONE OTHER Japanese meal that sticks in my mind from the summer of 1982. Wendy and I had our wedding dinner at Katsura, at the Prince Hotel in Don Mills, with her four closest friends and her mother and stepfather in attendance. I wasn't really thinking about food that evening, but it did seem odd that the chicken teriyaki came with home fries and steamed cauliflower. An early example of Fusion cuisine.

Ours was a fairly traditional modern suburban wedding. The service took place in a windowless room in North York City Hall, conducted by a rather hip, female Unitarian minister.

"I like that passage you chose," she said, before we all signed the register. "Where's it from?"

"The Bible."

"Really!"

I thought she was going to add, "I must get around to reading it some day." Then it was on to Edwards Gardens for the ritual photographs on the quaint wooden bridge, dinner at Katsura, and a twelve-hour honeymoon at the Windsor Arms. After that, we fled the country. Tired of surviving on banquet burgers, and dreading the thought of another winter in St. James Town, we had opted for early retirement – not for ever, perhaps, but certainly for the foreseeable future. To do so while we were still in our twenties and fully able to enjoy it seemed eminently logical.

LOVE IN IDLENESS

IN OUR IMAGINATIONS, Wendy and I had envisioned a life of ease: a Greek island lulled by the gentle zephyrs, a remote mountainside, an ancient stone house, a room with a view. It took us five days to find one, and five months to organize its purchase. The island was Corfu, the house a two-storey building, two hundred years old, with an acre of olive and almond and plum trees. It had no roof, a dirt floor, no electricity, and water had to be carried from the well on the other side of the village, but the view was indeed spectacular. I had only to lay down my pickaxe and glance up from the septic tank I was excavating out of the marble hillside to see tens of thousands of olive trees sweeping down to the coast. Beyond the cobalt Ionian, two miles away, soared the stark, jagged peaks of Albania.

We got the roof finished before the first storms of winter came thundering down from the

Adriatic, and by March we had fitted windows into the upstairs rooms to discourage the swallows from nesting. Wendy spent her eighth month of pregnancy carrying furniture down the mountainside, or on her hands and knees, sanding the cypress floors until the wood glowed like gold. We slept in our overcoats, creeping downstairs at dawn to light the tiny woodstove and the Calor gas ring for the kettle. The front door was on and the track that led down to the house almost finished by the time she went into labour, counting contractions as we hurtled around the mountain roads in our ancient Land Rover at three o'clock in the morning. The sky was pale as we reached the clinic in Corfu Town.

In the years that followed, we came to appreciate the backbreaking effort that underlies any primitive rural idyll, but our life was not without compensations. The beach was a forty-five-minute walk away (when measured with stroller and baby); Venice was two days by boat. We took that cruise only once. Part of our reason for choosing Corfu was to use our new home as the base for extravagant expeditions – down the Nile, up the Bosphorus and round the Black Sea, all over the Middle East – but we slowly lost interest in travel. As our Greek improved, the life of the village changed from a silent movie into cinéma-vérité, rich in its endless feuds and alliances, its profoundly rooted traditions, its festivals and its feasts. While I tried to master the vocabulary of the building trade, learning the words for various grades of gravel and sand, wire and cement, Wendy was being inducted into deeper mysteries by the young mothers of the hills. She would return from afternoons in their company dazed by gossip. None of the plot-lines and dramas that we had invented about our neighbours were half as bizarre as the truth.

The villagers, in their turn, found us curious and amusing. The men were scandalized when Wendy decided to rectify thousands of years of gender inequality by taking their wives to a discotheque on the coast for a girls' night out. The women thought it the funniest thing in the world when she told them I did all the cooking. For weeks after that little bombshell was dropped, visitors appeared at our door just before dinnertime to see if it really was true. They never interfered or offered advice to me, but the next day they spoke to Wendy, and a culinary tip or recipe usually found its way into the conversation. I was sincerely grateful. Though my mother always smuggled down treats in her suitcase whenever she came out to stay – pork pies and bacon, Cadbury's chocolate, a jar of Branston pickle – our ideas about food were rapidly changing. During our first year on the island, I had to learn how to cook all over again.

At first, it was a question of ingredients. Things we had always taken for granted – bananas and mushrooms, for instance – were simply not to be found; neither were onions one winter, the whole local crop lost to rain. Next, it was basic techniques: cooking with olive oil rather than butter, acquiring the patience to simmer a soup or a stew for six hours on the gentle hot plate of the woodstove and figuring out how to bake in its fitful oven, learning to leave well alone when faced with the island's marvellous produce. Eventually we realized that our whole attitude towards food had altered. It no longer bothered us that our fridge lacked a freezer: like our friends and neighbours, we ate only food that was fresh. What that food might be on a given day could only be guessed. Maybe the vegetable man would drive up the mountain in his heavily laden truck, bringing things that did not grow at this high, dry altitude: lemons and oranges, melons and vegetable marrows, fresh chickpeas and bunches of rock celery. Perhaps we would hear the drone of a moped in the silent afternoon: a fisherman with a crate of fresh mullet or plump little sardines, caught that morning down in the bay. There would always be things we wanted but could not have. I missed soy sauce, of all things; Wendy developed a desperate craving for black jujubes during her second pregnancy, a need that was only exacerbated by the sight of the tiny black lianolia olives on our trees.

There is no better way to learn about food than to grow it on your own land. We were absurdly extravagant with our water by local standards, always pouring it onto the ground, but the small crops we grew were as precious as treasure trove. Beyond the vegetable bed, the wild garden flourished unaided. In April the air was heavy with the sweet scent of purple iris; in October the dun-coloured tussocks of grass were jewelled with pink Persian cyclamen. If we ever thought of Canada, it was only to fantasize about washing machines and furnaces. Sometimes, late at night, I would pick up a static-infested broadcast of a Blue Jays game on the shortwave radio, relayed to the American air force base on the heel of Italy. Occasionally friends from Toronto would come out to stay, and we would listen politely to news of the city, news that seemed as insubstantial and irrelevant as the gossip of ancient Rome.

No doubt our guests found us profoundly insular and self-involved, for our lives had slowed to a barely perceptible pace. Projects were planned in terms of years – the construction of drystone walls, the nurturing of three elderly vines from which to make wine, the gathering of next winter's firewood that began when spring arrived each February and lasted all summer long. Through it all, there was the absorbing sight of our sons growing up. Joe turned three in 1986, Ford was eighteen months old, and we looked forward to the coming summer as a glorious emergence from the tyranny of the diaper. We wrote, and sometimes sold short stories to publishers in England. We baked cakes and bread and bartered them with our neighbours for eggs and fish. We made oil from our olives and picked herbs and wild plants on the sun-parched peaks behind the village. We learned how to dive for octopus, where to dig for clams on the sandbars, how to judge when the quinces were ripe on the gnarled old tree in our garden. When we needed a little cash, we would dress up in unaccustomed finery and drive down out of the mountains to the elegant casino outside Corfu Town, multiplying our small investment at the roulette tables on the moonlit terrace. We took our luck for granted and gave no thought to the future or to the past.

The summer of '86 was particularly beautiful on Corfu. Our acre of land was flourishing after four years of effort, and while the olive trees still worked to their own ancient agenda, the damson orchard brought forth a record crop of dusty amethyst fruit, oozing sweet, tangy juice that dried into resinous gems. "It's a plum summer," said Joe one July afternoon as we laboured over the jam-making, but for the three of us the sunlight was black.

Earlier that year, in April, Ford had suddenly stopped being able to walk. The local doctor diagnosed the problem as psychosomatic and suggested discipline would bring him to his senses. Instead, we took him to England, where it was discovered that he had leukemia. After six weeks of suffering, our little boy died. We buried the tiny casket that contained his ashes under an olive tree in the garden and lingered nearby for the rest of that fecund summer. Our Greek friends, with their fatalistic, unsequestered emotionalism, helped us to mourn him. In the fall, however, we finally conceded defeat, fastened the shutters, locked the front door, and moved back to Canada.

My wife had spent part of her childhood in Scarborough, and it was to Scarborough we returned – to a room in the Howard Johnson's on McCowan, to be precise. On our first evening we went down to the dining room and the three of us sat at a table for four. We ate hamburgers that tasted of sour white bread and the salty liquid that seeps out of cheap Canadian bacon. We made an effort with a salad, but the iceberg lettuce turned to cold water between our teeth and the tomato had the texture of cloth. For dessert, Joe chose a bowl of lime green sherbet. We were back in North America.

5

ᛥ CALITALIA ᛤ

Turning points in history, like other moments of truth, are often easier to recognize from a distance. Desdemona drops her handkerchief, but the audience only notices when Iago picks it up. Toronto did not step out of the shower on January 1, 1980, and decide it would instantly reinvent the way it dined out. There was no single defining moment when the new rich discovered that novelty had its own kind of status. Nevertheless, if you give or take a year, the turn of the decade had more than its share of beginnings. While Wendy and I were still living in London, gorging on cockles and curry, John Maxwell opened Joe Allen, Michael Carlevale gave us Carlevale's, two young chefs called Jamie Kennedy and Michael Stadtländer burst into the public eye at the newly created Scaramouche, and Franco Prevedello left the employ of John Arena to open first Biffi Bistro and then, a few months later and just across the road, Pronto.

In their own ways, each of these restaurants would influence the way Toronto thought about eating out in the years that followed. Exactly how and why is a matter of opinion. The Bonapartist school might argue that this talented group of individuals seized the city in their strong hands and squeezed it into small-restaurant consciousness. The Republican view might be that Toronto was changing anyway and that these chefs and restaurateurs were lucky to find themselves hoisted onto the shoulders of the new idea. Certainly Kennedy, Stadtländer, Prevedello, and, later on, Susur Lee achieved the sort of stardom that is accorded to few public servants. Like basketball super-stars, they became known by their first names, within and outside the industry. People who had never set foot in their restaurants were aware of their achievements, through word of mouth and through the reviews of Joanne Kates in the *Globe and Mail*. Merciless, opinion-ated, and entertainingly written in the sensual style of *New York* magazine's Gael Greene, Kates's weekly report was a dispatch from the front, devoured by her fans and her detractors.

Publicity is a curious implement. Chefs and restaurateurs respond to it in precisely the same way as actors and impresarios – or anyone else, come to that. If a review is good, they smile modestly and take it as their due. If it is bad, they present umpteen excuses and justifications, which may or may not be valid, but which are always irrelevant after the fact. They generate lashings of self-promotional hyperbole, but they have no respect for a reviewer who merely regurgitates such pap. Whenever a new play or a new restaurant opens, it is the ruthlessly independent critic's opinion that is turned to first. Because we are conditioned to believe what we read in the newspapers, the mere fact that the critic's judgments are set in type gives them authority. In his wise and funny book *The French at Table*, Rudolph Chelminski describes how two Parisian journalists, Henri Gault and Christian Millau, coined the phrase Nouvelle Cuisine, systematically set about glorifying its precepts, and then rode to fame and fortune on the bandwagon they had constructed. It's a tight little system of cause and effect. The food writer glorifies the chef; the chef becomes a celebrity; the food writer's judgment – and job – seem suddenly more important.

During the eighties, certain chefs and restaurateurs became stars. The way they cooked and the mood of their establishments reflected the values of that small section of the population who had decided that spending the evening in an expensive and sociable restaurant was exactly what they wanted to do. The food and the wine were important, of course, but so was the endless party. It began to matter whether one had been to the newest, most extravagant restaurant, had tasted the latest exotic ingredient, could spell its name. An element of snobbism oozed into the scene, with a hint of the sort of hysteria that always accompanies hero worship. For a restaurant to excite and entertain the fans it had to have a particular style, a glossy cachet that matched the public's increasingly narrow expectations.

There is nothing intrinsically wrong with this sort of adulation, I suppose, except that there are victims. When novelty is the watchword, the restaurant that cannot keep up, or chooses not to, seems suddenly unattractive. Consistent quality, the single most difficult achievement within the restaurant industry, is no longer valued. And woe betide the young couple who open their own little place based on notions of hospitality that do not match the mood of mode or the taste of the trendsetters.

In the boom time, a small group of high-end restaurants picked up speed and veered out onto the fast track of the fashion industry, with its exaggerated enthusiasms and its built-in obsolescence. Lacking the basic engineering to handle such speed, many crashed and burned, but enough survived to keep the race endlessly fascinating. And for most of the decade one man held the lead.

The restaurant as automobile is Franco Prevedello's metaphor. It is an image that pleases him, and he falls back on it tirelessly in his conversation, sometimes for fun, sometimes to sidestep too penetrating a question. Once, in the early days of his fame, a *Globe and Mail* reporter took him literally and informed her readers that he had been a racing-car driver back in Italy. Not quite, though he drives like a demon up the winding hill roads near his home town of Asolo, an hour or so northeast of Verona. I saw him once in Verona, in a sumptuous little restaurant called I Dodici Apostoli, near the old heart of the city. A compactly built man with curly black hair and a thick moustache, he sat at the head of a table of twenty men, the gracious host, charming them all with his stories.

"I was there," Michael Carlevale told me years later. "I had travelled with Franco to visit Vinitaly, the wine fair at Verona. Going through it with him was like walking with a demigod. He knows everybody."

Any attempt to understand Prevedello, his energy and motivation, his triumphs and his mistakes, the consummate skill with which he works a room, begins with Italy.

"He's a Venetian," said Carlevale. "What does that mean? Masks. Obfuscation. Mischief. And also money. The Venetian culture revolves around money the way other cultures revolve around violence. He comes from an ancient race of traders, and in his family, among his cousins, is unspeakable wealth – private jets, Palladian villas. I don't think his side of the family was ever that wealthy, but they were definitely people of standing in their community. They still are."

I once asked Prevedello himself about Asolo. It was early in the morning, the summer of 1990, and we were alone in the small upstairs dining area of his flagship restaurant, Centro. Images of the town surrounded us. At the mention of its name, Prevedello's guarded smile broadened. The lines around his hooded eyes vanished. He leaned forward in his chair, putting down his coffee cup to leave both hands free for talking.

"Asolo? Asolo is ... fan-tas-tic! A little jewel up in the hills. Unspoiled. It's a small walled town – an interesting town – small and big at the same time. My family has lived there for ever, and my mother, my brothers, and my sister still do. We are all very close. I call my mother religiously every Saturday night. By the time I finish work here it's two or three in the morning, so it's nine o'clock on a Sunday morning there. My mom brings me up to date with everything that's going on. She knows who everyone is and was, who married who, who killed who ... all the history. To have that sense of family and place – it's always a part of your life, a reassurance of the continuity of where you have come from, what you're doing, where you're going.

It lets you take risks, makes you more secure, more aggressive. You say to yourself, What can really go wrong?"

Prevedello gives an interview in the same way he works a room: with relentless energy. He talks quickly, placing the emphasis on favourite adjectives – fantastic, spectacular – and has something to say on any conceivable subject. His manner towards the press is usually one of professional deference, distanced sometimes by a hint of the gracious patrician. That morning, however, I saw nothing but passion and enthusiasm.

"Asolo … Asolando! I go back two or three times a year. My brother picks me up at the airport – Venice is only an hour away – and drives me home. I have to go home first, in case my mother finds out from someone else that I'm back. Then I head for the square, to the Caffè Centrale. Life revolves around the cafés in a small European town, and the Caffè Centrale is a mecca. Sooner or later everyone arrives.

"A week goes lightning fast. It's far too short a time. When my brother gets me to the airport, I'm exhausted, and so is he, because his pace of life is so different. You need more than a week to relax. Then you begin to gain calmness, strength. Your facial expression changes. You become aware of the smells. Walking through the town, down the Via Roberto Browning, you can smell where the bakery is, and the butcher, and the grocery with its aroma of cinnamon and coffee. Or go out in the countryside in October when the smell of winemaking is everywhere. Or in the winter when the small farmers make their own grappa in the hills – you can smell it a mile away. It's illegal but nobody bothers them."

The vivid images bubbled out. One of them in particular stuck in my mind. There had been a time of misjudgment before the Second World War, when all the family's assets had been turned into cash. Then the war came. Prevedello remembered sitting on the carpet as a child, playing with bags of bankers' drafts that were worth nothing. It was a good way to eliminate the mystique of money, reinforced in the years that followed. Prevedello's father was a merchant and young Franco often went with him to the market.

"He was never afraid of making or losing money," explained Prevedello, "buying, selling, bargaining, purchasing. Our lives were a roller-coaster of ups and downs. He died in a car accident when he was only fifty-two. That was in 1967, the same year I first came to Canada."

Six years earlier, at the age of fifteen, Prevedello had left home to train at the hotel school in Stresa, John Arena's old alma mater. He wanted to see the world, and the hospitality industry was the best available ticket. He found a job as a steward on passenger ships, working all hours, came to Toronto, where his sister was living, and eventually reached Montreal. Expo 67 needed professional personnel, and Prevedello ended up managing a dining room at the Ontario pavilion. It was there he met his wife, Barbara, the daughter of Ernie Jackson, one of the prominent Ontarians who had bought shares in Arena's Winston's. She was working at Expo as a hostess, and when the fair was over they married.

What did the twenty-one-year-old Italian waiter make of his wealthy London, Ontario, in-laws? What did they make of him, come to that? "I did what I wanted to do," said Prevedello with a shrug. "I had travelled, I understood what makes things happen, what doesn't make things happen." He spent a summer working for his sister's husband in the construction industry, then took a job as a waiter down at the Westbury Hotel, where Tony Roldan was chef. Within a year, he moved on, first to the Lord Simcoe, then to the Hyatt House. Colleagues were puzzled by his restlessness, but for Prevedello, the joy lay in the challenge of problem-solving. When the day-to-day operation became too smooth and easy, his instinct told him to leave. "With me, instinct is everything," he explained. "I've never done a market survey, a forecast, a business plan. My wife supplies the logic. She does all the bookkeeping and keeps the money straight. All my decisions are based on feeling and balance – like walking at night and not bumping into the furniture."

In 1974 Prevedello joined John Grieco's La Scala. His sights were set on a junior partnership, but he soon realized he had entered a family situation. Grieco's son Charles would eventually take over, and there was no opportunity for advancement or innovation. After a year, he left.

"I wanted freedom. I wanted to do something, so I went out and bought Quo Vadis on Church Street. The place was as dead as a doornail, and ugly! Completely different from what I wanted it to be. But I worked hard."

A year later, Prevedello was once again free. By his account, he had turned Quo Vadis around; others have called it a frustrating false start. Either way, he sold the place for what he had paid, and went to work for John Arena, as a maître d' at Winston's. Though they have had their differences in recent years, Arena found him an exemplary employee.

"Yes, he did a good job. He was never strong on the flambé cart, but he was a good orchestrator at sitting people down. He knew what to recommend, what not to recommend when the kitchen was under pressure, when to move in and out of conversation. But he was only at Winston's for a few months. Then an opportunity came up at Trillium in Ontario Place, and I put him in there as the catering director. A difficult job. You had to be able to take care of two thousand people, and on the same day look after the party of fifteen members of Parliament. He did an extremely good job for me over three or four years in several locations, and left of his own accord. After that, I think he became engulfed in what he was doing in the city, and perhaps he forgot some of the friends who helped him along the way."

Michael Carlevale was also working for Arena at the time. "That's how I first met Franco," he told me. "I remember him conceiving Biffi, scribbling that famous logo on a napkin. The modern Italian restaurant was invented in Milan and shipped throughout the world by other people. It was Franco who codified it for us in Toronto, first at Biffi, up on Mount Pleasant, then at Pronto. He had been away from Italy for a while. I see it as an original act of creation. Those two restaurants galvanized society. There was a polish, a product, an attitude, that everyone had to be part of."

"Biffi!" To this day, Prevedello cannot say the name without a nostalgic smile. "There was a magic to that place! I just wanted to do a small restaurant with a lot of soul. I'm driving home, see the little building, think it's going to work, go in there and try it, and design it upside down, with the kitchen in the front, a skylight at the back rather than the usual way around, and the little piano bar upstairs where Hagood Hardy used to play jazz every Monday. I think in one way Biffi was the breakthrough of the small restaurant. It wasn't the first with an open kitchen, but it was one of the first of the high-end restaurants to do it. We scraped and borrowed from friends and family, put together some money. My partner was Corrado Furlanetto, who was also working for Arena, though we had met in 1972 at Hyatt House. After a while, Raffaello Ferrari came over from Italy and took over as chef. A few months later, in 1980, we opened Pronto, just across the street."

As ever, Prevedello's timing in opening Biffi and Pronto was instinctive: "Nothing is guaranteed. You just think, Let's try it!" It was also right on the money. Press and public loved the New Italian cooking, with less emphasis on the big sauce and more on prime ingredients, good healthy olive oil as a condiment, the grill rather than the frying pan. The uptown location was quirkily attractive – closer to Forest Hill and the well-heeled enclaves of Hoggs Hollow, Lawrence Park, and the Bridle Path than any of the restaurants previously patronized by the rich.

But perhaps the real innovation was one of mood. Somewhere early in his career, maybe at Winston's, maybe before, Prevedello had absorbed the fact that customers liked to bask in the reflected status of an ostentatiously successful restaurant. Biffi was witty: customers did a double-take when they realized they could actually see into the kitchen. Pronto's look was success as defined by the eighties – the glamour of mirror, oversized floral displays, the hot glow of red neon signage, the whole effect coolly assertive, the antithesis of stuffy. Above all, there was Prevedello himself, svelte in shirt and tie, working harder than anyone else, meeting and greeting, muttering instructions to the waiters, recommending a wine, changing an ashtray, pausing for a moment to boost a customer's ego with words of recognition, a joke, a touch on the arm. He was the owner, not an employee, a fact that resonated in all sorts of discreet ways in any conversation with a customer. And his energy was contagious, dazzling when compared with the stately progress of the traditional European maître d'.

In spite of the success of Biffi and Pronto, the partnership with Furlanetto eventually ended in rancour. He kept Biffi, Prevedello kept Pronto – and chef Raffaello Ferrari. "In our industry," Prevedello once philosophized, "partnership is such a delicate thing, because it's such a personal business. Sometimes it ends up in shambles because ego becomes more important than day-to-day business, and then more important than the financial side. People get carried away. They forget that it's always one, two, three, a hundred pennies in a dollar."

For Prevedello, those dollars began to accumulate. Pronto doubled in size, but soon its owner was once again growing restless. He embarked on a series of projects designed to satisfy his urge as a builder, a creator of restaurants, without stretching himself too thin or tying himself down for too long. Buying and selling real estate has always fascinated him, and has always bankrolled his restaurants: very few people know the full extent of his properties in Toronto and the Veneto. The 1982 mini-recession and its aftermath offered irresistible opportunities. Prowling his Lawrence Park neighbourhood, he spotted a Greek restaurant called Elios, bought it, renovated, and reopened as Bindi, with Jack Guenzi as partner. When success was assured, he sold most of his share of the business to Guenzi, retaining a small percentage and receiving the rent. In 1983 he repeated the process when he bought a veteran restaurant called Le Gourmet, on Yonge Street below Hoggs Hollow, and leased it to chef Gary Hoyer.

The Prevedello connection ensured newspaper coverage and the curiosity of his fans, but it was nothing compared with the press he received for Expo 86 in Vancouver. He had already contributed advice about fitting a practical restaurant into the Ontario pavilion – "a beautiful building, but a nightmare operation." Now, as other Toronto restaurateurs, including John Arena, gathered to present their detailed bids for the project, he sat down at the back of the room and listened.

"At the end of the day I went home and wrote a very short proposal on a piece of paper – I will do this for this amount, this percentage of sale, no basic rent, I'll find my own apartment, don't worry about me. I put it under their door." The proposal was accepted.

If there was a certain satisfaction at beating Arena to the contract, a sense of supplanting the established master of high-volume catering, Prevedello was far too busy to dwell on it. He moved out to Vancouver with a kitchen and service team of 130 people, and Raffaello Ferrari as chef, flying in Ontario produce from goat cheese to lamb to Inniskillin wines.

Serving eighteen hundred people a day, seven days a week, Expo was a personal triumph for Prevedello, and also an invaluable dress rehearsal for the next venture he had in mind. His return to Toronto could have been an anticlimax, but there was no question of resting on laurels. Before leaving for Vancouver, he had sold Pronto to Peter Costa, Leslie Kubicek, and Mark McEwan, the hot young chef from the Sutton Place Hotel. He had also acquired the lease on a carpet showroom at Yonge and Castlefield, and in February 1987 he started work on the property, excavating the basement himself with the help of such friends as Ferrari and Al Carbone, later the owner of Kit Kat. Publisher Al Cummings would show up with take-out lunch from Grano, Roberto Martella's restaurant, where Prevedello was landlord and avuncular adviser.

In November 1987, Prevedello opened Centro, his magnum

opus. Its design resembled a cathedral, complete with a columned nave, a gallery, a private chapel by the door, a sheet of plate glass like an altar screen, behind which the gastronomic mysteries were celebrated. The walls were all hung with pictures, but not of the saints. Adding humanity to the in-your-face opulence were photographs of Asolo, of people Prevedello had known all his life. His inspiration was his home town's Caffè Centrale, the social hub, transposed through some millions of dollars into a three-level space of glass and bright colour where his clientele could feel just as much at the heart of things.

"It was a calculated act of hubris!" exclaimed Michael Carlevale. "To establish a city-dominating restaurant in that part of town ... No one goes to Yonge and Eglinton. But Franco said, 'This is the centre! This is where you will come!' And they did."

Centro was an extrapolation of Pronto and the Expo adventure, with a peppering of the Veneto, and a splash of the food and mood of California stirred into the mix. Perhaps Prevedello was not the first Toronto restaurateur to bring the Cal-Ital ethos north, but he was the first to import upscale San Francisco and announce the fact, loud and clear. He loved the notion of a restaurant that was beautiful and luxurious but also fresh and informal, where people could show up in jeans or in a tuxedo and order pizza with a $150 bottle of Sassicaia. That was the goal; that was the achievement, especially in the downstairs piano bar. Prevedello liked to use the space as a venue for tastings of the fine wines he imported privately from Italy, another line of business that had a significant impact on Toronto's increasingly well-informed, ever more Italianate tastes. It also became quietly renowned as a meet market for suits of both sexes. Everything, in fact, was absolutely fabulous, except perhaps in the kitchen.

Prevedello's rages with employees were legendary. Over the years, many a cook or waiter walked out of a job, unable to cope with the boss's temper, the yelling and screaming, the attitude. His ability to switch from one mode to the other in the time it takes to walk from dining room to kitchen used to astonish Michael Bonacini, the tall Welshman who was Centro's co-chef from 1990 to 1993. "I'd go out to chat with a guest and Franco would always come up and squeeze my arm and say, 'Michael, can I get you a glass of Champagne?' With total sincerity. And I'd think, Two minutes ago the man wanted my balls!

"My years there were among the most exciting of my life, but it was survival of the fittest. I come from a traditional European background, where to have someone shouting in fury in the kitchen was a normal event. But you'd get these young Canadian cooks and waiters, and they'd fill their underwear. I think those that stayed found it an invaluable education. Being yelled at by Franco ought to be on the George Brown curriculum. And alongside the terrorism goes a remarkable generosity. He would literally kick you in the arse and curse you all night long because you broke a wineglass, then he'd slip one of the cleaners $600 to have his teeth fixed because the guy didn't have the money."

Over the years, a fair number of friends and acquaintances benefited from this unpublicized streak of charity: advice, money, inspiration, freely given. For most soldiers in the restaurant business, however, Prevedello was always a faraway figure with a famous temper and a much-envied share of the limelight. "He could have been a leader within our industry," John Arena once suggested, "an ambassador, a teacher."

"Teaching? That may come," replied Prevedello, without much conviction. "But you know, I'm already in the training business! You work for me, you may think I'm crazy, you may like me or dislike me, but at the end of the day you will have learned something. As for the organizations of restaurant owners, they come and go. I'm happy to lend my name to a good cause, but I don't like the politics that goes on. I don't have time for that. It's just that my head is always busy, always putting things together, a winery here, a restaurant there, a little real estate. Ideas for new places are coming into my head all the time. It's a continual evolution. Architecturally, as soon as I finish one restaurant I want to burn it to the ground and start all over again. I would have liked to have been an architect. I can't draw, I can't do any of that, but it fascinates me. It comes from growing up in Asolo, from being surrounded by fantastic architecture, Palladian villas, buildings from the fifteenth, sixteenth, seventeenth centuries. You take them for granted, but somehow you absorb them. You may not realize it's there, but you carry a sense of dimensions inside you. It's part of what you are. At Centro, for instance, to create the feel of a piazza took me two seconds because the feel of it was already there inside me."

Is that what drove Prevedello through the eighties: the restless creative urge of the builder? Or were there other sources of motivation?

"He loves work," was the explanation I heard from Michael Bonacini. "It's that simple. At Centro, he had a routine. He'd be there first thing in the morning, tinkering around with things, fixing drains, repairing refrigerators, changing light fittings, then he'd have an afternoon nap. At seven, he'd come back, all charged up, ready to go. Little problems would be solved when most of the staff had gone home. My co-chef Marc Thuet and Franco and I would stay up talking until four or five in the morning, maybe planning new menu items. Franco has certain dishes that constantly come back because he loves them – polenta and liver, veal chop and porcini sauce. He'd say, 'How about we do some beautiful liver, caramelized with butter and oil, with soft polenta?' We'd say, 'But we did that last winter,' and he'd say, 'Yeah, but it's beautiful, spectacular, a little mascarpone ... stupid simple!' That's one of his lines. It means any idiot can do it. Only no one could ever do it exactly the way he wanted."

Bonacini was right, of course. Prevedello loves work. He also enjoys success, not because it can buy him freedom or time, but because of the status it brings, in Asolo as well as in Toronto. Is money also a motive? If it were that simple, he would surely have chosen a field with better returns and more security. I asked him if risk was part of the plea-sure. "Maybe," he shrugged. "Maybe it's that immigrant feeling. I think an immigrant always has a certain insecurity concealed within himself. I never want to lose that spirit of saying, 'If I want to, I can just pack a suitcase and do it again somewhere else.' It's almost a test on yourself to see that you're not frightened of moving. It's part of you. Part of doing."

LATE IN THE WINTER of 1995, I interviewed Prevedello again. He had proposed a meeting at Acqua, his one-year-old restaurant in BCE Place, on Front Street. As always, at lunchtime, the place was packed, with jovial downtown suits lined up three deep at the bar, tucking into olives and almonds while they waited for tables. In a blue shirt and crimson silk tie, Prevedello was guiding a party of four through the crowd, telling a waiter to clear a plate as he passed, to bring water here, over there a bottle of wine. His daughter, Barbara, appeared: a telephone call. "Take a message." Behind her, a customer hovered, his uncertainty turning to preening gratitude when Prevedello paused to greet him before darting behind the bar to make espresso for eight. I wondered if Franco had chosen the time and place of our rendezvous as a way of showing me that Il Padrone's legendary powers were still undimmed.

There was no hiding the lines of exhaustion around his eyes as he joined me at last at a table. His fiftieth birthday was approaching rapidly, but the stress came from other quarters. Five years had passed since we had sat down together at Centro and talked about Asolo. Today, there were other, more difficult questions on his mind and on mine: matters to do with a sudden reverse in his fortunes, with errors of judgment and restaurants that had closed unexpectedly. Like the circus performer who sets plates spinning on rods, Prevedello had seemed to defy the gravity of the recession, bringing on chefs and managers to keep the crockery airborne, taking the bows to sustained applause. Then his hands-on attention had strayed. The last twelve months had been a financial disaster. He had lost Terra, Acrobat, Acrobat Bis. There had been heckling from the industry, even the press. Voices hitherto silent were suddenly calling "I told you so," with barely disguised satisfaction.

There are low points in the careers of most restaurateurs, moments when news-hungry editors scent blood and release their hounds. It's the one repellent aspect of my particular job, and I frequently try to postpone the distasteful phone call until the deadline has passed. Often my embarrassment is mitigated by the victim's reaction. Some are gracious in their dignity. Others are filled with rage and resentment, directed not towards me but against some real or imagined enemy. They are eager to tell their tale to whoever will listen, cursing absconded partners, ignorant customers, a conspiracy of municipal tax collectors, or just the vindictive Fates.

Prevedello, as it turned out, had no wish to blame anyone for recent events, not even himself. We both knew the issues that would eventually have to be discussed, but he began by diverting the conversation onto happier subjects. Centro was doing well. Bonacini had left in 1993, but Marc Thuet, a man whose robust energy and cheerful, generous spirit match his enormous talent, had stayed on as executive chef. Thuet and manager Tony Longo, who had joined the restaurant as a waiter in 1988, had clubbed together to buy 50 percent of the business for a substantial sum. The negotiations had been typical of deals that involve Prevedello – everything agreed in three seconds flat, then fifteen months of ulcer-inducing legal nitty-gritty – the prevarication that Bonacini once called the Prevedello Dance. "Lawyers," grumbled Franco. "The evil of the twentieth century."

As for Acqua: it was coming together after a shaky start, and Prevedello still owned the option on a rented property down in Palm Beach – "a spectacular building, very high ceilings, just off Worth Avenue. It was once the Rolls-Royce showroom." Plans for a restaurant in the space, with Georges Gurnon as possible partner, were merely on hold. He had acquired the Canadian rights to Replay jeans (the high-end pants owned by a young man from Asolo) and was constructing a store on Queen Street West in which to sell them. The upstairs floors would be offices for his wine agency. He had finally disengaged himself from the lease of the massive stone Ombudsman's Building at Bloor and Avenue Road – another stillborn project – and three days earlier he had bought a couple of buildings on Yonge Street, one of which housed the restaurant Azalea.

"So you see, I'm keeping busy." He smiled, his hands smoothing the air, stroking the sides of an invisible object. "There are times for sitting back a little, taking stock. Maybe this is such a time. It's true that I lost some millions, but I can still eat. As a small businessman, you have to be flexible. You get up in the morning. You say, 'Okay, it's another day, let's carry on.' You can't grow if you stay still. Acrobat cost me money; the space is still costing me money, but I'm not going to walk away. The location is great, the space is great. I love a high ceiling. If I have that, I can work with anything else."

Prevedello had opened Acrobat in August 1992, in the old premises of Noodles at Bay and Bloor. Nightclub maestro Charles Khabouth was the collaborating partner, and the extravagantly over-decorated room was split down the middle with a restaurant on one side and a bar on the other. It might have worked, but while Prevedello's customers came to eat, Khabouth's equally recognizable, totally different clientele came to drink and hang out. The oil and the vinegar failed to form an emulsion. As Tony Longo defined it: "When a guy who has spent a thousand dollars on dinner goes back the next night in leathers and jeans and the doorman won't pick him out of the lineup, that's not Toronto." In the end, Khabouth walked away from the project; Acrobat teetered for months and finally closed. But Prevedello refused to admit defeat. He hired Claude Bouillet as chef, with Georges Gurnon and Marcel Réthoré to manage the front of house, and reopened quickly as Acrobat Bis. Nobody came. The experiment collapsed in a matter of months and Prevedello was left with a dark property and an unbreakable lease, paying out a fortune each month in rent.

Terra had been terrific when it opened in June 1993, a suburban version of Centro, designed to attract the well-heeled denizens of

Thornhill. This time, Prevedello's hands-on partner and executive chef was his old friend and former right hand, Raffaello Ferrari. There had been bad feeling around Ferrari's departure from Centro in 1990. First, Michael Bonacini and Marc Thuet arrived and joined him in the kitchen. After an increasingly uncomfortable couple of months, Ferrari moved out to work in the dining room. There was talk that he might partner Prevedello in a new project on Harbord Street, to be called Splendido, but instead Franco brought in Arpi Magyar as chef (he had cooked at Pronto in the old days) and one of Centro's managers, Paolo Paolini, to handle the front of house. It was another inspired idea, but it left Ferrari feeling unwanted. He finally left the fold for John Maxwell's Orso, where he cooked brilliantly, then suddenly took off for California. In 1992, he reappeared in Thornhill, as partner and co-chef with Gary Hoyer in a colourful little Italian restaurant called Tutto Bene. He was still there a year later when Prevedello brought him on board at Terra.

Friends warned that Ferrari was prey to persistent addictions, but Prevedello decided to risk it, for old times' sake. At first, all went swimmingly. The modern Italian menu at Terra was a triumph. Then Ferrari's demons once again sank their teeth into him. The drugs that fuelled his after-hours parties and which always seemed to be available when there was cash in the till were no longer recreational. He stopped coming into work, was seen here and there along Queen Street. Friends such as Albino Silva, owner of Chiado, tried to talk him down. Al Carbone, always ready to lend a hand to a chef in trouble, gave him a job in the kitchen at Kit Kat, but Ferrari was slipping beyond their reach. A charming, talented, much-loved man, he was only forty-one when he died of an overdose.

Terra had already closed. This time, however, Prevedello was able to divest, selling the business and the name. "It's doing well now," he pointed out, "which is a good sign that the basics were right. The location, the design. The car was good; it just needed a different driver. Acrobat? Maybe the same. Why, what, where, who is to blame? Maybe I am to blame as much as anybody else. It's like playing billiards. You take your eyes off the ball, it's no good. All of a sudden you're not there and it gets very tricky. Other people have made the same – not 'mistakes,' the same moves that I made. I don't call them failures. I'm still here, still keeping going. Financially, I don't make a step unless I know I can carry it through. I always put myself under water a little bit, but not so far down that I can't resurface."

An image bubbled up in my mind: the young Prevedello watching his father wheel and deal with the traders of Asolo, revelling in the ups and downs of commerce. Much more than any abiding reverence for the hospitable soul of the restaurant industry, more than any love for fine food and wine, more than the showmanship and the social status brought by success, it has always been the entrepreneurial action that moves Prevedello to passion, the achievements of his career far less compelling than the ceaseless act of achieving.

Through his energy and attention to detail, his instinct for what his public wants next, his intuitive sense of what makes a restaurant work, he gave this city an unparalleled series of spectacular restaurants. Their looks and their internal operating systems, their menus and wine lists, inspired countless imitations. They did not add up to an empire, for each was too individualistic in its conception, too reliant upon the ever-present hand. There was never anything corporate about the merchant-adventurer.

I asked him if he had any regrets. He could have stayed at Centro, grown old there, spent a little more time with his family. "Or I could have stayed at Biffi, or Pronto. Or just concentrated on the wine business. But where is the challenge? What am I going to do? Retire? Play golf? I don't know how to play golf. Retiring to me would be having the freedom to do what I want to do – which is to do more, more of the same."

ONE YEAR after our meeting, Prevedello sold Acqua to the restaurant's chef, Rob Buchanan, and general manager, Helder Carvalho. Eight months later, in June 1997, he sold his remaining 50 percent of Centro to his partners, Tony Longo and Marc Thuet. Prevedello was still their landlord, as he was to so many restaurateurs in the city, but suddenly, for the first time in twenty years, he had no restaurant of his own in which to perform. His wife, Barbara, seemed slightly stunned. "I'm hoping we'll have a chance to do some travelling," she told me. "Franco wants to expand the wine agency's portfolio, and the Replay jeans franchise will keep him busy."

Six months went by before I saw Prevedello again. A grey October afternoon found us at Splendido on Harbord Street, standing around near the bar in a throng of chefs and caterers, journalists, and photographers. It was the media preview of a charity gala, raising funds to send students from the Ontario College of Art and Design to Florence. Prevedello was chairman of the event, but he seemed to have other things on his mind. He took me by the arm and led me aside.

"Have you heard about my hotel?" he asked. "The plans are coming together. We're breaking ground early in '98, down at the corner of Charles Street and St. Thomas. It will be a fantastic little hotel."

Ever since Centro's sale, foodies of a speculative bent had wondered when and where Prevedello would reappear. We had grasped at the rumours that he was about to create a highly sophisticated boutique hotel called the Florian a stone's throw from the old Windsor Arms. Now he filled in some gaps: the names of architects and designers from Toronto and New York, some dimensions, some details. A beautiful bar – spectacular. His voice fell to a murmur. And he was thinking of bringing Wolfgang Puck up from California to collaborate on the hotel's one-hundred-seat restaurant. I asked why he felt he needed a collaborator. He shrugged. The idea of creating restaurants on his own no longer excited him.

"Where is the challenge these days?" he growled. "At one point, in this city, the standard of restaurants rose very far and very fast, but for years now, it has been flat and level. I look about me and I see nothing new, nobody taking the next step."

What might the next step be? I wanted to ask Prevedello, but he was leaving for Asolo that evening and could not linger. "I'll keep you informed," he said.

☜ THE CALL OF THE WILD ☞

THE OLD GUY pulled off his tartan hat and scratched his head, pulling a face of comic quizzicality. "Ya lived in Greece, eh?" he repeated. "Seems to me, Greece is what I fry my bacon in!"

Guffaws.

"Don't mind him," advised the woman behind the counter, chuckling as she refilled our cups with the sweet brown water she called coffee. "That's just a joke."

I guess it was just a joke – in the same way that the room in which we were sitting just qualified as a restaurant, as well as a beer and pool bar, TV room, and lodge for the scattering of snowed-in summer cabins on the property. It was November 1986, a month after our second return to Canada. As a break from looking for a place to rent in Toronto, we had come north to stay with Wendy's mother and stepfather in their beautiful home in Muskoka. We had driven over to this little resort to use its laundromat, and while the washing machines shuddered and shook and the industrial-sized dryers churned static into our long-suffering clothes, we stamped across the parking lot in search of lunch.

The frozen North. Frozen burgers and frozen fries. If they were lucky they were introduced to a skillet before the final indignity – tossed into a basket lined with a paper napkin. If not, they were doomed to the three-minute purgatory of the microwave, simultaneously thawed and "cooked" in a grim parody of the culinary process until the telltale bell put an end to their suffering. Ask not for whom the microwave dings: it dings for thee.

Like many a landed immigrant, I had once harboured visions of the matchless produce of the Canadian wilderness, a land teeming with game, each swollen lake and stream coruscating with fish, every forest glade abundant with berries and rare mushrooms, fiddleheads, wild honey, wild ginger, and wild leeks – the bounty of the inexhaustible hinterland. There must be dozens of charming restaurants in Muskoka, I imagined, where dedicated chefs worked with such fascinating ingredients, to the delight of the wealthy Torontonians who owned cottages in the area. No doubt that explained why there was no decent game in Toronto: the good stuff was all ending up in the kitchens of these little rural gems.

It didn't take long to shatter that particular illusion. Muskoka was muffin country, the land of the cheeseball and the dip, the burger and the barbecue. Each small town had its quota of fast-food franchises, its Junk Chinese restaurant, its quaint tearoom where the fruit pies and quiches were good but anything more complicated was a disaster. There was excellent cooking going on at the most exclusive resorts, but we could not afford to eat there, and though friends and relatives spoke enthusiastically about Gladys Fraser's idiosyncratic, deliciously domestic restaurant, Spot on 7, they felt obliged to add that it had closed some years before and the excellent Ms. Fraser had passed away. Now there was nothing left on the slipstreams between city and cottage country to compete with Paul Weber's burger stand. For us, the only good meals north of Barrie were the dinners my mother-in-law cooked with vegetables from her garden and fish we caught ourselves in the lake at the end of her lawn.

Such treats provided considerable consolation, but they could not make up for the one overriding irony: in a land of forest and wilderness, why was the game presented in restaurants so profoundly dull? That corner of the menu should have been a place of pilgrimage, where culinary art embraced the province's most delectable aboriginal and pioneer traditions; instead, it was a desert of disappointment. Chefs bent over backwards with marinades and fortified pan juices, spices and fruits, but their venison still tasted like beef. Their pheasants may have looked like bona fide English ringnecks in life, but they tasted like tough old capon on the plate.

One reason has to do with hanging. For a mature pheasant to develop the delicious pungency proper to a game bird, it should be hung, undrawn and unplucked, for eight or nine days at cellar temperature. Ontario's early settlers knew this and wrote with relish of many a well-hung brace. These days, farm-reared birds are hung for a maximum of an hour before being packed off to a processing plant. Expert opinions differ about why this is the case. Some shrug and say North Americans just like their meat squeaky clean. Others blame government paranoia, the same ill-informed, paternalistic hypochondria that recently threatened our supply of raw milk cheese. In fact, bacteria perish in a properly roasted bird. The most likely explanation is that wholesalers prefer not to tie up their production lines with a warehouse full of stationary fowl.

The short-hanging theory explains why our pheasant are such banal eating, but where animals are concerned, it's only a part of the story. There are butchers in Toronto who hang their venison properly, for ten days or so, in the fur. That would certainly be long enough to coax out some flavour, were it not for the fact that the deer are farm-raised. The flesh of game birds and animals that live on manmade feed ends up unnaturally fatty, often pallid and invariably bland. Again, the problem lies with the law. Chefs and butchers alike find their hands are tied as tightly as a trussed grouse by bureaucratic red tape, because the province insists that all game meat sold in our shops and restaurants must be farm-reared and must come from animals not indigenous to Ontario.

"It's for the best," Wendy's stepfather, Weldon, told me. "Otherwise, you'd have every guy who owns a gun emptying the forest to feed Toronto's greedy gourmets." As it is, hunters are forbidden to sell their tiny quota of wild meat: they must either take it home and eat it themselves or give it away. "A lot of it gets donated to the Shriners," mused Weldon, "for the Beast Feast. I could get us a couple of tickets if you'd like to go."

THE BRACEBRIDGE CENTENNIAL CENTRE was a stark, utilitarian hall, but the local unit of the Shriners Rameses Temple had gussied it up for the annual November Stag Night (a term they preferred to Beast Feast). Paper-covered trestle tables, a coupon bar, door prizes, and four blackjack tables lent the place a party atmosphere, as did the Shriners themselves, resplendent in red or tartan jackets and fezzes glittering with jewelled scimitars as badges of rank. The Shriners are senior Freemasons who use their spare time to raise money for charity. The Bracebridge unit had a muster of about 150 active members, and this was one of three regular fundraising events, eagerly awaited by the community as both a social and a culinary spree.

In charge of the centre's tiny kitchen was Max Beaumont, affable and unflustered as he checked a brim-full twenty-gallon cauldron of rabbit stew and fourteen saddles of beaver roasting slowly in the ovens. Most of them were "blanket beavers," their hide measuring seventy-two inches by sixty-five, big enough to have earned a native trapper payment of a blanket, once upon a time. Beaumont had personally removed the musk and castor glands from the saddles. One year the cook forgot to do it and the meat smelt so high no one would touch it.

There was no room here for larger game, so the Shriners used the huge teaching kitchens of the local secondary school, where John Hudswell ran the food technology program. Weldon and I drove up before the feast began and found him instructing eight of his ninety students in the art of carving moose. The meat looked deliciously tender. It had been marinated for thirty-six hours in red wine and olive oil and then soaked overnight in buttermilk to temper its gamey flavour. Roasting time had been precisely judged. Although local tastes insisted on well-done meat, wild game is low in fat and dries out quickly if cooked too long.

The bestiary of the Stag Nights had dwindled in recent years. Bear, once a staple, had been banned because the animals foraged around garbage dumps and their meat contained the pork bacterium *Trichinella*. Deer liver was another traditional treat until levels of cadmium in the organ rendered it potentially dangerous. No one knew where the heavy metal was coming from, but sources at the Ministry of Agriculture suspected it leached naturally from the ground. Despite such restrictions, there were plenty of other wild delicacies to please the Shriners: five hundred pounds of meat among three hundred men. John Hudswell supposed there might be enough left over at the end of the evening to fill a small paper bag.

The party was well under way by the time we got back to the Centennial Centre. Shriners from Caledon and Parry Sound had arrived in force, as had the Tecumseh men, complete with accordion fanfare. Tables were filling up with local fathers and sons, big bellies and baseball caps, sweaters and plaid. Old acquaintances were renewed, and old jokes revived to considerable hilarity. I took a place near the kitchen and found myself seated with a policeman, a conservation officer, a Crown attorney, the man who played Santa Claus during the summer at Bracebridge's local theme park, and a musician called Ike Kelneck. Ike had run a trapline for years and the novelty of wild meat had worn off long ago, but he was keenly looking forward to his share of fifty dozen New Brunswick oysters served on the half shell.

Other hors d'oeuvres were available at the buffet: tangy Nova Scotia kippers called Digby chicks, plates of crudités served with a light mayonnaise dip, and mountainous troughs of moose nuggets. These turned out to be small pieces of moosemeat sausage, spiced with pepper and garlic. The Shriners and their guests stood about like jugglers, each balancing a plastic glass, a paper napkin, and two or three nuggets, reaching over periodically to dip them into a bowl of sickly-sweet Oktoberfest honey mustard.

Finally the big game arrived. There was beaver, moist and delicious, textured like a turkey leg with a rich, sweet flavour that reminded me of kid. There were thick slices of venison and moose, their densely fibred but tender meat only hinting at the aromas of the wilderness. One tray was piled with hunks of chucker, a species of woodcock, and another with crudely dismembered pheasant. These last began life as farm birds but were purchased by the township and released into the wild for the benefit of local sportsmen. Unless they stock the forest with an annual quota of two hundred birds, townships are forbidden to charge for gun licences. Perhaps it was too early in the season, but I'd hoped for more flavour from the pheasant. Another minor disappointment was the rabbit stew, marred by what Ike Kelneck called industrial dipping gravy, but baked whitefish from a native reserve on Georgian Bay were superb, quietly stealing the show. To provide the feast with a much-needed respite from protein, the Shriners had broken with tradition and added coleslaw to the menu. For dessert, Max Beaumont brought out a brigade-sized pot of sticky baked beans in molasses, known in these parts as Muskoka caviar.

The banquet proved immensely popular with the hungry men of Bracebridge. Santa Claus warned me that beaver meat could be indigestibly rich. "It's the beer, not the beaver," quipped his neighbour, the cop. A bagpiper appeared, to wild applause, prizes were auctioned off, and the smile beneath each gem-crusted fez grew increasingly good-humoured. But there was more to the evening than moose meat and making merry. "Our unit raises about $35,000 a year," Max Beaumont told me, "and it all goes to the Shriners' Hospitals, twenty-two of them across the continent, for burned and crippled children."

Weldon and I had such a good time that he promised to keep an ear open for similar events. Two months later, he called to say he had found one, the annual shindig organized by the Hill and Gully Riders, a snowmobiling club based in Port Sydney. Driving north from Toronto under a bruised and snow-laden sky, I wondered what I was in for. That winter there had been several stories in the newspapers about drunken fools wrapping their machines around a tree, or going through the ice on a lake. The press seemed to see snowmobilers as some sort of snowbound Hell's Angels gang, and as I drew into Port Sydney I had visions of flickering flames in the benighted forest, dangerous, beer-basted men tearing at hunks of charred meat, and Ski-Doos careering across the ice like the motorized hordes of Genghis Khan.

The Hill and Gully Riders, I discovered, weren't like that at all. The club was one of the oldest in Ontario and was run by dedicated volunteers who were as careful about law and order as they were about grooming their 180 kilometres of immaculate trails. With thirteen hundred members from all over the province, their patronage kept tiny Port Sydney going during the endless Muskoka winter.

To accommodate the five hundred expected guests, the club had rented the Granite Ridge Lodge on Lake Devine, a forty-minute snowmobile ride from the town. It was a lonesome and peaceful spot, an old pine lodge surrounded by cabins in eighty-eight acres of unspoiled forest. I arrived at three-thirty, as the daylight was fading, and parked under the trees, my car outnumbered a hundred to one by snowmobiles. Behind the main building stood four massive charcoal barbecues. Two Riders wearing black leathers and chef's toques stood in the gently falling snow, turning mooseburgers and venison steaks and putting the finishing touches to foil-wrapped lake trout stuffed with lemon.

Inside, down in the lodge's games and recreation rooms, the mood was that of a huge family gathering. Children and grandparents, husbands and wives crowded tables before a cosy open fire or waited their turn at the buffet. The meats and fish came in from the barbecues in a steady parade, backed up by a roast of beaver, cauldrons of moose-meat chili, a dreadful chicken curry, hot dogs, salads, and rabbit stew. Five dollars bought me all I could eat – which turned out to be a lot, for the game had been beautifully prepared and skilfully cooked.

"It's all butchered and hung by the trappers who donate it," explained Fred Rogers, one of the club's oldest members, "and hung for a good long time. The venison's wild and it's had two weeks in the fur. That's why it's so tender you can cut it with a fork." The cooks outside had told me they just slapped the meat on the coals, but that was no more than macho bravado. The beaver meat had been mari-nated in water and vinegar, the larger joints of venison were fragrant with garlic, herbs, and wine, and the rabbit stew was a thoroughly pro-fessional job, the meat tender, the vegetables still fresh and firm.

"People up here recognize good cooking, but they mistrust exotica," said Geoff Ivany, the resident chef at Granite Ridge but a guest that afternoon. "Last week I put a new dish on the menu: grilled breast of duck in a sauce of bourbon, shiitake, and lettuce mushrooms. I couldn't have moved it if I had called it that. I just wrote 'duck' on the menu and we sold the lot."

Almost anywhere in the world, beaver would seem a good deal more bizarre than a shiitake mushroom. Adventurousness is relative, I suppose. Fred Rogers remembered the year a whole goat was donated to the Beast Feast, butchered and served up beside the beaver and moose. "An elderly lady asked what it was, and I told her it was wolf. She came back for four helpings, but I don't believe she'd have touched it if she'd known it was goat."

Like the Shriners' Stag Night, the annual Beast Feast of the Hill and Gully Riders was more than a meal made up of gastronomic curiosities. Walking back to the car, long after nightfall, with the snow falling in the silence, I could still feel the warmth and hear the music and laughter of the gathered community. For one night at least they had drawn close to Canada's past. The abandoned braziers glowed crimson in the darkness. Far away to the north, very faintly, wolves were howling.

6

CANADIANA

"WHAT WERE Toronto restaurants like," I asked Wendy once, "when you were growing up? What was the heritage, the true Canadian cuisine?"

She looked at me pityingly. Suburban families in the sixties did not eat out often in those days. To go to a restaurant was a significant event, tied in with some major celebration. She could count the restaurants of her childhood on the fingers of one hand. The Ponderosa for steaks, the

CANADIANA

Old Mill for wedding receptions, Sai Woo or Lichee Garden for the exotic flavours of soy sauce and sweet and sour pork, Captain John's for seafood. Not a sensationally daring repertoire. But daring wasn't the point. When embarking on an expensive adventure like dinner, the suburban family preferred to know where it was going and exactly what it would find when it got there.

"But what about the romance of the restaurant? What about candlelight?"

Romance was also covered. The most sophisticated date was dinner at La Chaumière, Toronto's first French restaurant, famous for its hors d'oeuvres trolley, checkered tablecloths, and air of Gallic savoir-faire. Opened in 1939, a year after Oscar Berceller founded Winston's, it was familiar to Wendy's parents' generation and therefore an acceptable destination for teenagers who were in the process of making the tricky social leap from mall rats to restaurant-goers. Its owner, Alice Bianchi, and her husband, Sam, had bought the place in 1950 from the two ladies who created it. When Sam died, Mrs. Bianchi remained as beloved patronne until the restaurant finally closed in 1988. Business had declined in its latter years. The petit-bourgeois menu seemed too commonplace, the ambience too old-fashioned. When Wendy and I had dinner there soon after our return to Canada, it was only the knowledge of its past that lent the food any savour at all.

Having lived here for almost fifty years, Mrs. Bianchi was entitled to think of herself as Canadian, in spite of her Italian name and English ancestry. But did that make La Chaumière a Canadian restaurant as well as a French one? What is a Canadian restaurant, anyway? Suddenly, towards the end of the 1980s, the question started to matter.

The assertion of a national or regional cultural identity is usually a reactive gesture, a response to some real or imagined threat. In Canada, the threat of Americanization is real enough, but the reaction seems to be more a quest than an assertion. A Canadian restaurant? That looming adjective is always burdened with provisos, semantic quibbles, and demands for definition. Ask what it means, and then take your choice of platitudes for an answer.

The multicultural riposte insists that any dish is Canadian, be it bannock, bigos, or borscht, so long as it's cooked here, by Canadians, using our own local ingredients.

The aboriginal lobby restricts the term to dishes made with indigenous (in other words, pre-European) ingredients. Canada recently sent a separate team of First Nations chefs to the Culinary Olympics, where they performed brilliantly, and yet there has never been a native Canadian restaurant in Toronto.

The official government approach, based on the menus prepared for banquets of state in Ottawa, seems to limit Canadian gastronomy to salmon, wild rice, fiddleheads, and maple mousse. The regionalist manifesto, meanwhile, denies the existence of Canada altogether, dividing the country into distinct local pockets and arguing that no single cuisine can hope to represent so vast and scattered a nation.

The debate was in its infancy at the tail end of the seventies, when the first generation of young Canadian chefs emerged from their apprenticeships and started to look for ways to make names for themselves. In Europe, top chefs were redefining and refocusing national culinary identities in the wake of the Nouvelle Cuisine movement. In California, a local style was gathering momentum, and its success would prompt other regional expressions in the Southwest, New

England, and eventually Miami. Why couldn't something similar happen in Toronto? Christopher Boland, fresh out of George Brown College, was working at Fenton's as a salad-maker in 1978 when a dish he called Upper Canadian vegetable terrine won a prize in the Wiser's Deluxe Culinary Classic.

"I went to Montreal for the final," he told me. "I remember sitting with the other chefs at a press conference, and one of them answered a reporter's question by saying, 'Of course, we're all European here.' I said, 'Now just a moment ...!' But the restaurant business was like that in those days: a single European fraternity."

Boland's generation would fracture that hegemony. Many of the young chefs who emerged during the eighties were Canadian-born. They had their triumphs and their failures. They survived the too-affluent boom time, when flattery and easy money threatened to inflate their achievements to bursting point. They survived the recession in their own particular ways. Many of them have reappeared in recent years, charged with a new confidence and discipline. I used to think of them as a sort of culinary equivalent of the Group of Seven, but the analogy doesn't hold water. There was never a common manifesto, never a sustained, shared effort to find a uniquely Canadian style. In this city, every restaurant is an island, and every cook far too busy (that is the excuse they always give) to find time for brotherhood.

It is simplistic to try to trace such growth back to a single root. Nevertheless, I would argue that if Scaramouche hadn't existed, in its first, fascinating, energetic, self-indulgent incarnation, if its owner, Morden Yolles, hadn't decided to risk his restaurant on the talents of Jamie Kennedy and Michael Stadtländer, two young chefs barely out of their teens, the quest for Canadiana would not have developed as it did. And where did Scaramouche begin? Fade to 1977. Herbert Sonzogni's kitchen at the Windsor Arms. A quiet, serious-minded young cook called Jamie Kennedy stands at the grill. He is tall, slimly built with tousled black hair, fine features, and piercing blue eyes. Born in Toronto and trained at George Brown, he will soon complete his four-year apprenticeship ...

It was probably one of the most purely European educations any Toronto chef could have had. Looking back on it, Kennedy remembered being the only man in the entire Swiss-dominated brigade whose first language wasn't German. Sonzogni was a distant figure, but his sous-chef, Ulrich Herzig, took a liking to the young Canadian's attitude and work ethic. When Kennedy expressed an interest in gaining further experience in Europe, Herzig promised to see what could be done. That summer, Kennedy left to work at the Windsor Arms' latest project, the Millcroft Inn, but he was not forgotten. When George Minden mentioned that he needed someone to cook at his private chalet in Gstaad for the following winter, Sonzogni replied that he knew just the man for the job.

"So I flew out to Switzerland," recalled Kennedy. "It was my first experience of running a kitchen on my own, and it was a lot of fun. I could do whatever I wanted, running up accounts at all the stores in the village, playing with some pretty specialized ingredients, no matter what the cost."

In the New Year, Sonzogni came out to stay with Minden as a guest, and one afternoon he took Kennedy off to visit the chef of Gstaad's Palace Hotel. Old cronies, they spent the afternoon drinking, swapping memories, but at some point, Kennedy realized they were discussing his future. In that little world, when a colleague asks another colleague a favour there is no question of any refusal. A call was made to the Grand Hotel National in Luzern, where Gustav Partsch was the chef. At the end of the skiing season, in April 1978, Kennedy reported for work as an apprentice.

His years at the Windsor Arms had equipped him for the rigid hierarchy of the Hotel National's kitchen. Auguste Escoffier himself had once been chef there, and the brigade was still strictly modelled upon the system the great man had established. Chef Partsch was a German, while his immediate subordinates – the sous-chef, the chef garde-manger, and the saucier – were all Swiss. The rest of the team was a virtual League of Nations: a couple of Canadians, an American, some Germans, some Dutch, an Italian. French was the official language of the kitchen, but everyone seasoned it according to their background, creating a bizarre Esperanto patois.

Maintaining discipline seemed to come naturally to Partsch. There was no latitude extended to the apprentices, no question of self-expression. Kennedy accepted the situation as part of the learning process, but it irked one of his colleagues, a very tall, very serious-minded young German called Michael Stadtländer, who had started his apprenticeship on the same day as Kennedy. Stadtländer had just finished his national service in the German navy, an experience he had loathed, and he was in no mood to jump to attention at the bark of a command.

"Michael had so much imagination," explained Kennedy, "way out in left field, but he possessed such great mechanical skills that he was a real asset to the brigade. Partsch never could understand it. It confounded him that Michael could be so talented and at the same time such a freak, and he reacted by making him a whipping boy.

If it hadn't been for the sous-chef, Michael would never have finished the season."

Kennedy and Stadtländer's friendship grew throughout the summer. They spent their spare moments talking, went camping together, discovered that they were kindred spirits in the kitchen. Stadtländer came from a small, rural village on the outskirts of Lübeck, close to the Baltic Sea and the East German border. His father was a milkman, a man who took pride in the self-sufficiency of his farm; his mother filled their cellar with jars of preserves. They had had little time for young Michael, and his childhood was spent running wild with friends in the forest, camping out by the stream, catching eels and selling them by the roadside. Formal education was at best a distant distraction, but the Cold War seemed close and real. Stadtländer dreamed of getting away from that fear, and his dreams were fed by mythic images of a wild, pristine Canada culled from National Film Board clips. Long before he met Jamie Kennedy, he had sewn a Canadian flag onto his Levi's jacket as a token of his ambition.

Sustained by his friendship with Kennedy, Stadtländer stuck out the season, though neither of them found much inspiration in the kitchen. The National was a resort hotel, and all summer long the brigade was required to pump out simple, American-plan menus for two hundred guests a night. Chef Partsch, one suspects, was as frustrated as his apprentices. Then, in October, at the very end of the season, a different opportunity presented itself. Most of the cooks had already left on vacation; only Partsch, a couple of chefs de partie, Stadtländer, and Kennedy had stayed to close down the kitchen. It was then that they learned that a team of French hotel critics were planning to visit the hotel.

"Partsch prepared this incredibly lavish five-and-a-half-hour banquet for them," Kennedy remembered. "We worked for three days and the quality was amazing. So was the level of tension. The whole thing was exhausting, but for us it restored the thrill, reconfirmed our choice of career. Then the very next day, it was over. The hotel was open only during the summer. People took six weeks off, and then the kitchen brigade moved to another hotel in Davos for the winter. I decided to join them, but Michael had had enough. He told me he wanted to go back to Germany."

But first, there was time for a holiday. Stadtländer took Kennedy home to visit his family for a couple of weeks and showed him all his old haunts. They went to Paris and stayed with Kennedy's girlfriend. They hitched out to Normandy and went up and down the coast eating oysters and drinking wine, postponing the parting of the ways. It was there that the telegram reached them.

Morden Yolles was the owner of One Benvenuto Place, a ritzy residential apartment block on the brow of the hill halfway up Avenue Road. The restaurant in the building had been impressive in its day, but its traditional menu had become seriously outdated during the last years of the seventies. Now Yolles and his wife, Edie, wanted to brush the cobwebs away and create something new, a restaurant that would bring European Nouvelle Cuisine to Toronto. He had friends who knew George Minden, and two of them had been out to stay in Gstaad the previous winter. They remembered the dinners prepared by the young Canadian cook at the chalet and recommended him.

Yolles's telegram was essentially an invitation to audition: come back to Toronto for a week, cook us a meal; if we like it, we'll build you a restaurant. "Okay," replied Kennedy, emboldened by the craziness of it all, "but only if Michael comes too." The Yolleses agreed. At the end of the meal, they told the two young men that the deal was on.

Kennedy had to go back to Davos for the winter, but the following spring he returned to Toronto, went on half salary, and finally started to develop the idea of Scaramouche. Morden Yolles had gutted the restaurant, and everything was to be created from scratch: the design of the room, the angular wooden furnishings, the construction of a new kitchen along European lines, with free-floating hotplates set in a central island. There was resistance from Toronto's fire officers, problems with air movement laws, workmen who said it couldn't be done, but at last Kennedy had his way. The whole process took a year and a half.

Stadtländer, meanwhile, stayed in Europe, waiting for his application for landed-immigrant status to find its way through the narrow, tangled tubes of Canadian bureaucracy. To improve his English, he spent a miserable, rainswept couple of months as a pastry chef in a hotel in Bournemouth, then fled back to Germany, working at a tiny restaurant called the Postillion, outside Stuttgart. There chef Vincent Klink spent his days perfecting the clean, refined, ingredient-driven precepts of the new German avant-garde, a way of cooking that Stadtländer found inspiring and shared with Kennedy when he finally reached Toronto in August 1980.

Scaramouche opened that summer, just as Franco Prevedello was opening Pronto. The critics interpreted its cooking as French Nouvelle Cuisine, something many had heard of but few in Toronto had tasted. Interest within the profession was intense, at least among cooks of Kennedy's generation. Christopher McDonald, then an apprentice at

Sperling's, an up-market take-out-cum-restaurant at Yonge and Eglinton, remembered meeting Stadtländer at a party.

"We all knew he was really, really good – everyone wanted to work in that kitchen for free for a couple of days just to see him in action. It was the team of Michael and Jamie equally, but Michael was more exotic to us because he'd just come from Germany, as if he were some kind of special force brought in to do something terrific. I told him I thought it was quite interesting that he was considered the guy who does Nouvelle Cuisine better than anybody else, because it means that if he undercooks, say, a green bean, the public will then consider that that's the way beans should be cooked. His English wasn't so good in those days, but he seemed quite interested in the observation."

Green beans aside, Stadtländer was less than thrilled with the quality of ingredients available to restaurants in Toronto. He built a miniature smokehouse on the hillside below Scaramouche to cure eels and fish in his own way. He was delighted one morning when an artist named Whitney Smith, who ran a small company called Forest Foods, showed up at the kitchen door with a basket of wild leeks, fiddleheads, and other indigenous exotica. These were the sort of wild and wonderful foods he had dreamed of finding in the Canada of his imagination, a Canada that seemed increasingly distant from his high-pressure urban life.

"Those wild plants just blew Michael away," said Kennedy. "But the whole two years was wild. The Yolleses gave us the opportunity to do whatever we wanted. We were the enfants terribles; we weren't reined in at all. The hours were unbelievable: nine to three in the afternoon, then back at six until closing. Michael was pastry chef during the morning and saucier at night; I did the administration and the pass during the evening. We had an à la carte menu with new additions every night, and a prix fixe as well – a tremendous amount of focus and concentration. The menu was printed up every day and we signed each one just before seven o'clock in the evening. A continual challenge."

The public was impressed by Scaramouche's cooking, though not by the eternity of waiting that too many of the dishes demanded. Everything was created à la minute, and it was left to the waiters to explain to customers why their order was two hours in coming. Such delays eventually had a detrimental effect on a business already stretched by high food and labour costs.

After two years, Morden Yolles decided that perhaps the wunderkinder had played long enough and that a little return on his investment might be in order. Kennedy had recently married and was planning an extended honeymoon. Stadtländer wanted to try something on his own. Having sustained such an extraordinary level of creativity for so long, the chefs were also in need of a break.

FOURTEEN YEARS LATER, I sat with Michael Stadtländer across a polished farmhouse table, drinking hot tea on a cold autumn morning. Through the window, grey clouds were blowing across a wet white sky, bearing the rain over forested hills towards Collingwood. A distant voice in the kitchen asked whether anyone had fed the pigs yet.

With his long legs stretched out into the room, and one huge hand holding his three-year-old son Hermann on his lap, he was taking his ease. He seemed every inch the farmer in his heavy denim dungarees, outlining plans for a new plantation of conifers and for drainage of the pond he had excavated on the eastern edge of his hundred acres.

As he talked of the crops he intended to sow on an unplowed meadow behind the barn, his big face was suddenly animated by a smile.

"The work here will never end," he exclaimed. "That's the beauty of it. Everything takes so long. Sometimes I think I haven't done anything at all."

Eigensinn Farm will always be a work in progress, but it was already a masterpiece: a home, a community, a source of inspiration, and a uniquely conceived restaurant where Stadtländer offered his inimitable cooking to a dozen or so customers at a time, three or four times a week. Most of these pilgrims drove the two hours from Toronto, bringing their own wine and confident expectations. They parked in the farmyard, avoiding the hens and Rouen ducks, and entered the house through a muddy boot room, where Günter the dog wagged an affectionate tail. At this point, first-timers had been known to wonder whether they might be the victims of an elaborate joke. Then Stadtländer's wife, Nobuyo, led them into the dining room. Wood-panelled walls, candlelight and firelight, soothing classical music, only two or three tables beautifully set with linen and crystal, sculptures of driftwood and found natural objects, deep colours, delicate shadows – the effect was enchanting. But the real magic began when Nobuyo brought out the preliminary amuse-gueule.

"Seven o'clock is showtime," said Stadtländer. "I think of the evening's menu during the day. At some points in the year, we are almost self-sufficient, with our animals, the things we grow or gather in the forest. Our fish comes from Georgian Bay, beef and lamb, venison, goat, an occasional mallard, and some vegetables from local organic farmers. They are all friends. And sometimes friends of my elder son bring us the things they find. A boy brought a beautiful white puffball yesterday. I gave him $15 and served it with the lamb."

Stadtländer smiled again as Hermann climbed down from his lap and ran into the kitchen in search of breakfast. Working so closely with the land, improvising superb meals for a devoted and appreciative clientele, disappearing sometimes to spend a couple of days on his own in the deep forest of pine, tamarack, and wild apple at the back of the property, the chef had found the Canada he had dreamed of as a boy and had established his own place within it. To me, his entire career seemed to have been leading up to this point, or leading back to it, for the parallels with his liberated childhood on the farm and beside the forest streams in Germany were obvious.

After Scaramouche, and a brief stint as chef at the private club 21 McGill, Stadtländer found himself fancy-free. He was young, well known within the industry, and eager to do something on his own – perhaps make ice cream commercially, using fine natural ingredients, and sell it to other restaurants. At that time he met Jean Boutrot, owner of two bakeries called the Upper Crust, one in Forest Hill Village, one on Yonge Street. Boutrot wanted to expand into catering, and the two men decided they might be able to work together. They bought a huge, very expensive Italian gelato machine and then set about looking for somewhere to put it. The place they found was the Cow Café on John Street, just north of Queen, a second-floor space with a high ceiling, high windows, and a high rent, and from the moment he saw it, Stadtländer's plans changed. It would be a restaurant, or something more European, a mixture of café and restaurant, where people could come for a meal or just for coffee and cake, stay the whole afternoon, talk about life ... Call it Stadtländer's. Boutrot agreed. He found investors from the textile business, and in 1984 the restaurant opened.

The ice cream machine ended up in the dining room as a dessert station.

It must have been an extraordinary experience working with Michael Stadtländer, day after day, in the long, narrow kitchen he called *das Boot*. Almost all the members of the young brigade he assembled went on to make a significant mark in Toronto's restaurant industry. Bryan Steele was sous-chef; he became chef of the Old Prune in Stratford and an instructor at the Stratford Chefs School. Christopher Klugman, with no formal training and nothing on his CV except a brief stint at Scaramouche, would later be chef at Karin, Bistro 990, King Ranch, Oro, Rosewater Supper Club, et alii. Chris McDonald went on to be chef-patron of the excellent Avalon.

"Stadtländer's was so exciting," McDonald once told me, "so spontaneous, so difficult! Michael was not exactly an articulate teacher, you just had to learn what he wanted by observation and memory. There were five starters, five main courses, five desserts, lunch and dinner, changing every day. Michael would put together the menu in his almost illegible handwriting, based on whatever he found in the market that morning: sweetbreads, calf's brains, veal tongue. The restaurant was too big, but there was nowhere else in the city where a cook could learn how to work with products like that, and certainly nowhere that customers could go to eat them. People were tasting these things for the first time in their lives."

McDonald left after eight or nine months, and his place was taken by Paul Boehmer, an eager young giant of a man, twenty years old, whose only experience of the restaurant industry had been to work as a nightclub bouncer. He too would go on to cook at half a dozen of the city's top restaurants and later became chef at Opus.

"My very first week," he recalled, "I had to clean a shipment of salmon trout that Michael had flown in from Norway. I was so scared I'd screw it up! Next I had to butcher some whole suckling pigs, break the carcasses down, waste nothing. At first, I just didn't get it, and it didn't look as if I'd last, and then all of a sudden everything just kicked in. It was amazing, like a big family, with all of us learning together."

Stadtländer would brook no compromises in the cooking, sometimes scrapping an entire menu and a day's preparation at four in the afternoon if new inspiration struck. "I wanted it to be successful," he shrugged. "But the business side of things got so complicated. The investors were losing money. I was still young, inexperienced, intolerant, and very stubborn. I would not change the way we worked." The restaurant closed.

Jamie Kennedy had gone into private catering after Scaramouche, and had then opened his own successful restaurant, Palmerston, in June 1985. Stadtländer decided he too would try catering, in partnership with Chris Klugman. They printed up business cards with Stadtländer Klugman Presents in proud letters and prepped six-course meals out of Klugman's home, finishing them in the customer's kitchen. Then Stadtländer received a phone call from Sinclair Philip, owner of Sooke Harbour House, the famous hotel and restaurant on the coast of Vancouver Island.

"That was the first time I saw British Columbia," mused Stadtländer, "the first time, really, I came to Canada, the way I had always imagined it. Sinclair is a man who knows everything about everything. He loves to use local ingredients, organic meats, everything from the ocean and the seashore, from his gardens. He reminded me of my father, the way we used to grow our own produce, make preserves, make hams from our pig."

To this day, Philip chuckles when he remembers the frighteningly busy summer of 1986, with Expo in full swing and Sooke Harbour crammed with a hundred customers a night for months on end. "It was wonderful working with Michael," he told me. "I remember one of his first days here we went out walking on the beach, and he picked up a limpet and took it out of its shell and ate it raw, and I knew from then on that he would be right for this place. He loved to work with seaweed, crustaceans, beach barnacles, anything that came from the woods. It fitted in perfectly with our own philosophy. He likes a very simple, direct approach, but he also has a deep understanding of flavours and colours, and his plate presentations are his own.

"So he cooked with us for that season. The numbers we served in July and August were probably a little hard on him, day after day after day. When November came around, we asked him to stay, forever if he wanted, but Michael's a guy who likes to explore. Then there was his marriage. Michael and his first wife were in the final stages when we knew them. It's hard for a person who wants to lead a normal, stable Canadian family life to be married to a busy chef. In the end, she moved to Australia with their two children, and he drove back to Toronto, with the trunk of his car full of preserves."

In spite of his success at Sooke Harbour, Stadtländer felt mightily disillusioned with the restaurant business. Somewhere between B.C. and Ontario he made up his mind to get out of it altogether, to go travelling, or maybe to return to the land as a farmer. But once again a new friendship brought about a change in his plans. He met a young chef from Hong Kong called Susur Lee, who was then cooking at

Peter Pan on Queen Street West. The two men decided to go into partnership. Calling themselves Rice and Potatoes, they took their act on the road, borrowing a quiet little restaurant such as La Bastille for a couple of nights and cooking a six-course meal, with each chef preparing alternate courses.

For people lucky enough to hear about them, the Rice and Potatoes evenings were a revelation. Lee's style already reflected his genius for combining Asian and European techniques and ingredients; Stadtländer's cooking was full of the natural Canadian exotica he had discovered in British Columbia. For a while they considered leasing a permanent location, a restaurant called 414 on College Street, but their enthusiasm dissipated in the face of legal problems with lease and licences. They decided to spend the money they had saved on a trip to Europe, and when they finally returned, their search for alternative premises was never much more than half-hearted. Eventually, Stadtländer found a tiny café on Tecumseth Street, an unfashionable residential backwater north of King and west of Bathurst, but they both felt the kitchen was too small to accommodate two co-chefs.

"If you don't want it, I'll take it," suggested Lee. "I'll call it Lotus."

FRANCO PREVEDELLO had found a new mood in Toronto when he returned from the Vancouver Expo and set about building Centro. Michael Stadtländer had the same experience. Seeds that he had helped to sow at Scaramouche and Stadtländer's through his enthusiasm for indigenous ingredients were beginning to show signs of growth. It was a time of discovery, for learning new names, new cuisines, new combinations of the extravagant. The city's food consciousness had reached adolescence at a time when people had money to spend, and the growth spurt was prodigious.

In the midst of the Cal-Ital hurly-burly, those who cared to listen could hear Canadian voices. In 1985 Christopher Boland and his partner Chris Grammatis, having cooked together at Telfer's, opened Trapper's, in Le Gourmet's old location below Hoggs Hollow. Boland called his menu "contemporary continental North American with a Canadian flare" and made telling use of traditional Ontario preserves (most of them drawn from his grandmother's recipe book) and fine Québécois produce such as smoked trout and maple-glazed Laurentian hams from Val David. He was also perfectly prepared to borrow ideas from cosmopolitan Toronto's extraordinarily rich gastronomical pool. "Our contemporary Toronto cuisine draws from many sources," he explained. "We're not defined, and that is a huge opportunity. Diversity is part of what we are."

Christopher Klugman was also busy exploring the possibilities of a regional way of cooking, especially during his short tenure at Karin on Scollard Street in 1987. "We debated for a long time about how to describe the things we were doing there," he said. "We felt it really was a Toronto style, a reflection of what was available here, cooked by Canadians. In the end we called it Fresh Market cuisine. I had never heard the term. I don't know if we coined it."

Fresh, healthy, local ingredients, an imaginative freedom to borrow inspiration from the city's myriad ethnic restaurants, a general feeling that haute cuisine might at last be able to shed its formal, European mysteries ... Cheered on by the press, Toronto's hot young talents seemed to be moving in the same direction, creeping towards some sort of recognizably regional gastronomic consensus. The flag had been hauled up the pole; two new restaurants set it waving.

The first was Metropolis. Its chef and co-owner was Mark Bussières, a George Brown graduate whose first full-time job had been in Chris Boland's kitchen at Telfer's. From there he moved to a small hotel in Collingwood, and then spent two years as chef in the rural isolation of the Benmiller Inn, near Goderich, where he taught himself to smoke fish and grow herbs and passed the long days devising marvellous recipes for breads. In 1987, having found the right partners and a prime location on Yonge Street near Cumberland, he opened Metropolis as an adventure in independence.

The name was a pleasant irony, given a menu that was unabashedly based on rural Ontario's culinary heritage. Bussières's salt-crusted sage loaf and pepper-studded cornbread opened proceedings in the long, sometimes noisy room. Rabbit appeared in a moist terrine, served with tart, spicy cranberry-citrus marmalade; Ontario-raised guinea hen was stuffed with pecans, wild rice, and flecks of Huron County lamb. Desserts featured the sort of hearty baked goods that sometimes appear (if you're lucky) at country fairs: chocolate pound cake with dark chocolate sauce, or a wonderful pie of sweet carrot and parsnip spiced with ginger and cloves.

The other restaurant that typified the quest for Canadiana was Nekah. Through 1987, Michael Stadtländer had kept himself occupied cooking occasional one-night benefits, most famously at Karin, where he shared the kitchen with Christopher Klugman. He had also started a one-man catering company called I Like to Cook at Your House, spreading the word by means of postcards printed with a picture of vegetables and a fish.

As the months hurtled by, it became clear that he could be doing more. Years earlier, at Stadtländer's, he had toyed with the idea of a farm-cum-restaurant somewhere in the country, but he had no money for such dreams. And besides, Toronto seemed an exciting place to be. All his old friends and disciples were busy. Jamie Kennedy's Palmerston was in its third triumphant year. Paul Boehmer had worked for a moment at Karin before going on to Scaramouche; Christopher McDonald was cooking with Raffaello Ferrari at Centro. Chris Klugman had left Karin, paused briefly at Panache, but was now talking about his plans for a new restaurant to be called Bistro 990, financed by Tom Kristenbrun, owner of Toby's Good Eats, Perry's on Wellington Street, and a string of fashionable restaurants.

Klugman suggested that Kristenbrun might also be interested in putting something together with Stadtländer; another friend mentioned that Perry's was not doing well. Stadtländer took a look, loved the space, and by the time he met with Tom Kristenbrun, the whole image was formed in his mind.

The concept was in many ways a summation of his career. He would offer two six-course menus every night, the format he had perfected over the years when catering meals with Klugman and Lee. The actual dishes would change nightly, the menu decisions depending on what he found in the markets each morning. He would make maximum use of small, local, artisanal suppliers. As for the look of the restaurant: "We did it ourselves," says Stadtländer. "When Perry's closed, we just set to work, finding the fabric for the walls, all the driftwood, that kind of wild B.C. look. We put jars of preserves on the shelves – it reminded me of my mother. During the winter we could open up one of those jars and there was Ontario summer."

The name he chose for his restaurant was Nekah, an Ojibway

word for goose, symbolic of freedom of the spirit and of wild, remote places. Such romance was symptomatic of his post-Vancouver mood, but at Nekah, it was to be tempered with a philosophical asceticism. At that time, Stadtländer was studying the precepts of Zen Buddhism and thinking a lot about the precise, intricate naturalism of Japanese food. These were the thoughts on his mind one afternoon when he went down to Susur Lee's Lotus and fell into conversation with a young woman called Nobuyo. Lee had set out a couple of tables on the little patio in front of his restaurant, and the place had become a favourite hangout for chefs in the late afternoon, somewhere to meet for a glass of wine or a quiet beer before the evening's work began. Nobuyo came from a tiny island near Okinawa and had studied law in Tokyo, paying for her tuition by working as a pastry chef. Realizing that a knowledge of English would help her law career, she had come to Canada on a working visa and ended up as pastry chef at Liberty. She and Stadtländer became friends, then roommates, and eventually husband and wife.

Meanwhile, Nekah was almost complete. Part of the vision was a wine list deliberately assembled to complement the food perfectly, a list that would require the services of an expert sommelier. Stadtländer placed a want ad in the newspaper and Andrew Laliberte, once the barman at Fenton's, answered.

"Putting together the cellar was a real adventure," he remembered. "Michael had this idea of matching a glass of a different wine with every course except the sorbet, and they had to be good wines. We also decided that we ought to have a Canadian house wine, which was a very brave and curious thing in those days. Things were still pretty raw in Niagara in 1988."

Inniskillin Chardonnay and Pinot Noir became the house wines, but the Nekah team found other surprises. At a wine and cheese show at Exhibition Place, they noticed a table with nothing on it but a bottle of Cave Spring Riesling. The winery was virtually unknown and Laliberte's interest brought forth excited invitations to visit the vineyards. There they met Cave Spring's owner, Len Penachetti, who was intrigued by the sight of Stadtländer picking chickweed from between the rows of vines while murmuring about salads. Penachetti took them to lunch at the Beacon Motor Inn, the only restaurant in the area. His embarrassment that day eventually led him to create On the Twenty, the winery restaurant that pioneered Niagara regional cuisine.

Nekah had already been open for months when Wendy and I first ate there, reviewing it for *Toronto Life*. Walking in, turning our backs on the after-dark, pre-theatre traffic of Wellington Street, we also left Toronto behind and entered a calm, serious space formed from Stadtländer's imagination. Ethereal flute music played (those interminable, liquid, New Age arpeggios were new to this city and still had the charm of novelty); exquisite native artwork and curiously beautiful natural objects, driftwood and beachwrack, picked up the muted earth colours of walls and surfaces. The room was large, with tall columns like the trunks of smooth, pale trees – the whole effect was as serene and impeccable as the open sky.

A woman led us to a table and brought us menus, handwritten on soft brown paper. It was then that we noticed there were no other customers in the restaurant. That night Stadtländer and his team performed for our benefit alone. The meal began with an amuse-gueule: for me, a tiny complexity of moist salmon wrapped around delicate sole mousse over a teaspoonful of intensely flavoured lobster sauce; for Wendy, a minuscule triangle of lamb and lentil tart, decorated with a cream of beetroot and yogurt and crisp, earthy radish sprouts, intricate but not fussy. There was a deep pheasant consommé the colour of topaz, sweetened with walnut and truffle. Then a coarse-grained salmon tartare, spiked with onion, speckled with beluga and salmon caviars, served on soft brioche triangles. Cold as the Arctic, cleansing the palate, a sorbet of bitter grapefruit and Gewürztraminer followed.

And so on through the evening. The service was flawless, the wines irresistible and imaginatively chosen; each of Stadtländer's six-course menus was a fascinating sensory progression, like a suite of chamber music full of surprises and unexpected thematic echoes. It came to a calm finale at last with a quartet of petits fours served on a cold stone strewn with tiny blue calendula petals.

Nekah was the most interesting, the most satisfying, the most memorable, quite simply the best restaurant I have ever been to. Others I know say the same. It's like being members of a small, select club, or like meeting someone who also found their life changed by your favourite book, but without the edge of competitiveness that creeps into the reminiscences of ageing groupies. We few, we happy few …

I saved my money and went back again twice. The place was always virtually empty, except once, towards the end, when a rowdy office party had taken a table for ten and was trying to drink the cellar dry. At other times, I ventured in and sat down at the bar, waiting for goodness knows what to happen. On one particularly silent night, I passed the alcove where the customers' coats should have been hanging and saw a tall figure in chef's clothing sitting on the floor like a broken marionette, a liqueur bottle in his hand.

"I was not very happy," admitted Stadtländer. "There was so much pressure. The biggest problem was the size: it would have been successful with thirty seats instead of seventy-two. And I hated the idea of people coming here before the theatre. I used to think, This is the theatre! Don't dance at two weddings.

"In the kitchen, it was more like an artists' troupe than an ordinary brigade. Each station had one person. I would be saucier most of the time. I let my sous-chef call the pass, something the chef usually does. But it was very much a one-man operation. We'd go to the market every morning. That was always my vision: to have a relationship with a network of organic farmers who would come to the door. David Cohlmeyer with his salad greens, baby vegetables, and edible flowers, the lamb people, the different summer vegetable farmers ... Nekah was a celebration of Canadian ingredients – a harmony with nature. I've been a forest walker, and a river walker. I think I always understood and appreciated the natural wealth of Canada."

Fiscal wealth was another matter. Creating two completely new table d'hôte menus every day from scratch was astonishingly expensive. Stadtländer might insist that every morsel and organ of a lamb be used in wonderful ways, but it still amounted to waste with the dining room empty. Andrew Laliberte gave me the figures. "From the beginning it was a hopeless project. We had a $160,000 rent plus a $25,000 maintenance fee, which meant we had to do at least forty dinners a day, five days a week, to break even. Our food and beverage costs were actually pretty good for the prices we charged. All our percentages were in line, but there was no way we could drive up the top line to hit the fixed expenses. Oh, we had our good nights.

Saturdays were always booked a couple of weeks in advance and we had some busy Thursdays, but during the rest of the week ..."

Occasional special promotions helped a little. Sinclair Philip came from Sooke Harbour and packed the room for three nights. Christian Vinassac was another guest chef. Used to Stadtländer's ethereal textures, the kitchen team gaped at the sight of the Frenchman lugging in ten-litre containers of 45 percent cream, but Vinassac's talent won them over. So many of Napoléon's former customers showed up that Christian had to return for a second night.

In whatever spare time their restaurants gave them, Stadtländer and Jamie Kennedy were once again working together intently, putting the finishing touches to Knives and Forks, an organization intended to help chefs and organic growers and farmers work together. The notion had started as a search on the part of the chefs for local ingredients of superior quality; the organic angle came later, after they noticed that all the artisanal producers they favoured happened to be farming organically. Gradually, environmental issues worked their way into the project, and Kennedy in particular seized the opportunity to use his fame and press coverage in a cause with a broader significance than cooking.

One of the early triumphs of Knives and Forks was the establishment of a weekly organic market in downtown Toronto; another was Feast of Fields, an annual outdoor fundraiser where growers, chefs, and Ontario's brewers and winemakers meet one another and the general public for a day-long picnic. The first Feast was held on some land up near Singhampton, and when it was over, Stadtländer went for a walk through the forest and over the fields of a neighbouring farm.

"I was thinking the time might have come to move on," he remembered. "I wanted to travel again, to go round the world for a year, to go to Japan. I thought I might give Nekah to Paul Boehmer, my sous-chef, and he could do what he wanted with it. We had Knives and Forks up and running; the market was in place. It seemed what I'd wanted to do in Toronto was all done."

Nekah was done too. For two years, Tom Kristenbrun had kept his part of the agreement, paying the bills, allowing Stadtländer to do as he pleased without pressure to compromise. Toronto's financial life, however, was not what it had been in 1988. The stock market had crumbled and all the bunting and banners, the carefree, spendthrift hobby industries were dragged down in the wreckage. There were plans to open Nekah for lunch, but a patch of gauze doesn't help much on a terminal wound. The precise details of the restaurant's demise remain muddled. Kristenbrun was told one morning that Stadtländer had gone back to British Columbia, and without a chef, he felt he had no option but to deliver the coup de grâce. Stadtländer thought his patron had simply decided enough was enough. The question is unimportant. On June 26, Stadtländer's birthday, Nekah closed.

It has not been forgotten. Talking to Jamie Kennedy recently, I asked him what he remembered of the place, and his comments were as good an obituary as any: "Every great artist experiments in the early days, plays with a lot of colour and a lot of texture, and in Michael's case with a lot of ingredients and a lot of techniques. Over the years, you simplify and the true lines that represent you start to emerge, the lines that people can identify as your own. For Michael, I think that started at Stadtländer's, but it became very identifiable at Nekah. He loves nature, and he loves what Canada has to offer. Perhaps it takes someone who is not from Canada to recognize the beauty of our indigenous things, to zoom in on them and to present them in a completely different context. Michael was able to do that at Nekah. It was urban, and cosmopolitan ... It was art."

THE RECESSION APPEARED to stun the burgeoning regional Canadian movement in Toronto's restaurants. By 1991 Karin had followed Nekah into oblivion. Jamie Kennedy had left Palmerston and was cooking at SkyDome's Founders' Club, beyond the ken of ordinary mortals. Mark Bussières had sold Metropolis and opened a bed-and-breakfast in Gananoque. Christopher Klugman was working north of the city at King Ranch, developing an extraordinarily flavourful and satisfying spa cuisine in that most hedonistic of health clubs, unaware that the ranch was itself on the verge of closing.

Almost all of the high-profile pioneers had departed Toronto's public stage, but not without leaving a legacy. It had become habitual for menus to name the provenance of local ingredients, furthering pride and recognition in Canadian products. Restaurant suppliers such as Cookstown Greens and Highland Springs trout farm were well established, while the growing fame and quality of Ontario wines continued to sustain interest in the province's overall potential.

Knives and Forks was still cutting the mustard, its original mandate working particularly well in such areas as Stratford, where Bryan Steele, once sous-chef at Stadtländer's, was now chef of the Old Prune. Each winter he met with local organic farmers to discuss his restaurant's needs and to plan what they would plant and grow in the coming year.

As Toronto's interest in the quest for a Canadian culinary

identity dimmed, Stratford's role seemed increasingly important. The reason was the Stratford Chefs School, founded in 1983 by three of the town's leading restaurant owners: James Morris of Rundles, Eleanor Kane of the Old Prune and Joseph Mandel of the Church (who soon sold his restaurant and dissolved his affiliation with the school).

An urbane, soft-spoken Irishman, Morris had worked at Winston's during the seventies, at the same time as Franco Prevedello and Michael Carlevale, and had left in 1977 to open Rundles in a converted boathouse by the river. But Stratford's peculiar demographics – packed with tourists for the summer theatre, sleepy and parochial when the season was over – had presented him with a problem. There was no way he could keep his restaurant open during the winter, and therefore no way he could keep a chef and key staff from one year to the next. Kane was in the same predicament at the Old Prune. The school was their solution. For half the year, their restaurants became classrooms and their chefs instructors; even their regular local clientele were brought into the act as occasional judges on nights when the students took over the kitchens for practical experience.

The Stratford Chefs School remains a model of its kind. As well as rigorous instruction in the classical basics of cooking, there are courses in historical and modern gastronomy, food styling, nutrition, kitchen management, various foreign cuisines, and wine appreciation (spiced with comical banter) under the expert nose of oenologist William Munnelly. Similar courses are part of the culinary management program at George Brown and Humber Colleges, but Stratford's tiny classes of six or seven allow the students' progress to be scrutinized in exceptional detail. What is more, they are being trained specifically for restaurant careers, rather than jobs in the broader food industry. At the end of their first fifteen-week program the students are apprenticed for nine months to prestigious restaurants, more often than not in Toronto; after their second term, they head out into the world, carrying the idea of a recognizable Canadian cuisine with them.

"It's one of the first subjects students tackle," Eleanor Kane once explained to me. "We explore with them the regional nature of cooking in Canada, and also the way it has been influenced by the various ethnic groups that have settled the country. We look at aboriginal cuisine, and at the contributions of the French and English cultures." In 1993 she helped organize a conference called Northern Bounty that brought together chefs, restaurateurs, vintners, food producers, journalists, and historians to articulate Canada's gastronomy. Its fruits were a book of the same name, edited by Jo Marie Powers and Anita Stewart (that charming and indomitable crusader for our culinary identity), and also the impetus to create Cuisine Canada, a nationwide network of food professionals dedicated, in their own words, to the promotion of "the growth and study of our distinctly Canadian food culture."

It was encouraging, in the late 1990s, to see a renewed interest in Canadiana gracing the menus proposed by many leading restaurants in and around Toronto. Avalon, Centro, Canoe, On the Twenty, Pangaea, Langdon Hall, Rundles, even the big hotels – the King Edward, the Royal York, Sutton Place ... There was a new sophistication in the way they made use of indigenous ingredients, integrating them into their cooking in a far less self-conscious way than seemed possible in the eighties. An Ontario duck could at last appear on a menu without announcing which lake it came from and who its parents were.

MICHAEL STADTLÄNDER had not left immediately for the coast when Nekah went under. Instead, he and Nobuyo had turned their tiny apartment on Bathurst Street into a private dining room, seating fifteen or sixteen people who brought their own wine. Word spread, and the living room was packed every night; every morning, the neighbours gaped at the bottles in the Blue Box. After two or three weeks, they had earned enough cash to leave town.

"We took off!" said Stadtländer. "First to Sooke Harbour, then to Australia, where my two sons were living with my first wife, then to Japan. There we went to work for Masanobu Fukuoka, a guru of organic farming. He teaches a very natural way of growing, throwing vegetables around to seed themselves, and what grows grows, what doesn't doesn't. No plowing. Disturb nature as little as possible. His philosophy is also based on Zen, and it took me a while to understand that when he urged a respect for nature, he was also referring to human nature. Yes, you have to adapt to your environment, but also to your own nature. When we left Japan, we went on to Germany, to study some old ways of farming and communal living, and to look into some primitive architecture. I had this idea we would come back to Canada and build our own place in British Columbia."

Penniless after their travels, the Stadtländers returned to Toronto in 1991. To raise money for their dream, they decided to re-create Nekah for a limited run of six months, and looked about for a location. Jamie Kennedy suggested they might get in touch with Marcel Réthoré, who was now running Palmerston and rumoured to be struggling. The collaboration was an artistic triumph, with Stadtländer and Réthoré cooking in the open kitchen, Nobuyo waiting table, and Andrew Laliberte back in the role of sommelier. No one grew rich on the proceeds, but the Stadtländers saved a little. After six months, they packed everything they owned into their Volkswagen and headed west.

The plan was to settle somewhere on the ocean and establish a cooking school for young chefs, a place apart where eager students could study gardening, how to gather and cook the foods of the forest and the sea, perhaps even invent a whole new cuisine. Nobuyo wrote endless letters to the provincial government but no one was interested in providing the financing.

They visited Sinclair Philip at Sooke Harbour House. "We employed Nobuyo, who was an absolutely fantastic person to work with," he recalled. "She was tremendous at pastries and desserts, and she also prepared a number of Japanese village specialties which were extremely good, quite unlike the familiar Japanese restaurant dishes.

"Also, her feet were solidly on the ground: a good counterbalance to Michael's artistry and imagination. But Michael didn't stay. If he had owned land here it might have made a difference, but I think Ontario was where he felt the most happy. He had a big following there and could always make ends meet if he had to."

But it was more than security that drew Stadtländer back to Ontario. "We were lonely," he says simply. "The people out west are not like people I'm used to. I didn't feel comfortable. I missed the Ontario people, with their more European sensibilities, rather than the New Age westerners. I'm not a New Age person. And the ocean and the forest and the mountains out there are beautiful, of course, but I realized that it was more a place to go to for answers and inspiration than to settle. The answer I found was to come back to Ontario."

The Stadtländers returned via Germany, and there the old vision of a farm-cum-restaurant was suddenly rekindled. An aunt had been left a sum of money by some elderly people she had cared for and, impressed by Nobuyo's practical common sense, she offered to lend them the down payment on a farm.

"It was all because of Nobuyo," admitted Stadtländer with a grin. "The money is all in her hands."

It only remained to find the ideal piece of land, and that task did not take long. By a highly improbable but poetically satisfying coincidence, a hundred-acre farm outside Singhampton was for sale – the very same property across which Stadtländer had stalked after the first, triumphant Feast of Fields.

So there we sat, finishing our tea, on a rainy morning, in the dining room of Eigensinn Farm. This time the name had come from a Hermann Hesse book; one might translate it as "I did it my way." Stadtländer raised his eyebrows. "This was meant to happen," he said. "We sustain ourselves, and others. We pay the mortgage and have a great life. It keeps us busy."

"Us" was a team, an extended family, a community where everyone had a role to play and also helped out on the farm. There was the chef's apprentice, David Jones from Splendido. Marc Lapointe, once sous-chef at Langdon Hall, Ontario's most elegant country-house hotel, lived in the barn and baked the breads. Nobuyo's teenaged niece from Japan was housekeeper and helped to wait table; Stadtländer's sixteen-year-old son by his first marriage was an occasional busboy. Transient house guests swelled the numbers: student chefs who stayed for a couple of days to watch and learn, young people from around the world who belonged to an organization called Willing Workers on Organic Farms, working their way across Canada in exchange for room and board.

Only once has the idyll been threatened. In the fall of 1997, an overzealous LCBO inspector who had never been out to the farm persuaded the Ontario Provincial Police that the whole operation, especially its strict bring-your-own-bottle policy, sounded too virtuous to be true. One night two police officers, disguised as a couple celebrating their wedding anniversary, arrived for dinner, but without any wine. They begged Nobuyo to take pity on their plight, and eventually she sold them two bottles she had been saving for Christmas. Days later, the cops raided the farm and charges were laid. To Stadtländer's fans, it was a clear case of entrapment, of the artist bullied by the philistines. Renowned lawyer Clayton Ruby rode to the chef's defence and a non-punitive settlement was eventually reached before the appointed court date. The Stadtländers dealt with the ordeal philosophically, building a bonfire on the lawn outside the kitchen door and burning all the anxieties of the last six months.

"Come on," said Stadtländer, draining his tea. "Shall I give you the tour?"

We began with the kitchen, a room as unlike a restaurant kitchen as a restaurant kitchen can be. Instead of the noise of compressors, Mozart played; in place of stainless steel racks, the well-used whisks and ladles hung from the bough of a tree that arched over the work surface, an irregular slab of polished granite, like a pool of black water.

The previous night, Wendy and I had tasted the food, sitting at an impeccably formal table while the flames flickered in the old grey fieldstone fireplace. The meal began with the delicious crusty rye bread baked in the kitchen that morning – the perfect way to blunt the edge of hunger. Then Nobuyo brought us each a tiny salad, describing its elements with pride: grated beets and apples from the garden dressed with oil pressed from roasted sunflower seeds, and a morsel of pork tongue from one of their own pigs. Two hours earlier, just before dusk, Stadtländer had gone out into the garden looking for inspiration for the evening's soup. He came back with a basket of Jerusalem artichokes, cooked them and puréed them, dressed them with fried sage leaves and fried onion threads, small pieces of barely sautéed foie gras, a teaspoonful of peach compote ... the balance of flavours and textures was Elysian.

Stadtländer's cooking had evolved since Nekah days. Although his presentations occasionally referred to Japan in their refined simplicity, he had eliminated the exotic Asian ingredients that he liked to use in Toronto. "Here," explained Stadtländer, "I do bio-regional cooking. I can identify with this bio-region very well, and relate to the ingredients, because it's so like northern Germany. It's looser and less detailed than it used to be when I had five or six people cooking with me. I like the food to fall naturally on the plate."

The fish course brought a supple fillet of fresh Georgian Bay catfish, lightly smoked in the oven, sharing the plate with sweet roasted red pepper, watercress picked that evening from the stream, a hint of balsamic vinaigrette with the faintest prickle of wasabe, a garnish of whitefish caviar. The ingredients were impeccable, the technique discreet, the subtle balance of bitter and sweet a delicious dissonance.

There was a sorbet of pickled plum, and then a few slices of roasted duck breast prettily arranged on an exquisite plate, the meat juicy and sapid, though not particularly tender, moistened with a raisin-cinnamon sauce. Its vegetables were roast squash, roast celery root, and a tangle of greens in which the potent flavour of spinach was dominant.

The main course was lamb, bought from a neighbouring farmer:

a chop, a slice of the shoulder, a kidney, served with sautéed wild mushrooms and soft white chunks of the wild puffball fungus from the
woods. Green beans and potatoes fried with bacon reminded me for
a moment of Germany.

For dessert, an ethereal cake of maple-hazelnut mousse, crowned
with a maple-hazelnut tuile, lapped by raspberry coulis and wild blue-
berry compote. Much later, over coffee, Nobuyo brought out a quartet
of chocolate truffles, arranged as in Nekah days on a flat cold stone
and garnished with tiny white petals.

"Where do your ideas come from?" I asked Stadtländer next
morning.

"I sit and drink tea for a couple of hours when the first chores
are done, and think about that evening's menu. Or I go out and think
about it while I'm working."

He led me outside. The drizzle was barely noticeable, more of a
mist – what the Irish call a fine soft day. Moisture glistened on herb
beds and blackcurrant bushes; there were puddles in the fieldstone
foundation of the half-finished smokehouse. In a muddy corner of a
field, a massive brown boar hurried out of its sty and pressed against
the enclosure, grunting a greeting. Stadtländer picked three or four
apples from a gnarled old tree in the hedgerow and tossed them into
the pen as he made the introductions.

"This is Arnold. We've had him three years – since we first moved
here. He's getting too heavy for the sows, and he's not as productive
as he was. Still, it's going to be hard castrating him." Nature also has
its painful side.

We left Arnold and headed for the new pond, still a half-empty
crater dug from the hillside. The following year, it would be stocked

with speckled trout and bass for the table, and also handy for midnight swims on hot summer nights when the guests have gone. On the crown of the hill, three years of wine bottles had been neatly stacked to form a low wall, encircling a space for picnic tables. The view was spectacular, but Stadtländer's eyes were fixed on his own hundred acres of meadows and forest, the farmhouse and barn, the tiny metal hut where his apprentice lived, the unplowed fields that might one day provide fodder for his animals and rye for a bakehouse.

Total self-sufficiency. Not just Canadian ingredients, but ingredients from a single organic property, interpreted by a singular man who saw and understood what Canada has to offer better than any chef I have ever met. I was about to ask him how it felt to be the guru of all those others who strive to represent this country's cuisine, about his own sense of being Canadian, but he spoke before I could.

"That's another thing," said Stadtländer quietly. "Here I find that I can be German. Much more than anyone can be in Germany. That's really important to me."

PACIFIC OVERTURES

THE FIRST TIME I sat and talked to Susur Lee I almost succumbed to hypothermia. It was in January 1994 – a bitterly cold Monday morning – and Lotus looked even smaller and more austere than usual in the dull grey light that crept through the windows from Tecumseth Street. On the plain wooden table between us, two cups of coffee were rapidly cooling. Lee switched off the heating on Sundays and Mondays when Lotus was closed, as a way of saving money. His tall, muscular frame was bundled up in a scarf, hat and overcoat. His breath formed clouds in the air.

"This reminds me of Hong Kong," he said with an illuminating smile, "like eating at street food stalls by the Kowloon ferry, sitting on a stool with a bowl of those little snails in hot broth and a cold wind blowing and the steam coming off the food."

I had glimpsed Lee often over the years —

in Lotus's cramped kitchen wearing his chefly whites; in other people's restaurants, dressed in the layered, charcoal-on-black livery of his Queen Street West neighbourhood. With his smooth, unlined skin and high cheekbones, he could have had another career as a photographer's model. Thick black hair tied back in a ponytail, moving with the poise of a cat, he certainly looked the part. It surprised me, when I got to know him better, to see how he doted on his children and to learn that he was a very big fan of Mr. Bean.

"I'm going back to Hong Kong next week, for the first time in four years, and I've had many dreams about it. I dream of arriving by plane and watching the city appear beneath me between the hills. You can almost see its energy, like heat waves on a highway in summer. Kai Tak Airport is right in the heart of the buildings – houses piled up on either side of the runway like the nests of bees, covered in those big, big Chinese signs advertising medicines. Then they open the door of the plane and the Hong Kong smell hits you – a unique smell, a mixture of kelp and pollution."

The idea of Susur Lee leaving Toronto for even a short vacation prompted a pang of dismay. Ever since Nekah had closed, Lotus had been the undisputed source of the most interesting cooking in the city. Its name had virtually entered the language as a synonym for marvellously accomplished Fusion cuisine, and any chef who ventured into that territory did so in the knowledge that his efforts would be compared with those of Susur Lee. Unique in its breadth, his repertoire encompassed the full range of Chinese and Western European traditions. Some critics described his dazzling cooking merely as East meets West, but that was like calling opera acting with songs. Night after night, Lotus's constantly changing menu showed his intimacy with the ingredients and his mastery of the technique of both cultures, but it was the wit, the imagination, and the instinctive aesthetic with which he merged them so seamlessly that set him apart as an artist.

Lotus, to me, was always about more than food. It had come to represent much of what I most admired in the restaurant industry. Whenever I wrote about it, words like "consistent integrity" would spring to mind, and for once, discussions of the art and the philosophy behind a certain dish did not seem absurdly pretentious. The room was far from comfortable – too hot in August, drafty in winter – but I loved the minimalist rigour of its decoration: a few jars of preserves, some curious framed displays of dried sea creatures, tiny oil lamps that provided a romantic twinkle but occasionally set the paper menu on fire. Such asceticism contributed to the mystique of the simple shrine where the food on the plate was all.

The first thing I ever ate there filled me with admiration. It looked like a melting cone of blackcurrant ice cream on the plate but turned out to be a salad of crunchy zucchini and golden beets formed into a ball and covered with tissue-thin slices of smoked duck. The cone was a spiral of sesame pastry so light that it crumbled at a touch from the fork; the melted ice cream, perfectly matching the colour of the meat, was a black and red raspberry vinaigrette. It sounds contrived, but the real point lay in the way the lucid flavours and contrasting textures balanced each other, the whole even greater than the sum of the extraordinarily delicious parts.

I don't think that particular recipe ever reappeared on Lee's nightly menus. His imagination renewed itself daily as he prowled the Food Terminal at dawn (one of only a handful of chefs who made the effort), seeing what was fresh and good and inspiring – the autumn's last case of passionfruit, a bushel of hollow yellow tomatoes, perfect for stuffing, a box of organic broccoli. Only Susur could take a couple of discarded broccoli stalks and turn them into something crisp, succulent, and unrecognizably wonderful. Only Susur would have thought to try.

The roots of that inimitable imagination lie in the densely populated Ching Sen Road area of Kowloon, where he was born forty or so years ago, the youngest of six children. His parents came from southern Canton, but there had been family problems and they never spoke of the past. His father was an accountant who took a masculine pride in flagrant womanizing; his mother worked as a tea lady for the British army. Childhood, he explained, was a matter of survival rather than of joy. Significantly, perhaps, the only positive memories he has of those years have to do with food: waking at four o'clock on New Year's morning to the sounds and smells of his mother preparing the family's annual banquet, or stuffing himself with delicious dim sum at a teahouse in Mong Kok while his father sat for hours behind a newspaper, studying the horse-racing pages. Such moments ceased as the young boy grew older.

"My mother took so much abuse at work, and she transferred it onto us, waking us up in the middle of the night and yelling and screaming, beating up on my sisters. She wanted the family to do well, to work hard, but she didn't know how to make it happen. None of us did well at school. The mental and physical abuse drove my brother and sisters away before they were fifteen. I left home when I was thirteen and got a job as a busboy in a coffeehouse, across the harbour in Hong Kong Central. I hated that work, being at everyone's mercy."

Tall and mature for his age, he moved into the room his brother rented in Kowloon's old theatre district. He spent all his time on the streets, haunting the neighbourhood's dark, pungent back alleys and making money by scalping tickets. Craving power and self-respect, he found a measure of both as a student of martial arts.

"Once a year my master would take a group of us into the New Territories, between Kowloon and China, for the festival of the buns. All the martial arts dragons, the teams, would be there, in a field, and there'd often be fights to gain face, to see who was most powerful. The New Territories were basically farmland back then, before the highrises were built, and every house would be hung with huge bamboo canopies in orange, red, green, such fantastic, strong colours, and with Buddhas and flowers and all the old Chinese heroes. For the festival, there were mountains of small steamed buns, like a giant croquembouche, as big as a two-storey house, and the martial arts teams would race to climb them and reach the package of money that lay at the top. My dragon won once."

Lee hardly ever came home to the room they shared and eventually his brother kicked him out. He found a job as a wok-washer in a Pekingese restaurant called Star House near the old ferry station in Tsimshatsui. He had no thought to be a chef, but he could eat there for nothing and hang out with guys who were older than he was. It was only when he was promoted to the water table, gutting and cutting fish and seafood all day long, that he started to pay attention to the work going on around him. Ironically, he knew far more about Pekingese cooking than his own Cantonese cuisine. By the time he was fifteen, however, he was ready for a change. A friend was working at the Peninsula Hotel on the Kowloon side, and he liked the sound of the clean, organized kitchen and the better hours – only twelve hours a day instead of fifteen. He applied for a job in the kitchen and was accepted.

Lee worked hard at the hotel, in spite of the haughty racism of the European executive chef and the problems involved in learning alien Western cuisines, but he continued to lead a double life. During his few hours off in the afternoon he would rush to the port and catch the forty-minute hydrofoil to Macao, the old Portuguese enclave on China's mainland, famous for its casinos. He would gamble for an hour, and then race back for the next shift. After work, he hit the streets. "I was a playboy back then, with lots of girlfriends lined up, and a bunch of guys who did what I told them. The girls were impressed when I took them to theatres or restaurants and did not have to pay, like a hot shot. We partied all night long and kept the gangs out of the area I controlled. Today I'm not proud of it, but I guess it brought me the attention I wanted."

Everything started to change when he met his first wife, a twenty-eight-year-old Canadian called Marilou Covey, who taught at the university. By then, Lee was eighteen, held the rank of saucier, and frequently cooked at a flambé cart in the dining room. Covey and her boyfriend, a self-important dentist from Shanghai, were regular customers, but after a while she began to come in by herself. One night, Lee was on the ferry back to the Hong Kong side, and she was there too. She spoke no Cantonese, his English was virtually non-existent, but they stayed up all night talking, drawing pictures, and laughing.

"She asked me to show her Hong Kong, and I took her to all the really gutsy, dirty, red-light areas, even to Kowloon Chai, the independent walled area inside Kowloon. You almost need a passport to go in, the police stay away, and it's very big for heroin and opium, full of junkies sleeping on wooden benches. She found it all fascinating.

"In return, she began to show me another side of Hong Kong that I knew nothing about. On weekdays we would go up to the top of the peak and sit there, watching the ocean. 'Just relax,' she'd say, 'look at everything.' 'Relax' wasn't in my vocabulary! Or we'd stay for a couple of days at a Buddhist monastery in Shatin, sleeping on hard wooden beds, getting up at dawn, and cleaning or cooking with the monks. It was so peaceful, on a mountaintop."

Lee saw little of his old cronies. Sometimes he met them by accident in the street and they would flatter and tease him and try to persuade him back to his old, wild ways. It was tempting, but he knew he had changed. He and Marilou had moved out to the unspoilt, mountainous countryside of Lamma Island, a forty-minute ferry ride from Hong Kong. It was a place where Westerners and teachers lived, and a few of the Hakka Chinese who had farms there. She bought him cookbooks and taught him how to take notes and write recipes. From their house on the hilltop they could see the ocean and the early-morning mist rising over the sea. There was a temple nearby, and sometimes the chanting seemed to fill the whole island, echoing off the mountains, especially on the night of the Ghost Festival, when the living appease the dead.

"If I had had an Oriental wife, we'd never have dreamed of living there," said Lee quietly. "We'd have been too busy working and making money. Marilou showed me a different way to live, how things should be. Then one day she asked me if I wanted to go to Canada. We took nine months to get here, travelling through India, the Middle East, Europe. I learned so much."

They arrived in Toronto in 1978. Marilou went back to university to finish her PhD, and Lee supported them both, holding down two jobs simultaneously, working as a baker in Hazelton Lanes from five in the morning to two in the afternoon, and then as a cook at the Westbury Hotel from three to eleven at night. He remembers running through the snow from one kitchen to the other, wearing sandals and a shirt, wondering what the hell he was doing in Canada.

Gradually he made friends in the Chinese community and got over the cold and the culture shock. He found better-paid work at Le Connaisseur and then at Le Trou Normand on Yorkville. Nevertheless, they were both delighted when Marilou was offered a full professorship back in Hong Kong. They made plans to buy a houseboat and live on it. Marilou flew on ahead. On September 2, 1984, she was on board the Korean airliner that veered from its flight path and was shot down by Soviet fighters. There were no survivors.

Lee's response to the tragedy was to lose himself in work. He took the first full-time job that presented itself, as chef at Peter Pan, the hip little diner on Queen Street West, grateful for the distraction of long hours and the demands of a kitchen of his own.

"It was there I met my wife Brenda," he recalled. "I thought she was weird, like a punk. She had never even tasted broccoli before. She introduced me to the modern, artistic Queen Street scene which gradually became the other great inspiration of my cooking – all because of Brenda. After a year we started going out together, and later she began to design clothes, starting her own company, Bent Boys, in partnership with Jamie Kennedy's wife. They were very successful, very hard-working. I went travelling with Michael Stadtländer, and then later, when I opened Lotus, Brenda and I moved into the apartment upstairs. One beautiful Sunday morning she said, 'Wouldn't it be nice to have a little kid rolling around on the bed.' Now we have two sons, Levi and Kai."

Lee laughed as he poured fresh coffee into the stone-cold contents of our mugs. "You know the rest. So now I'm going on my vacation, back to Hong Kong. I want to see what is left of Ching Sen Road and the old concrete ping-pong tables where I spent so much time, and to smell the alleyway where I lived. I want to see the young people and the way they behave nowadays. Maybe they're more mature now that life is not such a struggle. Maybe I'll even catch a glimpse of those strong, loud, tacky colours in the New Territories, and the red ribbons with lucky mirrors in the middle, flashing in the sun."

SUSUR LEE took his vacation. Then he came back to Lotus and took up where he left off, adding to his reputation, still combing the Food Terminal in the early morning, still balancing the yin and yang of his ingredients as he invented dazzling recipes. He was busier than ever, slipping away for weekends in the States, a guest chef in famous kitchens. Rumours that a very important New York restaurateur was eager to set him up in a business were legion throughout 1996. There was alternative backing offered in Toronto, but with every night busy at Lotus and months spent consulting at the Metropolitan Hotel, he felt too harried to pause and consider his options.

Lotus closed in the summer of 1997. "I need time to think," said Susur, then he flew off to Singapore to consult on a new restaurant and to study the precepts of the new Chinese cooking. The months went by. The investors in New York and Toronto continued to hope they might coax him back into a kitchen of his own, but Susur was enjoying the life of a freelancer, the chance to spend time with his family. As I write, he is thinking still.

7

❧ LA BOHÈME ❧

Simon Dorrell.

AT SOME POINT in my middle teens, I realized with a start that I would never be cool.
My parents were cool, my brother was cool, even
some of my friends were cool, but not me. When
I tried to look cool, I only gave the impression of
anxious preoccupation.

I did not go down without a fight. As soon
as exams were over, I quit the school orchestra
and started a rock band, singing and playing sax-
ophone under the compelling personal soubriquet

of Johnny Eagle. My act was the epitome of mid-seventies cool, but no one was fooled, not even the lads in the band. Before a gig, while keyboards, lead guitar, rhythm guitar, and bass were off being very cool indeed, the drummer and I would be trudging back to the venue through the rain, having spent our appearance fees on a hefty Cantonese meal.

"We're not cool, are we, Olly?" I'd say.

"No, mate," said Olly. "Frankly, we're not ... But we eat well."

Being uncool ceased to be an issue after the band broke up, only to reappear many years later, in 1987, when I went down to *Toronto Life*'s offices on Front at Church to meet Tim Blanks, then the editor of *Toronto Life Fashion*. He was thinking of broadening the magazine's range by adding a food column, and the interview amounted to an audition.

"Have you been to Stelle?"

"Er, no."

"Lotus?"

"No."

"Centro, then?"

"Not yet ..."

I sensed I was making a less than convincing impression as a man about town.

"You've been here six months – where have you eaten?"

"Red Lobster?"

After leaving Corfu, it had taken some time to assemble a life in Toronto. We rented a house in the heart of suburban Don Mills, bought an ancient Honda, and passed the first bleak winter in a myopic daze of bereavement. Our neighbours found us highly anti-social. Before our son became ill, we had started to write a book about the culinary traditions of the village in Greece where we lived. Now we sank back deeply into the project. Outside the window, passing cars sprayed dirty slush over snow ramparts on the sidewalk; we closed our eyes and tried to conjure up the tastes of sea water and summer herbs, the scent of the irises on the steep hillside of our rocky Ionian garden. The book was published in April, within days of my becoming a landed immigrant, and though eating in restaurants was not really part of our budget, we celebrated with a meal at the local Red Lobster. Not long after that, our daughter, Mae, was born, and spring came again to the obsessively verdant lawns of Don Mills.

Finally able to work without breaking the law, I went downtown with my books and short stories and began to pester editors in the hope of freelance assignments. The newspapers were dismissive, but *Flare* magazine eventually granted me an interview. I was handed an article someone had written about Greek food and asked if I'd care to comment in print and in detail on the author's disparaging remarks. "Be as critical as you like," said *Flare*, with a mysterious glint in its eye. When my story appeared, I was dismayed to see they had changed the text slightly. I had referred to the author as Ms. Kates, but the magazine had cut out the Ms., which seemed to me to be a tad disrespectful. Nevertheless, my paycheque was in three figures, and Wendy and I toasted what we hoped was a foot in the door of Canadian publishing with the rare extravagance of a bottle of wine.

"Red Lobster ..." repeated Tim Blanks. "You know, you might want to try one or two other restaurants if you intend to write about food in Toronto."

His magazine never did get its food section. There was a feeling that food lay outside its bailiwick and that to write about it would encroach upon the territory of *Toronto Life* itself. The two pieces I had already written for *Fashion* – articles that now seem full of pompous generalizations and hobbled epigrams – ended up in a drawer in the desk of *Toronto Life*'s food editor, Joseph Hoare. I guess he saw enough in them to consider adding me to his commando of anonymous restaurant reviewers, and after a discreet assessment over lunch at Café Victoria in the King Edward, I began my probation.

Years later, a young chef asked me, completely sincerely, whether Joseph Hoare really existed. He imagined the name was some sort of nom de plume, masking the composite mind of a team of writers, editors, and researchers. "None of us has ever seen him," he complained.

Ah, but they had. Joseph travelled the city, usually on foot, always incognito. He affected no disguise. Neat in a cashmere sweater, dark overcoat, and striped scarf, he had the air of a university student. His dark, curly hair was flecked with grey but his face was perpetually youthful. Though his manner might appear fastidious, there was a mischievous twinkle behind his spectacles, hinting at a sense of humour that occasionally bubbled up into abstruse puns or hilariously surreal pranks. That side of his nature did not impinge on his professional life. Seeing all and missing nothing, he dined in any restaurant where some controversy demanded his personal opinion, usually reserving a table in the name of Julian Barnes. He was the conscience of those who wrote for him, and from the moment I put on *Toronto Life*'s invisible livery and went out to eat professionally, he became my mentor and eventually my closest friend.

Joseph's knowledge of Toronto's restaurants was encyclopedic, his objectivity irreproachable, his integrity absolute. When Mark

McEwan made the cover of *Toronto Life*'s Restaurant Guide, he generously sent a case of delectable Italian wines to the magazine by way of a thank-you. Joseph couriered them back. When irate chefs and owners called to complain that their restaurant had lost half a star in the magazine's rating, his response was a model of beautifully phrased civility, but his will was adamantine.

Sometimes those chefs and owners attempted to bypass him, firing off indignant letters to the editor and the publisher, threatening to withdraw their advertisements from the magazine, then doing so when their blackmail was rebuffed. Within the office, such clichés as "the conflict of Church and State" then raised their grizzled heads, and people were heard repeating that the magazine's duty is to serve the reader, not the restaurateur. "We are an organ of criticism, not of publicity." Very few restaurants, need it be said, ever called to comment when their rating went up.

Joseph accepted it all with equanimity. His manners, like his dry wit, were the product of a more gracious time. He had been known to become flustered, his office was a mare's nest of papers (though he seemed to know where everything was), but he invariably found time to give detailed advice to the dozens of readers who called him each week asking where they could host a party for five hundred vegetarians, or where they might take their mistress's aunt for sushi, or where they could buy hen's teeth.

Keen to meet Joseph's high standards, it took me a week to write my first, probationary review. It was much too long and every noun was smothered beneath a garnish of adjectives. Struggling to find a happy medium between description of a dish and critique, I quickly discovered that English has a pitifully small vocabulary for literal food writing. Finding market-fresh synonyms for "delicious" and "flavour" remains a challenge. I can understand why so many restaurant critics succumb to the allure of metaphor, describing food in terms of music or painting or sex. Personally, I have no trouble telling the difference between chocolate cake and making love, but a surprising number of writers seem to get them confused.

I once sat on a panel for the TVOntario show called *Imprint*. Twenty-five years before, the host, Hargurchet Bhabra, and I had both been members of the same dining club at Oxford – a particularly self-indulgent University society called the Symbolistes – but he was too tactful to allude to our bouts of chartreuse-induced oblivion on air. "If the chef had used too much salt in his recipe, how would you describe it?" he asked. "Salty," seemed the obvious riposte. More often than not, the simple, utilitarian adjective is the most appropriate.

As the number of restaurants began to grow, the task of describing them became easier. Unlike some other publications, *Toronto Life* refused to hasten to a new restaurant within days of its opening. Waiting a month or two, maybe making a preliminary visit to see how things were shaping up, gave the place time to iron out inevitable problems or else, as was sometimes the case, to close. And Joseph was not interested in printing a review that merely demolished a lousy establishment. If a restaurant turned out to be truly appalling, it never appeared in the magazine's pages, taking up space that could be more usefully filled. It is easy to lambaste a restaurant for failing to meet one's expectations, to be wittily cutting at the expense of people who have different tastes from one's own. Being rude makes a writer seem clever and earns him or her a reputation for ruthless honesty. It was Joseph's view, however, that there was no sport in shooting fish in a barrel, or in trashing some hard-working but talent-free enterprise *pour encourager les autres.*

There have been many such duds over the years – and just as many pleasant surprises. One of the first restaurants I reviewed was Pantalone, a Venetian-style veteran on an unlikely strip of Bathurst near Lawrence. Co-owner and host Paolo Zane used to return to Venice annually and bring back trophies of the regatta to hang on his wall, as well as any recipes that caught his fancy. In 1987 his cherished souvenir was a fashionable dessert called tiramisù. I think Pantalone introduced it to the city – certainly, everyone in the restaurant ordered it on the night I was there and table after table dissolved into rapturous sighs of discovery. Was tiramisù a curse or a blessing? I have tasted hundreds of versions over the last ten years and have found that custom can definitely stale its infinite variety. The same is true of chocolate truffle torte, or double chocolate truffle cake, or double secret double chocolate truffle torte-cake. Whatever the handle, one forkful is all I want. Even crème brûlée, England's great gift to the world, vanilla in protective custardy beneath its brittle caramel meniscus, is not invariably irresistible these days. A good lemon tart is another matter.

As the months passed, I began to find my way around the city, at any rate after dark. Legendary areas such as the Beach, Queen West, and Bloor West Village became real as Joseph assigned me restaurants in those neighbourhoods. Seen by night and by car, they all shared a well-illuminated look: big on signage, lousy for parking. Toronto was a nocturnal city for me. I could not have recognized it by day. In the cold light of morning, I wouldn't have known Christie Pits from a hole in the ground.

There was one area of the city that seemed particularly hard to get to know: Queen Street West. The individual restaurants were as accessible as any others, but the neighbourhood itself was a challenge. The problem was my own, and it was an old one: Queen West made me feel uncool.

I have always loathed the image of the English fogy abroad, the plummy-voiced pontificator, studiedly eccentric, deeply self-satisfied, a phoney down to his brogues. I resented the fact that talking to some of the pierced and black-garbed Queen West potentates made me feel like a fogy myself. It had nothing to do with nationality. Nor was it an age thing: the hipsters were all a year or two older than me. It was more like the vague but unbridgeable gap that had slowly divided the friends of my youth into two groups, the cool and the uncool, like the faint, stale whiff of I-know-a-secret smugness that infiltrates the manner of people who do drugs when they talk to people who don't.

And yet, of all Toronto's neighbourhoods, Queen West reminded me most of the London in which I grew up: a little bit of Soho, a touch of the Charing Cross Road, of the Kings Road circa 1967. People who had lived and worked on Queen Street in the seventies referred to the past with a fierce nostalgia, as if they had once been pioneers who had watched their tightly knit settlement charted and subdivided by the developers. By 1987, I gathered, the golden age was over. Visits to individual restaurants for a couple of hours at a time in the late innings of the decade offered little insight into what had been. It was only in 1992, when I wrote an article about Greg Couillard, that I finally began to understand.

"GREG COUILLARD?" I have lost count of the food writers, editors, restaurateurs, chefs, waiters, and especially food suppliers who become indignant at the mention of his name. "How can you write about him!" they cry. "It's terrible how much ink he gets! The man's irresponsible, an egomaniac!" Etcetera, etcetera.

I understand the outrage of the food suppliers, several of whom were left with substantial debt when restaurants where Couillard cooked suddenly closed. Some of those other fingers, however, have less right to wag. Journeymen chefs who resent the publicity he gets should taste his food on a good night and see what all the fuss is about. Restaurant critics should count the column-inches they themselves have given him over the years and acknowledge that their praise may have contributed to the man's swagger. What matters more, especially to the public, is that Couillard can cook like a dream when he wants to, and he has wanted to often in the twenty-seven years since he turned his back on Winnipeg and came to Toronto. I'm a fan – have been since his Stelle days – and I should say right away that I also like the guy. Courteous and charming, he reminds me strongly of actors I have known, men who take a childlike pleasure in playing a part, off-stage, with such conviction that they become enthralled by their own performance. There have been times when Couillard and I have sat down together and conducted a mutually flattering little interview and it has felt as if there were four of us round the table. I watch myself asking the questions; he sits back and watches himself answer. Sometimes the watchers' eyes meet, and that's when the conversation becomes more interesting.

The Couillard saga had reached one of its more dramatic volte-faces on the bleak November night in 1992 when I set off to research the assignment. A cold wind gusted up Yonge Street from Davisville, scouring the deserted sidewalks, and the little restaurant on the east side looked decidedly warm and inviting. Through the window, candlelight gleamed on tables set for dinner; honey-coloured walls were flecked with golden stars. A few days earlier, the place had been known as Hudson, a suave two-storey boîte created by Jonathan Katsuras, better known as Johnny K, and his very young business partner and former waiter, David Kinnersley. Coincidentally, I had interviewed them both the previous summer for a different article about post-recession survival.

"This is the place of my heart," K had said then, leaning back in his chair, dressed all in black and smiling through half-closed eyes like a gunfighter at a poker table. "Hudson is stable. It's the nineties. High service, good food ... That's so much more important than flash."

"Definitely," Kinnersley had agreed.

Tonight, Hudson's signage was gone and the tables were empty. Only at the far end of the room, a dozen or so old friends were gathered around the bar to toast the future and Hudson's new incarnation as Avec ... Greg Couillard. Given Johnny's and Greg's sociable reputations, the opening-night hoopla seemed minimal, but the evening had been hastily arranged. Two weeks earlier, Couillard had been firmly ensconced in another restaurant called Notorious, a mile or so south on Yonge Street, cooking to packed houses and vowing to see out the decade in the tiny open kitchen.

"Then Greg suddenly became available," smiled Johnny, handing me a glass of Champagne. "So I invited him up here. Hudson didn't fold, but we decided to make a few changes out of respect for Greg. I'm just delighted to have his name on the façade." The smile broadened. "And I suppose if we ever have to, we can always white it out."

The kitchen at Hudson/Avec was upstairs, and I went up to see the chef. It was a hot, cluttered little space, but Couillard looked slim and happy, bright eyes shining under dark lashes, gold tooth glinting when he smiled, the trademark pirate bandanna wound tightly around his head, hiding his hair. He was cooking pierogies in Gorgonzola sauce.

"Well, here we go again!" he laughed. "And I feel great! God, I'm glad to be out of Notorious. I felt like a butterfly on a fucking pin in that open kitchen. And I'm in love again, for the first time in ten years. Did you hear Dave Nichol's bought the recipe for my Jump-Up Soup? I've been swimming and working out and I haven't had a drink in weeks!"

Couillard, it seemed, had bounced back. For him, the incident at Notorious – the drunken public fracas with a member of staff, the ensuing dismissal – was already ancient history. But not for Toronto's food writers. For a decade they had followed his career with uncommon diligence, astonished at the man's extraordinary talents, both for cooking and for getting himself into trouble. Other sudden departures had been reported almost gleefully, but this time the gossip was stiffened by an undertone of righteous indignation. Behaviour that in pre-recession days had seemed titillating, even appropriate in a temperamental artist, was now condemned as merely irresponsible.

Back downstairs at the bar, I noticed David Kinnersley, looking a tad shell-shocked by the sudden changes to his restaurant and once again very much the employee. Johnny K was telling his friends about plans for his next venture, "a classy cocktail bar at Adelaide and John." I wondered if Avec would make it to Christmas. There was something about this gathering that reminded me of the forced, over-eager bonhomie of the first-night party of an obvious theatrical flop, the hysterical mirth that would end suddenly at three in the morning when the early editions of the newspapers hit the streets with withering reviews. I was wrong. Avec survived for more than a year, and it was in the upstairs dining room, on several long, quiet afternoons, that Couillard told me the story of his life and helped me to understand his place in Toronto's foodscape.

He was twenty years old when he left Cecil Troy's restaurant in 1973, after two years of life as a kitchen hand. Becoming a chef was the last thing on his mind, but after a miserable stint as a post office worker he ended up cooking again, in the staff canteen of a ski lodge outside Huntsville. "That," he exclaimed, "was one of the scariest jobs I've ever had. We were twenty-five miles in from the nearest road and you needed a rifle to go to the bathroom in the outhouse. I'd be up at quarter to five in the morning, boiling water and whisking in powdered asparagus soup, cooking for workers who came in from making the snow and who all looked like they wanted to kill me. But I won them over, because I would find treasures like cabbages in the dead of winter and turn them into something better than the usual crap. When the season was over, I came back to Toronto and ended up down on Queen Street West."

It was there he met David Cohlmeyer, a friendly, soft-spoken American who had started a restaurant called Beggars Banquet. Cohlmeyer was looking for someone to help make soups and salads; he took a liking to Couillard's happy-go-lucky, hard-working attitude and hired him.

With its communal tables, avocado plants, and hip vegetarian food, Beggars Banquet was as innovative in its way as Troy's had been. Shabby, run-down Queen West had a resident population of hippies and artists who used the restaurant and approved of its four-course, fixed-price menu. Cohlmeyer changed the card daily, researching recipes from international cookbooks and passing his ideas into the kitchen, where an enthusiastic young New Zealander called Andrew Milne-Allan turned them into reality.

"It was a very happy place," remembered Milne-Allan. "Most of us had come from somewhere else, and we all felt like refugees in a no-man's-land. We had a great energy together. David's concept of a daily menu was a very daring one for the time and place – if it's Tuesday it must be Morocco – though somehow all the cuisines of the world ended up in his hands as a fairly homogenized vegetable stew."

"The atmosphere," said Couillard, "was simply bizarre. Cosmic karma, stuffed pumpkin that you'd share with eight people you'd never met before in your life. I was just coming out of my Gary Glitter period and I totally resented them, even though I'd been part of the flower power movement. But Andrew and his wife, Delis, were fascinating: two self-taught, very sophisticated young food fanatics, right out of an Iris Murdoch novel. In the fall of 1976, when Cohlmeyer decided to leave Toronto to become a farmer, Andrew and I bought the business."

They had fun with their new acquisition. The communal pine benches and avocado plants were the first things to go – ritually burned, according to Couillard, put out with the garbage, said Milne-Allan. They bought thirty chairs and painted them in primary colours. They put in a bar and an espresso machine to conjure up a chic Mediterranean atmosphere. Then they all went off to Europe for a month's vacation. When they came back, they changed the name of the restaurant to the Parrot and got down to business.

Within a year, the place had become an indispensable part of Queen West's carefree artsy scene. Milne-Allan did most of the cooking, putting together mainly vegetarian menus of Spanish, Moroccan, Italian, Caribbean, or French dishes, depending on his whim and whatever was fresh and good in the market. Couillard divided his time between the kitchen, where he specialized in soups and salads, and the front of house. His sister, Gay, baked the breads and desserts, while a procession of artists of every persuasion – including, at one time, all three of the Clichettes – waited table. The Parrot's weekend brunch was famous. Customers would line up on freezing mornings for eggs en cocotte, homemade bread, rich French toast, while regulars sneaked in through the kitchen door to grab their usual tables. At night, the room often dissolved into a party, led by Couillard, who was by now an occasional performer with a couple of local rock groups, Parachute Club and the Time Twins, dancing on stage when they performed and generally adding the party element. There were times when he seemed to be more interested in that than in running a restaurant.

By 1981 both Couillard and Milne-Allan wanted a change. They sold the business and went their separate ways. Couillard decided to take a break from Toronto and set off for New York, where he found work at a restaurant called the New Nile, run by Delis Milne-Allan, by then Andrew's ex-wife.

"New York was a ball," he said. "Like Scorsese's *After Hours*, except for me it went on for a year. We were doing a lot of catering – big razzle-dazzle production numbers for a highly receptive audience. I loved taking my bike over to the markets. They were full of food from Haiti and Central America. I've never been to Asia. The Asian influences in my cooking come via a long route, back through the Caribbean, and then later from living close to Chinatown here in Toronto. But it was New York where I started doing things like my Chicken Bangkok." By the time he returned to Canada in 1982, Couillard had made up his mind to be a chef.

But what sort of a chef would he be? Looking back on his formative years, it is as if the ingredients of his future career had already been gathered and set out upon the kitchen table. Couillard himself had no formal training; nor had Troy or Milne-Allan. His mentors were all gifted amateurs, in the best sense of the word, sensitive lovers of food who were able to parlay enthusiasm and natural ability into modest commercial success. Among such free spirits, Couillard's own talents had gradually blossomed. He knew nothing of business, large-scale food cost management, the handling of personnel, or any of the other thousand anxieties that confront an executive chef, but he had seen that instinct and hard work could effectively cover for the lack of an orthodox culinary education. He had learned how to shop and how to improvise; he had learned that a chef can take risks. Above all, he had discovered in himself that prescient imagination peculiar to chefs and sculptors that allows them to anticipate effect, to look at a basket of vegetables or a block of stone and see what it will become.

For Couillard, cooking was always an emotional, hands-on affair. He became famous for the juxtaposition of sweet marinades and hellish chilies, of fascinatingly obscure leaves and tubers, and for a deft hand at the grill. But dishes such as Slash-and-Burn Grouper, Shrimp Bangkok, and the famous Jump-Up Soup, masterpieces that recurred time and again on his menus under various names and disguises, were more than startling compilations. Their power came from his inimitable, instinctive ability to balance big flavours, like an acrobat juggling knives.

All this began to be apparent when he came back to Toronto in 1982 and took over the night kitchen at Emilio's, a funky, New York–style bistro on Queen Street East owned by Paul de Guzman, a native New Yorker and one-time lunch cook at the Parrot. "It was a new idea for this city," recalled Couillard, "a real light-a-fire-under-Toronto's-ass kind of place. Paul would jive the customers mercilessly, but everybody loved it. We felt that if we were working that hard, we could set our own rules."

His work attracted attention at Emilio's. It became the favourite soup-and-sandwich hangout for photographers, models, and the fashion fringe, but it was his next restaurant, Stelle, opened in 1986, that put him on the culinary map. Patrons from across the city queued up outside the intimate room on Queen Street West, while the critics cheered.

By now, Queen West had become a markedly eclectic restaurant quarter. The French were represented by the Parrot, Le Sélect Bistro, and Le Bistingo, Claude Bouillet and Georges Gurnon's sophisticatedly simple restaurant. The Bam Boo Club had opened in 1983, for great music, cocktails, heat, colour, and a hybrid Thai-Caribbean menu from chefs Vera Khan and Wandee Young. The Rivoli was another music club with creatively international cooking, approved by the art school crowd; Zaidy's was serving Cajun cuisine, then on the cutting edge of cool.

Well, not quite the edge – Stelle had the edge. The room was tiny, long and thin, with room for thirty customers. Its décor was basic white: white vinyl over corrugated metal, which was either post-modern sculptural or a camp take on a fifties suburban kitchen, depending on whom you asked. There was serious art on the walls, huge displays of exotic tropical flowers in heavy vases, vivid splashes of orange, purple, and green from gelled spotlights. It was tight, uncomfortable, service was extremely slow, and for three years it was one of Toronto's hottest culinary tickets. Here was Queen West eclecticism on one menu – Thai, Italian, Indian, West Indian, and North African influences – all juggled and set dancing to Couillard's instinctive rhythms. Presentation was dazzling (thanks in part to the talented, demon-driven chef Lee Bailey, who was also in the kitchen), but it was the way the potent, hot, and sweet elements on the plate worked together in the mouth that made the cooking so fascinating. Jump-Up Soup quickly became a legend: a rich, chili-hot bowl of soft vegetables and jerk chicken in a squash and tomato base sparked with cumin, allspice, Scotch bonnet peppers, and half a dozen other spices. Star shapes were everywhere: starfruit garnish for Shrimp Bangkok, polenta cakes cut into stars, sauced with cream, tomato, and three kinds of cheese, backed up by knobs of peppery fennel sausage. Couillard kept a toy Uzi machine-gun in the kitchen, in case a customer complained about the spicing.

"Stelle was payoff for me," he said. "People always thought I was the owner there, but I wasn't. Arthur Rowsell and another friend of his from the film industry owned the business and designed the room. We agreed from the beginning that I would cook there for a three-year run."

While Couillard's reputation as a chef soared, so did his rap as a guy who liked to party. David Cohlmeyer, now farming his famous Cookstown Greens organic seedlings and exotic baby vegetables and supplying them regularly to Stelle, noticed changes. "I'd seen him a few times before and thought he was getting a little cocky, but he was still a very pleasant person. At Stelle he was starting to seem wasted. Maybe it was the hard work. Maybe it was something else. I heard it was difficult working for him. Some days he was a wonderful person to be with; some days nothing was right."

Stelle's success was bringing Couillard other offers of work. First there was the Blue Room, an abortive attempt at a funky cocktail bar on King at Tecumseth. He never actually cooked there – how could he when there was no kitchen, just a four-ring electric stove? The sauces were made at Stelle and sent down, to be applied to the food in situ. The décor was also a problem. The ambience was so cool that even at lunchtime, customers felt as if they were in some dark and windowless Miami lounge at three o'clock in the morning. Mercifully, the place didn't last long.

Then there was the invitation from actor Robert de Niro to open his restaurant in New York. Rowsell had been working on the de Niro film *Stanley and Iris* in Toronto, and one night he brought the actors to Stelle. De Niro was impressed, and early in 1986, Couillard and Rowsell flew down to New York to take a look at the Tribeca Grill. "I wasn't very excited about going back to Tribeca," admitted Couillard. "I had actually tried to set something up there in 1981, with a friend who later died of AIDS. That had taken it out of me spiritually in New York. But I flew down to see the place. It must have been eight thousand square feet, with a kitchen staff of forty! Let's just say I was a little out of my depth. We shook hands and said goodbye."

By July 1989, his stint at Stelle was coming to an end. A new friend, nightclub owner Charles Khabouth, was wooing him for a project that he promised would be Toronto's most glamorous restaurant ever: Oceans. With Arthur Rowsell's blessing, Couillard arranged for his sous-chef, Michael Boose, to replace him in Stelle's kitchen. When the time came, however, Boose's health prevented him from obliging, and somehow the management company failed to find anyone else. One summer morning, David Cohlmeyer arrived at Stelle with his regular delivery of vegetables and found the back door open. "There was food in the fridge, and a lot of booze, even some money, lying around. The bread delivery was sitting on the doorstep. I guess they had a big party and just walked out. They never opened again. I was owed money from Stelle, though I have to admit it was nothing to do with Greg. It was the management company. They wouldn't even return my calls."

Couillard had moved on. For the rest of the summer and fall of 1989, he worked on the menu for Oceans. The room looked magnificent and Couillard was to have total freedom in the kitchen. It was the kitchen that was the problem – a room the size of a broom closet, stuffy and intolerably hot, with one wall that rattled and buzzed with the noise from the nightclub next door. Couillard hated it. "I was cooking for 120 people at 10 P.M. with each one of them wanting the full Greg Couillard fireworks in under an hour, and the temperature touching a hundred degrees. The hours were long, tempers flared. Even so, I could have done it with close coordination from the front of house, but it just wasn't there. I never went out into the dining room. I was too embarrassed! There I was, working in lime green bicycle shorts and a tie-dyed T-shirt and bandanna in a badly ventilated kitchen, and I didn't feel like walking out to shake hands with perfectly manicured women in Moschino dresses and Chanel suits. It was kiss-and-glamour, *Lifestyles of the Rich and Famous* out there. Not my style at all. Charles Khabouth and his partners were very hard-working and very efficient businessmen, but he thinks restaurants are all about riches and money and catering only to the wealthy."

For Khabouth as well, the relationship with his chef was turning sour. "In the beginning, you know, the whole thing worked like magic," he told me years later. "It was a perfect environment for him. He was making $90,000 a year for a five-day week. He was able to spend $2 just to decorate each plate! Then we began to lose customers because he didn't want to put someone's sauce on the side. Ridiculous! The customer has to get what he wants or you don't stay in business. But his philosophy is 'My way or let them go somewhere else.' Sometimes I'd go into the kitchen looking for him because food would be so late and he'd be in the walk-in cooler, smoking up ... We had a big argument and I told him things were not working out. Eventually he came across another opportunity. He gave me five days' notice and took all the staff with him. So unprofessional! I will say this, though. When he was working for me at Oceans he was cooking the best food I ever tasted in my life."

Did Couillard's departure lead to Oceans' closing, or was the restaurant doomed anyway, with lobster pasta at $42 and the recession taking hold? Khabouth reopened a month later with the pragmatic Susur Lee as chef, but he too left, after only two weeks. Alan Groom, brought over from England, cooked for the last few months of the restaurant's life. When it finally closed its doors, early in 1991, the city's food suppliers, some of whom were owed five-figure sums, were dismayed. Khabouth had no legal obligation to honour his debts, but he told the creditors they would all be paid eventually, and he proved as good as his word.

So glamorous, so expensive, Oceans seemed to me to be the bizarre apotheosis of the Queen West area's untutored, design-driven style in its decadent, late eighties phase. It certainly possessed all the Queen Street trademarks: enthusiasm, self-confidence, style, and hip hauteur. And yet it was so far removed from the mainstream that its memory has become dislocated from the history of the restaurant industry, surviving in anecdote as a hybrid and a curiosity.

Couillard too was rapidly acquiring that sort of reputation. By now it was common knowledge that he had a substance abuse problem, but that hardly made him special, either on Queen Street or in the restaurant world. He also had a precocious talent, and the combination of artistry and irresponsibility drew the attention of the press the way jam draws wasps. There were shades of Brendan Behan and Dylan Thomas to the phenomenon: as long as the artist continued to work, to astonish with his gifts, all was forgiven. "And then see what happens," complained the restaurateurs. "The press inflates the chef's ego to such monumental proportions that he forgets all concepts of loyalty and professional duty and comes and goes from one job to the next as he pleases." It was left to Joanne Kates to point out, in a cogently argued article in *Toronto* magazine, that it was the restaurateurs themselves who caused the problem, opening more restaurants when there weren't enough good chefs to go round, coaxing cooks away from other people's kitchens with offers of money and prestige.

In fact, both sides were right. In the late eighties, restaurateurs found themselves in the same position as the owners of baseball clubs. The league was diluted by expansion, but there were fortunes to be made if success could somehow be manufactured. Investors were waiting with wallets akimbo; all that was needed was a star chef, a name ratified by the opinion of press and public. So the chefs, in demand as never before, ceased to be artisans and invisible employees and became stars, free agents, flattered and wooed and paid handsomely by whoever could muster the dollars.

In Couillard's case, the flattery had come from the property developer Paul Oberman, a customer at Oceans who owned a location on King Street East, until recently the site of a decent Italian restaurant called San Lorenzo. Oberman needed a tenant, and he had proposed that Couillard leave Oceans, rent the space from him, and open his own restaurant there. He undertook to finance necessary alterations as a loan that would be amortized into the lease, and to subsidize the redecoration, an expenditure that would be paid back through a separate financial arrangement to be agreed upon later.

"It was a dream package," sighed Couillard. "Just like that piece of swampland in Florida. He wanted it open in five weeks. It was so exciting – the whole Judy Garland, Mickey Rooney thing – let's take a trashy but great set and turn it into Josef von Sternberg's *The Shanghai Gesture*. The lease allowed me a salary of $50,000, a lot less than Oceans, but that was okay. But I stipulated: I just want to do the food. I don't want to know about the business. Work me, exploit me, do my Blonde Ambition tour, but I don't want to do the bills!"

That was the first time I met Greg Couillard face to face. I was prowling the city streets late one night, still trying to familiarize myself with the restaurant strips and feeling like a cub reporter in the naked city, when I passed by the embryonic China Blues. The lights were on, the door was open: I went inside. Couillard was down on his hands and knees in T-shirt and baseball cap, hammering carpet to the floor. Another cook called Steve Potovsky was up a ladder, painting dragons onto the ceiling. They showed me around, explained the set-up, the main kitchen down in the basement, a semicircular cockpit like a bar where Couillard would cook in full view of the public, in touch with the customers in a way he had never been at Oceans.

Inevitably, the hammering and painting, the hands-on high spirits, reminded me of the theatre, of a stage crew constructing a set of canvas, wood, and paint that would look like marble and gold. The script, in this case, was the menu, a slim card of deep Oriental blue with a simple white insert, like a snowy cuff peeping from a silken sleeve.

Couillard always understood that a menu can be more than a list. The eighties had seen the rise of the recipe menu, where every conceivable ingredient was listed for every dish, a habit that had begun out of a desire for clarity but had sunk into showing off. Those were the days when it was cool to boast about the provenance of ingredients and to explain the way in which they were cooked. A typical example from a long-forgotten restaurant: "Free-range yellow corn-fed hen, split, pressed, rubbed with herb mustard and seared over mesquite coals." One can only hope the creature was dead before the ordeal began. I suppose it was more valid than the system it replaced, the classic French shorthand of naming dishes from an established repertoire: pêche Melba, chaud-froid Jeannette, dodine au Chambertin ... In the Escoffier era, sophisticated diners knew what they were ordering. Today, waiters would grow weary explaining that poulet Katoff was christened for a Polish city and not because Chef once found the family pet hunched over a chicken in the pantry. And yet the habit of dropping mysterious names persists to this day. What is Five Heaven

Phoenix Basket, tucked amongst the house specialties on the umpteenth page of a Chinese menu? What is a western sandwich, come to that?

At China Blues, Couillard had it both ways. He gave his creations amusing names such as Ruby Fong's Revenge – and then went on to list pertinent ingredients. Later, the pristine blue and white was replaced by a menu in a different style, created by graphic designer Laurie Siu. In Hong Kong, before coming to Canada, Siu had thought up exquisite menus for special events, such as a miniature gold and red paper fan, printed with the order of dishes and hidden inside a paper pouch. Knowing that Couillard's menu and wine lists were always changing, he devised for China Blues a beige-on-beige folder, decorated with an antique map of Canton and containing loose menu cards in five vivid colours. It was striking, practical, innovative – in other words, it stood out in Toronto like a palm tree in the park.

As a stationery obsessive, I have always relished an arresting menu, but 90 percent of the cards thrust into customers' hands in Toronto are utterly humdrum. Of the rest, half actually discourage ordering, either because they are stained and greasy or because their production values are so slipshod as to be offensive. Only a handful have ever been positively memorable.

The rarest attribute has always been beauty. Downstairs at Fenton's, the changing dinner menu dazzled with gorgeous water-colours of flowers. There was also a separate pasta card, and I like to think that this was as much to prevent the type from encroaching too clumsily over the illustration as to take advantage of market-fresh ingredients. The Avocado Club proposed the eponymous fruit, ripe, yellow, and good enough to eat, sketched by artist and filmmaker

Eugene Beck, who was also responsible for Beaujolais's grapes. They were definitely the exceptions to the rule of thumbprint.

"You like the blue and white?" Couillard asked. "Let's hope it's lucky!"

China Blues opened in September 1990 to triumphant reviews and sustained public interest. It closed one year later in a welter of acrimony and litigation. Exactly what happened in the interim is difficult to assess. I once spent weeks trying to get to the bottom of it, interviewing everyone involved: Couillard and his partner, Craig Howard, a young waiter from Oceans whom he had befriended and brought in to run the front of house; their lawyer, Jodi Feldman; their landlord, Paul Oberman; and a gallery of cooks, waiters, food suppliers, and general hangers-on. All parties had their own, very different versions of the progression of events, heavily laden with hostile allegations and innuendo.

Certainly the restaurant was successful, at least for the first six months. Money poured in and Howard paid the large staff handsomely, while both he and Couillard grew accustomed to living well. But, according to Couillard, there were also other expenses to be met (a claim that Oberman vigorously denied): "Soon after we opened, we found we had to replace every single bit of equipment in the place – plumbing, electrical, stoves, ovens, shelving, everything. But it was when I came back from a two-week vacation in March of 1991 that things started to get a little strange. I had my first look at the books and I flipped. There was literally nothing in the bank."

The bookkeepers hired when the restaurant opened had long since left, so now Craig Howard sought the advice of a freelance financial consultant, Tim Butson. Business matters were handed over to him, but as the months went by, China Blues' finances failed to respond to treatment. "Cheques were bouncing," remembers Couillard. "Suppliers were getting me on the phone, people I'd dealt with on friendly terms for years, saying, 'You owe me $30,000.' It just blew me away! Meanwhile Oberman was trying to get Craig and me to sign a financial agreement that would have given him complete control of everything if we ever went into default."

"The agreement was essentially a bank loan, with ridiculous insurance," said Jodi Feldman, "and as their lawyer, I absolutely forbade them to sign it. But Craig was very young and he was very scared, and one day he did sign it. Greg didn't, and without his signature it wasn't yet binding."

By the beginning of August 1991, it was clear that China Blues could not survive. Rent owed to Oberman was in arrears, debts to suppliers were piling up, and business was dropping off into its perennial August slump. On the afternoon of August 8, when the last lunchtime customers had left, Couillard gathered the staff in the restaurant for a meeting.

"They knew what was going on. I was very honest with them. Craig wasn't there and I was in a state of utter confusion, but I couldn't sign the next five years of my life over to Oberman. I was being forced out. I tore up the agreement and said, 'Now it's in the hands of the gods. Whatever happens happens.' We put a sign on the door saying 'Closed til the end of August.'"

"All indications are that they have abandoned the business," Oberman told the *Toronto Star* at the time. Attempts to contact Couillard and Howard were unsuccessful. The locks were changed.

"All I can tell you," he told me later, "is that we went to court, we were successful, we were awarded a very large judgment against Couillard, and he went personally bankrupt ... But don't be deceived. Don't for a minute think that this fellow is an innocent victim. I think if you look at the pattern, it's painfully obvious." Oberman had won his judgment in default. Couillard and Howard could not afford to litigate.

The aftermath rumbled on for weeks. Bailiffs arrived at Couillard's humble Queen Street apartment, looking for property missing from the restaurant, and took away an ornamental screen. This time, no attempt was made to reimburse the unpaid suppliers.

Oberman and Butson, together with most of the restaurant's original staff, quickly reopened China Blues, and the restaurant ran successfully until May 1992, when Oberman was finally able to re-rent the space. For Couillard, however, recovery was not so swift. "I was just dazed. It was like a movie where you're partying in a fast black and white car and there's a head-on collision and suddenly boom! It's over! People speculated that Craig and I had buried hundreds of thousands of dollars in numbered Swiss bank accounts. That August, we were spotted in Acapulco, Germany, San Francisco, Vancouver, in penthouse apartments, doing expensive drugs and drinking, living the high life ... Ridiculous. In fact, I was forced to go on welfare. Everybody knew my name, my reputation. Oberman had set up a *Toronto Star* article the following Saturday that completely damned me, including the photograph where I looked like everyone's Axl Rose nightmare. I can remember ducking when cars would backfire in Chinatown. My name was mud."

The success of China Blues had been a high point of Couillard's nine-year career as a chef; its failure marked an all-time low. A few loyal friends complained that he was a scapegoat, but most felt he had forfeited his right to any benefit of the doubt by his previous unexplained exits from Stelle and Oceans. The public latched onto the apparent pattern of the vanishing chef, while the food industry's own energetic network of gossip-mongers oohed and aahed at the scandal of a fallen celebrity.

The restaurant business is an odd demi-monde, as stressful and as self-involved as that of the theatre, but with more brutal hours. The big-time restaurateurs, like any other kind of impresario, need star chefs to draw in the public; they also need them to find the self-discipline to sustain their performance into a good long run. This always seemed to be more than Greg Couillard could manage, but a case might be made that at times he was miscast. His range may have been better suited to an intimate venue, such as the Parrot, Emilio's, or Stelle, than to a stage of the size and formality of Oceans or China Blues, where his lack of executive skills was most apparent.

In the end, it was Couillard's attitude that antagonized people. When things were going well, he revelled in any publicity, relishing and even embellishing the hearsay; when trouble flared up, he had a tendency to walk away, leaving the microphone to those he had angered, and half the story untold. Some saw such dramatic exits as symptomatic of an over-inflated ego; others, who had known him longer, interpreted them as signs of a deep-rooted vulnerability, necessary measures of emotional self-protection. Somewhere in the midst of the outrage and the adulation stood Couillard himself, fending off invitations to self-analysis with his motto of "no regrets," watching the movie of his life with wide-eyed fascination.

Throughout the fall of 1991, he lay low, living on welfare in his Queen Street West apartment. "Finally, after three months, I couldn't sit at home any more. I had my head shaved and put on a big cowboy hat, and went over to Johnny K's bar, Mrs. Smith's Cocktail Party on Queen Street. That's when I saw this guy smiling at me from the bar. He came over and I thought, Is he going to knife me for a bad debt? But it was Johnny. He said, 'There's no use trying to pull that alternative disguise; when I went down with Liberty I felt the same way.'

"I thought, Well, at least there's somebody out there with a sense of humour. I'd always found Johnny's places to be very hip and wry and comfortable. I'd loved Liberty and the King Curtis Room. He asked me to come and help out Lee Bailey in her kitchen at a new place he was looking after called Trixie."

And so, at last, the story approaches the point where it began, on the opening night of Avec ... Greg Couillard. A couple of restaurants still lie in between. Couillard worked on and off at Trixie until the spring of 1992, catering to a mainly gay clientele who were frequently disappointed at finding he was not in the kitchen. Then Johnny K opened Hudson, where a number of different chefs were assisted and eventually very ably replaced by K's wife, Laura Prentice, otherwise known as the lovely Lolita.

As for Couillard: with Trixie winding down, he was approached by Craig Howard with a new project. After China Blues, Howard had vowed never to open another restaurant as long as he lived, but time is a great healer. "I was driving by and I thought the place looked small enough, controllable ... I thought, Why not?"

Notorious opened on May 14, 1992, with Howard as manager, Couillard as chef, and enough of the old Queen West faithful schlepped north to Rosedale to bestow initial success. The tiny room on Yonge Street was beautiful, dark, colourful, and the menu offered fans another chance to taste revivals of favourite Couillard dishes, prepared in a minuscule open kitchen that gave the chef no chance to hide. Six months after the début, following a disgraceful attack on the young woman who worked there as maître d', and who was an old and loyal friend of his, Couillard was gone.

Craig Howard was spitting vitriol when I met him for coffee, days later. "Greg and I were very good friends for many years. He flushed it down the toilet and it was a very emotional thing for me. I wasn't about to see another restaurant go down. He abused customers and staff. He pushed me too far."

Couillard was more philosophical. Sitting with me one late afternoon in Avec's upstairs room, he came as close to self-analysis as I have ever heard him: "It's difficult working for people you've been partners with. Suddenly I was only an employee and was being made very aware of what I could and couldn't say or do. I loathed that open kitchen. My catch phrase at Notorious was 'I'm dancing as fast I can, Mr. Balanchine!' Within forty-eight hours of walking out I was saying, 'My God, I think I just saved my ass.'

"Which brings us all back to here and now, to Avec ... I'm getting real good at this. I used to wonder – maybe I can't keep a job. Now I *know* that maybe I can't keep a job. But I have no regrets. We've certainly had a lot of laughs in my kitchens."

And occasional fits of rage?

"Oh, I've thrown a few pans. Some would say with deadly aim, but I totally deny that. There was a story from Oceans that I was prone to throwing knives that would stick into the door at those waiters who were driving me mad. I never did that ... I may have brandished them – in a piratical sort of way."

Have drink and drugs damaged your career?

"Of course. But I would say enhanced, not damaged ... I've made up my mind not to deny myself any pleasures in this life. God knows, I've buried enough of my friends, and I would hate to be dying without having tasted a glass of Château Margaux just because I was on the wagon. I'd regret that. I'd be really pissed off. I work ridiculously hard. I have a huge clientele because they know me for what I deliver on the job. They're the reason I'm in this business. It's certainly not for the money, not so much for the glory any more. It's more that I love the restaurant life in its purest form, in the way Cecil Troy did, or Christian Vinassac, where you're living it ... I hate it when it turns into a business. If I ever did another place it would be me doing everything. No debts, no computers, just a pay-as-you-play situation, like Paul used to do at Emilio's. Maybe I'll take it on the road somewhere, go and cook in the Caribbean for a season, be a troubadour chef, go to Europe, Berlin ... I think if I hang around too much longer this city will get me. I'm going to be forty years old this summer. I'd like to start the second half on a positive note."

WHAT HAPPENED NEXT? Did Couillard take Berlin? Did Johnny K and Laura Prentice ride on to a date with destiny?

All three stayed at Avec until the summer of '94, when they left the premises suddenly, taking what they could, ripping doors off hinges and sprinklers out of the walls. Two weeks later they reopened as New Avec in hastily renovated but nonetheless handsome premises on Adelaide Street, back in the old Queen West neighbourhood. Almost simultaneously, K created a second restaurant, called Pan on the Danforth. It débuted to rave reviews, with Laura Prentice as chef.

"It's good to be downtown again," K told me one autumn evening at New Avec. "I was out of my element at Yonge and Davisville." Waiters were moving quietly between the empty tables, lighting candles, prepping the room for another busy night that would begin much later. Johnny K's clientele doesn't eat early.

Sipping a mineral water, looking decidedly clean-cut in T-shirt and denims, K presented a new, mellow kind of cool, befitting a man just turned forty. "I've been anti-dressing-up for a while now," he explained. "Mostly because I have a three-year-old daughter, which means stains on the shoulder." He smiled to himself. "She's won me over. Before she was born, if you'd told me I'd like staying home with a kid, I'd have said, 'No way in hell.' Well, I enjoy it."

I had to laugh. It was such an unexpected response. I'd shown up expecting to feel as uncool as ever in the face of K's gypsy disdain for the stay-at-home, and he'd turned the tables once again. But he has always cherished his lack of predictability. Since he opened the Queen Street Eatery at Queen and Logan in 1978, Johnny K has given the city more than twenty restaurants, clubs, and bars. They have had little in common, except that they always reflect his unerringly precocious taste. Such clubs as Crush, the Ballroom, 4th and 5th, King Curtis seemed to appear overnight and vanished as suddenly. There was little need for promotion. If you were cool, you knew where they were.

"That was the eighties," he shrugged. "Back then, nobody cared about money because everybody had it. So my clubs had a door policy based on attitude. We liked cool people, interesting people. You didn't have to be super-beautiful, or pull up in a limo, you just had to be interesting. Sure, the places came and went quickly. I was buying and selling a lot of real estate then and making myself my own tenant.

LA BOHÈME

It gave me the opportunity to create my little playgrounds, to have fun. And when the real estate sold, the place went.

"Today people are impressed by money again, so you'd have to spend a million bucks to get people in. That's why I'm not doing clubs any more. Besides, for a club to work, I have to be in there seven nights a week, to be part of it, and that means the outrageousness, the late nights, the non-stop drinking, the dancing up on the bar, the major flirting. In a restaurant it's a little more subtle – sexy in another way."

K's restaurants were always more conservative than his clubs. Down at the Beach end of Queen East, his eponymous bistro, Johnny K, lasted ten years. Liberty, on Richmond at Church, drew a corporate clientele who rarely recognized K as the owner, standing at the bar with long hair, a goatee, and a cane. He enjoyed the double life. It reminded him of the way he felt as Jonathan Katsuras, a Greek-Canadian kid racing home after school to change his clothes, running up the subway steps to get to the latest club. That was how he developed the instincts that guided his successes and his swift, occasionally fly-by-night exits. He had a low boredom threshold, a perverse antipathy to following fashion, and the confidence to trust his own feelings utterly.

Sitting there with him, I heard a small voice in my head: Where is it written that restaurateurs and chefs are required to be stable? Who says they have to stay put? If they want to wheel and deal like businessmen playing the stock market, why shouldn't they? The great blue- and white-collar majority of the restaurant industry can say it runs contrary to the time-honoured work ethic of the profession, but perhaps the majority are wrong. Toronto needs every free spirit it can muster, just to shake up the decorum. This city needs its Queen West.

"And have you seen Greg recently?" I asked. K smiled like a cat and slowly stroked a wrinkle out of the white tablecloth. He took a sip from the glass of mineral water.

"You might find him back where he started."

By the end of 1994, Couillard's career seemed to have come full circle. He was back at 325 Queen Street West, the property that had once been Beggars Banquet and the Parrot. Through the eighties, the restaurant had chugged along comfortably with owner-chef André Théberge at the helm. Chef Anne Yarymowich cooked with him there for a while before opening Mildred Pierce. In 1990 a new group of investors bought the place and imposed a number of different incarnations upon the tired old building before reopening in 1994 as Sanona, with Couillard in the kitchen. It didn't pan out. Some of the backers changed and so did the name, to Cool Yard, and then to Couillard's, all in the space of a year. There was also a month or two when the restaurant appeared to be closed but was actually running as an after-hours drinking club – probably the only time it turned a profit. Suppliers were complaining of unpaid debts yet again. The *Toronto Star* ran a story of a threatening late-night confrontation between some greengrocers and one of the owners. A spokesman for the restaurant called me up, full of indignation. "It gives us a bad name," he cried, "and it's so unfair! They weren't unpaid suppliers. They were just some guys who'd bought some bad dope from one of the bar staff."

Couillard also telephoned me occasionally, once at three o'clock in the morning. I went down to see him a couple of times. He seemed bored and tired and uninvolved, still cooking items he had developed in Stelle days.

In March 1996, the phone call came from a lunchtime Chinese-buffet-cum-karaoke-bar on Dundas West, right opposite the Art Gallery of Ontario. Ever curious, I hopped the subway, found Steve Potovsky once again up a ladder painting, and Couillard full of his usual new-location enthusiasm. There had been a quarrel down at Couillard's and he and Potovsky, who had been cooking famously at the Rivoli before moving up the street to join Greg as sous-chef at Couillard's, had moved on. I was introduced to the new partner, a tall, moustachioed police sergeant from 52 Division who owned the lease on the bar. He seemed somewhat dazed by all the attention, and my heart went out to him.

"Steve is going to remake the room with black lacquer, gold lamé, and purple paint," explained Couillard. "We're calling it Majic."

A few days later, I went back for the opening-night party. Four or five people were sitting around in the tacky purple glow. I stayed an hour and went home.

It was six months before I saw Couillard again – on a sunny autumn afternoon on King Street, outside the King Edward Hotel, with the cold wind whistling round the corner from Yonge. He wore a windbreaker and a baseball cap and looked ten years younger.

"I couldn't believe what I read in *Toronto Life* this summer," he began. "That I'd gone back to my parents' farm outside Winnipeg. They don't own a farm! They've never owned a farm!" Greg Couillard – ever the stickler for absolute truth. But he had gone back to Winnipeg, to his parents' house on the edge of the suburbs, and had made himself fit cycling thirty kilometres into the city and back every day. There, he explained, he had been fêted and hailed as a homeboy star by Winnipeg's burgeoning restaurant industry. He had cooked on television, guested in top kitchens, and spent time with his old friend

Dan Aykroyd, who was in the area making a film about the Avro Arrow débâcle.

"Anyway, now I'm back!" The eyes were shining. "And I'm opening a new place on Richmond West, a little place that reminds me so much of Stelle. I'm doing a whole new menu. We're calling it Sarkis."

A few days after it opened, and not without a certain feeling of déjà vu, I showed up for dinner. The room was good-looking, elegantly lit, and I wished there had been another two or three customers to enjoy it with me, for the menu was new and the food was wonderful. Tender little roast quail had picked up the sweet-tart spice of a marinade of lime leaf, lemongrass, and tamarind. Couillard served it with a glaze of grenadine and pheasant jus and an exuberant garnish of pomegranate seeds, pineapple, grilled oyster mushrooms, zucchini, crunchy raw okra, and pungent, fresh Thai herbs, making each mouthful a new adventure. A fillet of sea bass was poached in citric coconut milk until each juicy flake seemed to melt on the tongue; contrasts of texture and flavour came from a sweet, soft vegetable curry, crisp Chinese cabbage heart, green onion ribbons, and chrysanthemum greens. The carbo du jour was creamy scalloped potatoes, spiced with crunchy coriander seeds and star anise.

I waxed enthusiastic in my next *Toronto Life* column and received a ticking-off from a number of other food writers: How can you still give the man ink? Don't you know he still owes money to suppliers? Don't you care about how he has treated people in the past? I felt stuck in the script of *The Doctor's Dilemma*, only there was no dilemma. Judging the quality of a chef's work is hard enough; judging his or her moral rectitude is a little outside the restaurant columnist's mandate.

"**I** THOUGHT YOU WERE OLD!" she repeated in astonishment. "From reading your articles – I just assumed you were really old ..."

I didn't know what to say. We were standing by the check-in desk in Pearson's Terminal Three, on our way to a week's tour of Germany's heartland. She wrote for a Vancouver magazine; I was there for Air Canada's *EnRoute*. I still don't know if her remark was a compliment. The confusion faded as other journalists from across Canada joined us, introducing themselves, while a representative from the German National Tourist Office checked us in. It was to be a delightful week, cycling along the banks of the Main and the Neckar (some of the more sedate scribes followed in a coach), visiting moated villages and medieval banqueting halls, castles and vineyards, staying in very good hotels, tasting the region's finest food and wines. All that was required of me in return was that I should be a polite guest, a conscientious observer, and that I should share the experience with as many readers as possible when I came home.

For three or four years, soon after we came back to Canada, I led the charmed life of a bona fide freelancer, writing a restaurant column and wine and travel features for *Toronto Life*, a wine column and occasional travel features for *EnRoute*, and as many other assignments as I could coax out of a dozen or so publications in Toronto, London, and New York. Being persona grata with so many outlets put me on the lists of national tourist boards and public relations firms, and the invitations to travel and taste began to glide out of the fax machine. There are few better ways to see the world, but freelance travel writing isn't a job I would recommend to a family man. One is away too often from hearth and home. It also becomes apparent after a while that spending a week abroad, then a week at home writing the piece and organizing the next one, is no way to get rich.

Nevertheless, it can be done. The first thing you need is an angle, a reputation as an expert on something: green ecological issues, or skiing, or tigers, or golf, or perhaps food and wine. This is necessary in order to convince editors that you are the person best suited for the job. Next, pick somewhere out of the atlas that you want to see – Tierra del Fuego, for example – and spend an hour or two thinking of ways in which your particular angle can be applied to the destination; then pitch the story to the most prestigious publication you know. There will be no need to cover expenses, you explain. That's when they say yes, and you start making your calls: to the Argentine tourist board, the Argentine airline, the Ontario agents for Argentine wines, a brand-new resort hotel in Buenos Aires you have heard of from friends. You tell them all that you have an assignment from a prestigious newspaper. Accommodation and airline tickets soon follow. It's only a matter of brazen nerve.

Now you must make the project pay. Call up editors in other countries and tell them you're going to Tierra del Fuego: would they like an article, exclusive within their area, at no expense to themselves beyond your fee. The *Spokane Spectator,* the *Canberra Counterblast,* and *Yachtsman's Knitwear Monthly* all say yes. Add a further fifty bucks to each article if you know how to use a camera and can provide a picture. The trip is beginning to look like a nice little earner.

The next thing you know, you are sitting at dusk in the yacht club at the end of the world, watching a full yellow moon rise out of the Beagle Channel, while the lights of Ushuaia twinkle poignantly beneath the brooding charcoal silhouette of the Andes' southernmost peaks. It's March 21, the first evening of the antipodean autumn, and the kelp-thick water lies as sleek as a seal's back under the fading sky. Now all you have to do is conjure up a story that says marginally more than "Ushuaia, city of contrasts" and you've found yourself a career, or at the very least, a most entertaining sideline.

While travel writing broadens the mind, food writing tends to broaden the belly. Foodie trips demand just as much stamina as a hiking tour over the Hindu Kush. In France, in particular, the highly competitive restaurant industry vies for the appetites of visiting writers, striving to buy column-inches with more foie gras and ris de veau than you've ever seen in your life.

Such generosity! I remember sitting in the bright sun of a hotel garden in the Roussillon region, tasting thirty white wines, then tucking into oysters and pâté, olives and cheeses, and tiny fried fish tossed with onions and rosemary. "Leave some room for your lunch!" reminded our guide. It was as well that we did. Lunch was a magnificent cassoulet prepared by the wives of the vignerons of Limoux, surrounded by dish upon dish of local delicacies, preceded by a tasting of twenty sparkling Blanquette wines. Then it was on to the Minervois region to taste immature reds from the barrel before an eight-course dinner at the local two-Michelin-star restaurant.

A greedy man's fantasy vacation, but after a week of such treatment, the body begins to rebel. The intake of calories and cholesterol reaches toxic proportions and the brain begins to hallucinate about exercise and fasting. Towards the end of the Roussillon trip, walking into yet another Michelin-starred dining room and seeing each dinner place set with eight knives and forks and three spoons, the surviving journalists began to murmur of mutiny. There were fewer of us by then. Two of our number had begged to remain at the hotel, afraid that death by gastronomy was imminent. Nevertheless, we sat down, and the maître d' began his detailed litany of the ordeal that lay ahead – terrine of this and confit of that, sauces of cream and vermouth, glazes of meat juices and liqueurs, a turbot, a baby pig …

"Would it be too much to ask the chef," said the valiant Geraldine Rubino, wine writer and veteran of innumerable banquets, "if he could slip a simple green salad in there somewhere?" Our eyes shone with gratitude. The maître d' seemed nonplussed for an instant, then hurried away with the request. The thought of that salad sustained us through the first six courses of the meal. At last it appeared, but the chef had been unable to restrain himself. Tucked away, hidden beneath the glistening lettuce leaves on every plate, were tiny pieces of peach poached in Armagnac, and half a pound of impeccably cooked duck livers. The expression on the face of the maître d' was one of undisguised triumph.

WINE WRITING is the dream gig. Wine lovers assume that the claims of winemakers are not to be trusted, and that to find objective opinion one must turn to the writers. Winemakers know this, so they court and flatter and spoil the hacks, usually with the active support and financial backing of their board of trade and national tourist organization. Rescuing the whole situation from sheer commercialism is the fact that winemakers, without exception in my experience, are generous, civilized, congenitally hospitable people who enjoy it when strangers show enthusiasm for their creations.

So how do you become a wine writer? Step one is to drink a great deal of wine – rarely a problem for a writer. Step two is to develop a palate, which tends to come naturally if you excel at step one. Then you learn the mechanics of tasting like a pro (this takes about two hours) and familiarize yourself with the jargon (a week should be long enough). You read enough about winemaking to understand details of cause and effect and you cultivate a memory for smells and tastes and names. The writing bit isn't so hard. Simply follow the journalistic principles of looking and listening to everything that goes on around you, in the vineyard, winery, cellars, and tasting room. You learn by watching your peers exactly how to convey a sense of polite reserve when the winemaker opens the plonk. If you make the right noises, and maybe mention other wineries in the area you are thinking of visiting, the quality of the wines being opened for your inspection will miraculously improve.

There are one or two provisos. Most important, it is necessary to love wine. If you don't, you'll be bored out of your mind, and hiding it will prove impossible, especially when the oenologist pauses to bandy pH values or show off his new bottling line. For him, the rattling mechanism is so much more than a major financial investment. It is the place of the last farewell, the romantic envoi for a wine he has nursed since grapehood. Give him so much as a smile and he'll show you each tube and turntable, each individual device for applying label, capsule, and cork. The only escape is to reach out your hand as if to touch the beloved machine. In an instant, he sweeps you off to the tasting room.

The big test for the wine writer is the solo field trip. Suddenly there is no one else standing between you and the winemaker, no opinionated young colleague keen to do all the talking, no guardian angel from the public relations firm to make sure you find your way back to the coach. On such occasions hospitality can get out of hand.

Darko Dobrovic was my contact in Zagreb, a charming, slightly raffish character with short black hair and long black eyelashes who looked exactly like an English actor called Victor Spinetti. I was in Yugoslavia to write a travel feature for *EnRoute* and a wine column for *Toronto Life*, exploring the sudden renaissance in winemaking in the post-Tito era. Two Croatian wine importers in Ontario had set up the trip; Darko was their representative. He met me as I climbed out of the taxi from the airport and gave me five minutes to take my suitcases up to my room in the Hotel Esplanade. Then we drove off into the darkening, rainswept afternoon to the first tasting in a farm outside Karlovac.

"Are you hungry?" he asked, as we approached the town.

"Not really, I ate on the plane."

"A little, maybe?"

He turned off the road and into some wooded hills, coming at last to the Restaurant Dubovac, a locally renowned dining room in the turret of a decrepit medieval castle. The specialty was game, cooked in a distinctively Hungarian style, and Darko ordered a massive meal, rinsed down with the best wines in the cellars and a shot of slivovitz between courses to burn the palate clean. Hours later, bloated and creaking with heartburn, we resumed our journey. We finally pulled into the farmyard at about eight o'clock.

Our winemaker, Vladimir Nezic, was delighted to see us, and we waddled after him into the firelit parlour of the farmhouse. Steaming on the table stood a vast platter of sausage and fried potatoes prepared by Mrs. Nezic in our honour. "We must eat everything," whispered Darko. "It would be terribly rude to refuse." I did my best. Then the rest of the meal arrived: jugged hare, roast pork, a cauldron of heavy noodles in butter, many kinds of salad, grapes, cheeses, sweet pâtisseries filled with fruit jams ... It was only the extraordinary quality of Nezic's white wines – a fresh, full-bodied, botrytis-touched Neuberger and a rich, bone-dry, incredibly spicy Rotgipfler, a grape rarely found outside Austria – that allowed me to do my duty to his wife's magnanimous hospitality.

The rest of that sojourn in Yugoslavia was equally eventful. We nearly died in a sudden blizzard at midnight on a pothole-cratered highway in Slavonia; two days later, we almost passed out from heat prostration on the limestone karst precipices of the Dalmatian coast. We tasted ancient, heavily oxidized Rieslings in the Papuk Hills, wines that had been hidden from both the Nazis and the Communists in bricked-up niches, camouflaged with cellar mould.

We stood among vines, gazing through barbed-wire fences into Italy, and we surrendered our prized bottles of "red label" Babic, gifts from a kindly winemaker, to a carload of gun-toting traffic cops on a lonely coast road near Split. We drove far and slept little, struggling into early-morning tastings in moribund, state-controlled wineries, where the directors crowded around, chain-smoking black tobacco and drinking black coffee between gulps of their cooperative blended plonk. Many of the wines Darko showed me were astonishingly good, but it was other, incidental experiences that now seem more vivid.

"What are we drinking to now?" I asked Darko at two in the morning in the yacht club on the Dalmatian island of Korcula, as a rowdy gang of youths thrust yet another beaker of grappa into my hand.

"An independent Croatia," he answered.

"An independent Korcula!" one of the lads corrected him sternly.

In Slovenia, we stopped for lunch at a restaurant, and the usually gentle Darko got into a shouting match with the waiter. "Couldn't you tell!" he seethed later when we were back in the car. "The bastard was Serbian."

In the old port of Zadar, after Darko had gone home to Karlovac, my guide was an elderly and thoroughly urbane professor of modern languages. Together we explored the cathedral, the Roman forum, the church of Saint Donat that stood like a perfect cylinder, without foundations, on the two-thousand-year-old pavement. Then we wandered off through the crowded lanes of the old town. Everywhere, stallholders were selling the latest fad souvenirs: separatist bumper stickers bearing the letters CRO for Croatia, instead of YU for Yugoslavia. "I confess," said the professor, taking my arm, "that in a foolish spasm of nationalist feeling I too purchased one. Fortunately, rationality prevailed. I have not applied it to my car."

We finished our tour in the market, where amongst the colourful, fragrant mounds of fruit, vegetables, and fish we stopped to listen to two white-blonde pedlars trying to sell a tin alarm clock to a bemused audience. "They are Lithuanians," explained the professor. "People like them have been coming here for months now, driving down from the Baltic to sell cheap toys, second-hand clothing, hammers and nails, whatever they have. We don't understand them; they don't understand us. It's very curious. This country is changing, I think." Passing through a gate in the massive, sloping Venetian fortifications of the old city to where we had left our cars, we stood aside for a crowd of startlingly good-looking teenagers, their school binders decorated with the red and white checkered emblem of an independent Croatia.

The professor sighed. "Politics ... To tell you the truth, I am somewhat tired by the impulsiveness of Mediterranean life. As a journalist it is your bread and butter; but it is not my cup of tea. I dream of a small apartment in North London."

I noticed as he drove away that his car did have a bumper sticker after all. I had seen it before in Slovenia: EU, for a united Europe.

The professor's quiet rationalism did not prevail. Within two weeks of my return to Canada, Yugoslavia collapsed into atrocity. I wrote to Darko, but I doubt he ever received my letter. Bombs were already falling near Karlovac. In Toronto, restaurateurs were moaning about the high price of olive oil.

8

▧ COCOONING ▧

THERE HAD BEEN cheaper houses for sale
in Scarborough, but they were all located in
hydro fields or had walls made of asbestos and
urea formaldehyde. With our usual flair for
investment, we had set out to buy in 1988, at the
teetering peak of the real estate boom, and found
only one property that met our exacting financial
circumstances. It stood on a backstreet within
easy reach of the used-car lots of Lawrence
Avenue East. I think it was the same tree-lined

boulevard on which John from the Royal Alexandra had lived and barbecued, so many years before.

What we really bought was a garden. The house was incidental, a stolid, postwar brick cube made uglier by old aluminum siding and a drafty, unheated extension at the back. But the garden ... We saw it first in late summer, when the crabapple tree and the raspberry canes were laden with fruit, and thought the yard a tiny Eden, our unimprovable lot in life. By the time we moved in, winter had come and we could look left or right along the backyards of the whole street, a vista of mud and wire and rain-filled craters that would have squeezed a sigh of recognition from veterans of the Somme.

Five barren months of it. Then suddenly, overnight, around the middle of May: an eruption. Blunt, pale green shoots burst up in unsuspected corners; the tangled branches of the crabapple vanished beneath pink blossom. The scraggy sticks along the fence thickened into lilac bushes and forsythia. Within weeks, the garden was enclosed again, a private lawn surrounded by high walls of foliage that were impenetrable to all but the children, who found green tunnels in the bushes and hid in them like rabbits. On hot summer mornings, with the doors and windows open wide, the house and yard lost their distinct identities. The extension at the back, now my study, lay on that blurred frontier, a place of comings and goings. The traffic was busiest at lunchtime – small children passing through with rugs to spread in the bright sunshine, then back and forth again, more carefully, with plates of sandwiches and fruit, and finally, more slowly still, with brimming beakers of lemonade.

Joe's friends seemed to like spending the day on our gypsy property. Some of their parents, however, found our lifestyle disturbing.

In the evening, they would pull up in shining cars to collect their boys, stepping gingerly over the potholes in the driveway, looking askance at the tire swing. These were people who had bought monster homes on the treeless subdivisions to the north, investing to the limits of their lines of credit in the booming eighties, now consumed with anxiety as the recession swirled about their two-garage, mock-Georgian châteaux like the incoming tide around a sandcastle. They were mortgage paupers, as we were, but on a huge and terrifying scale. Haggard and exhausted, husband and wife pursued two separate careers to meet the payments on their echoing, broadloomed acreage. They had no time to live in the place, no money left to go out. The last vestiges of energy were spent on keeping up appearances and, in particular, looking after the lawn. To suburban men, an immaculate lawn is a complex symbol, expressing a public commitment to social values and also serving as a personal totem of manhood, its upkeep a measure of his powers. Priapus, after all, was also the god of gardens. No wonder they averted their eyes from our little patch, the anti-lawn, full of juicy clovers and merry dandelions. And when they had gone, our children toddled back around the house to invent new games in the flowerbed jungles, and the noise of their play made sense of our decision to move to the hinterland.

Because it sure wasn't for the restaurants. There were three within walking distance of our house. The first was a strip-mall "dining room" in the old-time Ontario sense of the term, a place for consuming ketchup and beer with eggs or bacon or goop cherry pie, fries and gravy being the compulsory side order. The second was Arax, a family-run Armenian restaurant which I enjoyed very much, but which left me reeking like an old garlic clove for days, so that our bedroom would be filled with a greenish fog when we awoke and even my son's pet newts backed away when I leaned over their aquarium. The last was a Greek restaurant, run by Greeks who found our Corfiot accent comical. We tried to make it our local, attempted to befriend the staff and to show an interest in the specials, but the kitchen, like a cheap soufflé, failed to rise to the occasion.

I don't believe any of our neighbours ever patronized these places. Their taste was for pizza or Swiss Chalet, or very occasionally for the food outlets in the great supermalls that stud Toronto's far-flung suburban ring from Mississauga to Pickering. Wendy remembers the impact that Scarborough Town Centre made on local sensibilities when it was built – something like man's first landing on the moon. Droves of architectural graduates were bussed in to witness the coming millennium; gangs of pre-teen mall rats went there to smoke forbidden cigarettes. It was a wonder of the world, vast, escalatored, tricked out in glass and marble, and set in a car park the size of the Gobi Desert. To me, it looked indistinguishable from a dozen other commercial labyrinths where suburban Canadians went to stroll for miles past fountained atria and dwarf trees that seemed perpetually in leaf.

Always searching for new restaurants for *Toronto Life*, I investigated every false rumour of gastronomic competence that emerged from these concrete hives, but found only terminal cases of mall nutrition, identical eateries that made a mockery of municipal boundaries. This was never obvious from the mall directories, those illuminated black obelisks by the entrance. The apparent breadth of choice bewildered the eye: six restaurants scattered about the aisles, or fifteen smaller outlets, gathered for the sake of convenience into a Food Hall, or Food Court, or Foode Fayre – tiny, over-familiar franchises, huddled behind the dazzle and subliminal buzz of a forest of wrought neon tubing. One sold hot dogs, another fries, one teriyaki, and another only salads; one offered nothing but cinnamon buns. Tables and seating were communal, a charmingly democratic idea; less attractive were the garbage bins at your elbow, and there were only polystyrene cups and dishes to be had, lending their uniquely inorganic flavour to everything, and plastic forks that were no match at all for a galvanized veal parmesan.

Back to the directory and a closer look at the six restaurants. Two were cafeterias, fine for lunch hours but hell for a solitary, heavily laden shopper or someone with toddlers in tow. Two turned out to have gone out of business or to be relocating to neighbouring premises. The fifth was part of a chain of pancake houses where even the bill comes wrapped in a flannelette crêpe, and that left only the one with the funny name that you passed on the way in and assumed, correctly, to be no more than a tarted-up tavern. It was as true then as it is today: if you've seen a mall, you've seen 'em all.

Thanks to my work, however, Wendy and I led a double life. The Don Valley Parkway was the great umbilical, the portal between penny-pinching daily reality and nocturnal extravagance. In the morning I would be queuing at cash register number one at the Kennedy Road Canadian Tire for a $50 advance on the store credit card – the only plastic that still worked. That evening, we might be tasting terrine of foie gras at Truffles, with *Toronto Life* footing the bill.

But man does not live by pâté alone. As the summer of 1991 opened like a rose, it became clear that our income would never keep pace with our expenses. Our bank declared record profits that year but was not lending funds to the self-employed. We felt we could not ask my beloved mother for yet another generous subsidy. Despair and disaster loomed. The solution was obvious: a road trip. A long one. "And when we come back," explained Wendy, "we can start all over again." It took months to organize enough assignments and then to finesse free accommodation for a family of four from the subjects of all those stories, but by the time we left for England in September, everything was in place for a four-month meander in a borrowed car down through Europe, on into the Sahara, and back again. We put our house on the market, committed our debts to posterity, and quit the suburbs forever.

BY AND LARGE, 1991 was not a good year for such irresponsible escapades. The banks shut up tighter than Rodney's oysters, and restaurateurs who had blithely signed absurdly expensive leases a year or two earlier found themselves looking for new careers. The rich and their imitators took to cocooning, holding tight to their wealth while great institutions cracked and broke like glacial icebergs and slipped into oblivion.

The Windsor Arms was one of the first to go. George Minden had sold it not long before, and his last two chefs, Michael Bonacini and Marc Thuet, leaped over to Centro just in the nick of time. Fenton's passed away amid much wailing and gnashing of teeth from customers who had forgotten to eat there during the last few years. Oceans dried up, and later, so did China Blues. The Sutton Place Hotel started its long, slow swoon into the arms of the receivers. It was byebye, Nekah, and so long, Noodles. The King Ranch spa became a training centre for bankers.

We returned from our road trip to a city still groggy from such devastation, and settled into a rented apartment near Yonge and Eglinton. Ironically, the closest restaurant to our new home was Centro – Centro the glittering, Centro the still glamorous, the holdout refuge of the big spenders – while just up the street was its equally glossy mirror image, North 44°. Sticking to his own defiant agenda, Mark McEwan had opened his restaurant in late 1990, and those of us who had raved about his cooking at Pronto (a lamb consommé, served in a golden bowl, lives forever in my heart as the very essence of the flavour of lamb) hoped he would make it. McEwan himself took a much more pragmatic stance. He knew Toronto's economy would eventually recover, and he wanted North 44° to be around and intact when that happened. Rather than compromise, he decided to make the maximum use of his resources, baking bread in the wee small hours when the kitchen was dark and wholesaling it to the city. He did the same with smoked salmon and then set up a catering company to keep his cooks and serving staff busy. In the years to come, these sidelines would be million-dollar addenda for North 44°.

But Centro and North 44° were the exceptions. During the early nineties, most restaurants were cinching their belts. Tablecloths were hidden beneath butcher's paper to cut the laundry bills. Menus were shorter and more reasonably priced as big-ticket ingredients gave way to the comfort cuisine of "peasant" economies: pasta and mashed potatoes, onions, root vegetables, beans and pulses. Owners with tens of thousands of dollars locked up in the inventory of their wine cellars unloaded what they could and stopped replenishing bins. Many people who were used to eating out three times a week found the habit was hard to break, but now they sought out places where they could relax without having to dress up or flaunt the flexibility of their credit cards, places that offered obvious value for money. Relative frugality was politically correct, which did not mean burgers at Fran's but might involve turning your back on Centro once in a while and crossing the road to visit Massimo Rosticceria, where Christopher McDonald was chef for three months in 1990.

Stadtländer's protégé had already assembled an intriguing curriculum vitae, with stints at Centro and a Tex-Mex restaurant called Santa Fe and a summer in Fort Belvedere, England, as private chef to Galen and Hilary Weston. He had travelled and worked in Italy, and the rosticceria represented the fruits of that particular sabbatical, not to mention his Stadtländeresque mission to mould the tastes of his public. Customers sat at communal tables and chose their meals from a very limited list of nightly options recited by the waiters. The marvellous spit-roasted, herb-dusted chicken on a Tuscan salad of bread, tomato, crunchy cucumber, and onion soon became famous. McDonald might frame it with a salad that Wendy and I had known and loved in our village in Greece, made with orange, onion, and olives, or else a simple celery soup. Fresh fruit and biscotti were the plain dessert, as often as not. If it all sounds a tad monastic – well, that was partly the point, but the cooking was good enough to make up for the fact that patrons might end up having to talk to strangers, an alarming prospect for many Torontonians. The critics raved, but the owners lost their nerve and changed the format to something far more conventional, and McDonald moved on.

Strolling up Yonge Street, through our new neighbourhood, it was clear that Toronto had entered the Bistro Age. Some blocks north of Lawrence, for instance, Da Dante had recently opened its doors. The Dante in question was Dante Rota, once executive chef of the

Windsor Arms and then owner and chef of Noodles. When Noodles closed in 1990, he had gone briefly to Orso to sort things out in the kitchen recently abandoned by Raffaello Ferrari. His son, Carlo, was working there as maître d'. But Dante wanted another place of his own, where he and his wife, Rina, could cook together. Thanks to the recession, he was able to buy the Da Dante building for half its original asking price.

If there is a more friendly, down-to-earth couple than the Rotas in Toronto's restaurant industry, I have yet to meet them. The whole family was busy repainting the cosy little premises when I dropped by, putting up shelves to hold boxes of pasta and bottles of oil (instant décor) and laughing about the new adventure. Verdi played on the cassette deck. We sat down around a table, a bottle of Chianti appeared, and Rina brought out photographs to show me, pictures of Dante fifteen years earlier when he was executive chef of the Excelsior Hotel in Hong Kong, surrounded by his kitchen brigade of eighty, pictures of the Windsor Arms, of Noodles.

"Now that really was an adventure," chuckled Dante. "Buying Noodles from Mr. Minden cost us every penny we had. If no one had walked in that first Monday we'd have had to close down."

"But a restaurant is like anything else you own," added Rina. "When we were first married, we had nothing. We saved up for each new gadget and appliance for our home, and treasured it because we had worked for it. Noodles was the biggest gadget of all, so we cherished it accordingly. It'll be the same here."

Dante asked if I was hungry. He and Rina were testing some recipes – penne with sausage and fennel, and delicate little agnolotti filled with fresh crab, bathing in a sauce of saffron, brandy, and cream.

While they went back to the kitchen, Carlo waxed philosophical. "A lot has changed since the eighties. At Noodles we had a $35,000 computer system to manage the accounts. Here we have an old tin box. But my mum and dad are happy; they like having us all together. I think this place will do well, because people are savvy now. They know what's important. There are plenty of things about the last decade that we all want to forget: how much we spent on stupid things. People are no longer impressed by glamour for its own sake. Looking back on it, I suppose Roberto Martella at Grano showed the way. These days, we all want good food and a good time, but it has to feel genuine and comfortable and real."

Grano exemplified those qualities. The smell of the bread baking in the basement, the inevitable queue impeding the view of people scouting the antipasto counter, Roberto greeting customers from his central position by the little horseshoe bar: even before they added the extra rooms, Grano was party central. In the eighties, the rich had found it all such fun to sit on hard wooden chairs and drink old Amarone from dime-store tumblers, to bring their children and raise their voices and point out the recycled olive oil cans that doubled as vases. In the nineties, the place came into its own, a model for restaurateurs instead of an eccentricity, a source of energy in timid times. Earlier they had reminded each other that Roberto was a close friend of Franco Prevedello, as if that lent Grano extra kudos. Now they took pleasure in the fact that the Martellas lived upstairs and that Roberto's wife, Lucia, was the chef.

Domesticity had become chic, but while bistros were a fashionable alternative for the wealthy, they were scarcely guaranteed money machines. The neighbourhood restaurant's traditional, middle-income clientele was eating at home. Night after night, walking the streets, peering through restaurant doors and windows like Wee Willie Winkie, I saw nothing but empty chairs and tables.

And yet people continued to open new restaurants, though I had to wonder why. One day I put the question to Brian Heaseman, hands-on owner of Cities, a much-loved bistro on Queen Street West, near Bathurst. He and his partner, chef Eugene Shewchuk, opened in August 1990, but the timing was coincidental. Heaseman had always intended to open a restaurant and had left his native Peterborough to study at Ryerson with that ambition in mind. Shewchuk was born and raised in small-town Manitoba but lived for much of his life in Paris, where he once had his own small bistro. Returning to Canada, he ended up waiting table at Auberge du Pommier, Peter Oliver's beautiful restaurant on Yonge Street near Highway 401. Heaseman was also working there as a waiter, and when he and Shewchuk realized that their ambitions coincided, they decided to pool their resources. Oliver gave his blessing to their departure, and they set about renovating the site they had found, a defunct old diner in dire need of repair. Shewchuk mixed the concrete and did most of the plumbing and wiring himself. They skimped on cutlery and plugged in a boom box instead of an expensive sound system. Décor consisted of little more than a lively orange paint job and a bust of Elvis on the bar. The two men were adamant that no debt would cast its baleful shadow over their enterprise.

"Creditors might have insisted we raise our prices," explained Heaseman, "and we knew we had to keep them low – soup at $2.50, appetizers under $5, a main course of salmon for $8. Eugene's idea was that dinner would cost people less than if they had cooked the same meal at home. We knew great value would eventually bring us a clientele, and we knew that if we were busy, we could succeed. A busy restaurant is cost-efficient."

It took tremendous dedication to stick to the formula. Producing the sort of value on the plate that lured customers meant food costs were running at about 45 percent, considerably higher than the industry average. To balance the math, they substituted hard work for other expenditures. For the first year, Shewchuk was alone in the kitchen and Heaseman was the solitary waiter. Each day began with Shewchuk's visit to Kensington market at seven and ended for both of them at two o'clock the next morning. Suppliers were paid cash on delivery and responded gratefully by agreeing to deliver unusually small orders on a daily basis.

"And so we developed a loyal nucleus of customers who understood what we were trying to do," said Heaseman. "It was a relationship of mutual trust. We relied on people showing up on time when they had a reservation, and not bringing two extra guests; we made sure we never did the eighties trick of double-booking and then keeping people waiting."

The plan paid off. Cities slowly became a more than local destination, and in the fullness of time, Toronto's critics made their way to the bistro, tasted, and found it good. Shewchuk's cooking owed much more to his Parisian background than to Toronto's neo-Italian, thrill-o'-the-grill bistro standards. Mushrooms and crunchy leeks were wrapped in a delicate crêpe beneath an unctuous, tangy goat cheese velouté. The flavours of a juicy, pepper-crusted sautéed salmon fillet were intelligently matched by a Basque-style tomato cream sauce. A cheese-covered, layered potato pie quickly became an accompaniment that could never be left off the daily menu, much to the satisfaction of the dishwasher, who made the pie himself every day.

Cities, to me, was the archetypal recession-born restaurant, a bistro created and sustained without pretensions or frills or folderol, with hard-working, hands-on owners, offering very good value to a neighbourhood clientele. Its continued success, with Heaseman as sole owner, proved the efficacy of the formula. Shewchuk went on to open a larger restaurant, Messis, on Harbord Street, but not before he had shared his philosophy and practical advice with several other alumni of Auberge du Pommier who also set out on their own in the first half of the nineties.

JOSEPH HOARE telephoned me one night in 1993 to say he had just been to a new restaurant on Yonge Street north of Lawrence, having walked past the previous evening on one of his exploratory strolls. The place had been open only a week, but Joseph was excited, sensing a new player in the park. It was ready, he thought, for review.

He was right, as usual. Service in the cheerful, orange and yellow painted room was smooth and friendly and the cooking subtly sophisticated. Appetizers seemed at first glance to be no more than the clichés of Toronto bistro – butternut squash soup, calamari, polenta with Gorgonzola sauce – but the balance of flavours and the command of textures was exceptional. Cumin and a hint of cinnamon inspired the silken soup; the squid rings were fried in a curry-scented tempura batter without a trace of oil; the polenta was crisp-edged and creamy-hearted, crowned with buttery grilled Portobello mushrooms and edged by the molten cheese, pungently aromatic as the plate was set down, but as smooth and rich as butter on the tongue.

Main courses brought more delights. Warm pheasant confit was succulent and tender beneath its crispy skin. The daily special was an old-fashioned classic I had never encountered outside Europe, a ballottine of chicken breast, stuffed with a feathery mousseline of leg meat, morels, and thyme, napped by a refined sauce of morels and cream.

And the desserts ... Bear in mind that the city still languished under the tyranny of tiramisù and the chokehold of chocolate mousse cake. Here the kitchen proposed a true French lemon tart, its curd sharp enough to startle the wine-cosy brain, or a loose-textured crème brûlée that tasted of egg and vanilla, deceptively light.

The restaurant, called Herbs, was a hit from the day it opened. Tony Nuth, the chef and co-owner, had trained in London with that formidable master Nico Ladenis. Eventually he bought out Richard Marshall, his partner and maître d', and later he opened a fine-food store across the street, also under the Herbs banner. The two businesses were enough to keep Nuth and his team very busy indeed.

Herbs was at the top end of my neighbourhood beat, just a block or two south of Da Dante. At the other extreme, down towards Davisville, was the former Hudson. Late in 1993, after Greg Couillard and Johnny K had fled back downtown, it was taken over by a New Zealander called Vaughan Chittock, who, like Eugene Shewchuk and Tony Nuth, had worked for Peter Oliver at Auberge du Pommier. The new restaurant's name was Otago.

I dropped by one night to have dinner, incognito, of course. The menu was ambitious, reminiscent of the Anglo-French avant-garde style then current in London, with no trace of homage to Toronto's Cal-Ital bias. There wasn't a single pasta on the card. Instead, Chittock offered a smoothly opulent chicken liver pâté paired with a savoury, bitter chocolate vinaigrette, crisp Melba toast, and iced grapes. A classic lamb navarin bathed slices of tenderloin, lamb's kidney and tongue, and two chops cut from the rack in a rich sauce of Merlot and meat juices. For freshness, there were little green peas, mushrooms, and crunchy rods of baby asparagus on the plate and a ravier dish of vegetables for everyone at the table to share: braised celery, carrots, and zucchini tossed with butter and masses of dill. He had made the effort to buy, cherish, and present a selection of excellent cheeses, something very few Toronto restaurants of any size were prepared to do in those days, and for dessert he suggested a miniature Grand Marnier soufflé, cooked and served in a long-handled metal pan, with a sweet caramel sauce poured into its heart.

A few days later, I went round to Otago to meet Vaughan Chittock. Twenty-five years old with tousled black curls and a dazzling smile, he talked and talked with all the dynamic energy that so many young men and women seem to bring with them when they leave the Antipodes in search of fame and fortune. He had moved first to England, where his work attracted the attention of the great chef and teacher Albert Roux, who put him to work in the Wandsworth pâtisserie that serviced his London restaurant, Le Gavroche. Later, when all the French cooks were suddenly fired, Chittock found himself elevated to sous-chef. Roux used his protégé at Le Gavroche and wherever else in his empire a fix of talent and energy was needed, and finally arranged a stint with Raymond Blanc at Le Manoir aux Quat' Saisons, one of England's most prestigious kitchens, as a goodbye gift.

Chittock arrived in Toronto with his Canadian wife and found a job at Auberge du Pommier, where he swiftly rose to the rank of sous-chef. He had met Tony Nuth in London; he met Eugene Shewchuk here: both men gave him good advice when he decided he was ready to open a place of his own. So did Peter Oliver.

"He taught me a lot," Chittock told me, "especially about business management and how to establish a relationship with your customers by remembering and using their names, things like that, things that are virtually unheard of in Europe.

"And Eugene has been a godsend. He saved me so much money. This place had been left in a disgraceful state by the previous tenants. They'd ripped out everything from fire extinguisher systems to the stalls in the gents and left a bloody great hole in the basement. Eugene showed me how to lay cement and do most of the work myself. He warned me how hard it is to open your own restaurant, and he was right. You've really got to want to do it, because it'll damn near kill you. The government and the LCBO will break your heart, your back, and your balls in one blow, they're so slow and difficult. So many bureaucratic problems. It took Consumers Gas six weeks to turn on my gas – they only managed it on the morning we opened. Of course it didn't help that Metro had cemented over the gas tap in the sidewalk outside."

Chittock had spent four months preparing an elegant financial plan, researching costs and making separate five-year budgets according to various volumes of business. He tried to anticipate every possible quibble the banks might throw at him and obviously read them perfectly, because he got the money he needed to open the restaurant in the blink of an eye.

In the end, Otago did not last a year. I stand by my assessment of Chittock's talent as a chef, and presumably the bank knew what it was doing when it okayed his business plan. No one could have worked harder to give the city something subtly different from the usual bistro fare. The problem, I guess, was location. Johnny K and Greg Couillard had failed to put bums on seats at 1995 Yonge; Otago was no more successful. Vaughan Chittock bounced back as chef at Ace Bakery Café and started his own catering company.

LOOKING BACK at the recession, the ruthless observer adopts a Darwinian stance. The sudden cooling of the economic climate killed off a number of dinosaurs and a good many of the flamboyant exotics who had spread their colourful wings in the booming eighties. The traditionally moribund months of January and August became deeper, blacker holes on the restaurateur's calendar, and those who had missed opportunities to buy the building they rented cursed the Fates and their landlords. But small, adaptable businesses came into their own, and friendly service and value for money took on a new importance. Survival, it turned out, was possible, while the bold and the lucky saw and seized new opportunities.

Peter Oliver is a businessman, and proud of it. Tall and fit, he glows with the robust self-confidence of a professional politician, a man of convictions with the charisma to back them up. He could do those motivational guidance spots on cable TV with his eyes shut. In 1993, when I heard he was planning to open a dazzling new restaurant called Jump in the heart of the downtown financial district, lost burial ground of the fine-dining trade, I admit that I doubted his judgment. Its instant and lasting success explains why he is a millionaire and I'm not.

Born and raised in South Africa, Oliver took a management degree at McGill before coming to Toronto. His first job was as a stockbroker with a company based in the great downtown towers of Commerce Court. Sitting at his desk one lunchtime, gazing solemnly down at the unappetizing sandwich he had bought from a local snack counter, it occurred to him he could do better. He went looking for premises, and in a matter of months, against all advice, he opened Oliver's Old-fashioned Bakery and Sandwich Bar on that busy stretch of Yonge that would later welcome Centro and North 44°. He was thirty years old, a hands-on proprietor, continually checking every detail of his business, from plate presentation to the colour of his waiters' socks. The place began to do well, expanding into the buildings on either side and sprouting Oliver's Bistro upstairs in 1982.

"We were very profitable," agreed Oliver, "because I was there all the time. That's the edge that makes the difference. Then you open another restaurant, but you can't be in more than one place, so you have to figure out how to get that same dedication to quality from your employees when you're not there. We're slowly finding the secret. It involves many mundane things behind the scenes, but success leads to success. Suppliers give you better credit, you can negotiate better deals with the bank, and in particular it gives you credibility with landlords. In this business, credibility is everything."

In 1986 Oliver opened Brasserie Bofinger at Yonge and St. Clair. A year later, Cadillac Fairview invited him to create the restaurant that became Auberge du Pommier. At first he said no. The property was interesting: two heritage cottages marooned in the forecourt of a grandiose new development just south of the 401. He could draw a wealthy clientele from Hoggs Hollow and from the hungry gourmets of North York – but he was already so busy. The offer became progressively sweeter, and eventually Oliver bit.

Auberge du Pommier turned out to be a good little earner, repeatedly topping readers' polls. A remarkably beautiful place to eat, it was decorated like a Provençal mas with whitewashed walls, terracotta-tiled floors, a terrace with a fountain, an intimate bar. For Toronto's restaurant critics, however, it never tasted as good as it looked. Very fine chefs have cooked there over the years – Arpi Magyar, Jean Pierre Challet – but have failed to give of their best. For years, the received wisdom within the industry was that Oliver may be a brilliant entrepreneur but he did not know enough about food to rein his chefs in. I have lost count of the times I have heard that little cliché, sitting up late with some chef or restaurateur, passing the bottle of grappa, discussing not only Oliver but anyone who has risen above the ranks.

"Franco is a great creator of restaurants, but he has no real love of food …"

"Carlevale understands service, but he knows less about cooking than he thinks he does …"

Sour grapes, but where Oliver is concerned the criticism has always proved particularly hard to shake. Particularly unfair, one might add. In 1987 Oliver's seven-year-old daughter was found to be a diabetic and the man took a four-year sabbatical from his armada of restaurants to concentrate on raising funds to fight diabetes. Without his hands-on presence, things started to drift apart. But he was back at the helm when I called upon him in 1993 to find out about Jump. Perhaps he too had listened to the critics, for he had taken on a partner for the enterprise: Michael Bonacini. It was an inspired choice. A thorough professional who had trained at the Dorchester under Anton Mosimann, Bonacini had reached a point in his career where he wanted more from life than a chef's toque. His long negotiations with

Franco Prevedello to buy part of Centro had come to nothing. Now Oliver promised him a partnership in Jump and even a role in the parent company, if all turned out well.

That "if," I suggested to Oliver, was the hinge upon which much was hanging. For the next hour, he enlightened me. The gospel according to Oliver begins with the understanding that opening a new restaurant is fraught with problems.

"It's the unforeseen expenses that bring you down," he explained. "The reason there's such a big casualty rate in this business is you get a guy who's been a waiter or manager or chef and he's got no experience of business or planning. He doesn't foresee that building permits cost you money. He doesn't know that contractors make their profit on extras, not on the initial contract. Then there are the costs. You lose at least 35 percent of your initial staff during the first few months of a restaurant's life. You have to budget for laundry, dishwashing chemicals, cutlery replacement, so many things beyond labour and food costs. It's a shark pool, and when some young guy asks me for advice, my first answer is, 'Don't do it.' On the other hand, that was me, sixteen years ago.

"So it's tough and challenging, but of course, that in itself makes it more rewarding. The more experienced you are, the fewer unforeseen expenses come along. As for the big decisions: I guess it all comes down to gut feeling. To tell you the truth, when the bank first came to me with the idea of creating a restaurant in Commerce Court, I wasn't looking for anything new. I was focusing on my existing restaurants and on eliminating my debt. But the deal we made was mutually advantageous. They liked my track record; I liked the fact that the project did not in fact add to my debt."

The idea of a bank actually commissioning a restaurant must seem like a fantastic dream to most would-be restaurateurs, cooling their heels in the bank manager's office, having offered to mortgage everything they own for the favour of a loan. For Jump, the tables were turned. The recession scoured tenants from millions of square feet of downtown office space, and landlords scrambled to attract replacements. Having a high-end restaurant on the ground floor was just the sort of lure to appeal to hungry young companies. The deal was done.

Jump came together extraordinarily quickly, a mere three months from conception to birth, opening just in time for the Christmas rush. Oliver and Bonacini had noted the success of Mövenpick's Marché in BCE Place and were buoyed by this evidence that maybe folks did eat downtown after all. Their plans, however, called for something on a considerably higher plane. Designer Robert Meiklejohn turned the glass and cement space into a chic modern hybrid of a conservatory and a conservative club. By day, the look changes according to the weather, lovely in sunlight or with snow falling outside, moodier when the sky is overcast. At night, when the long dark wood bar is lit by lamps made from cocktail shakers, it can even feel intimate.

Bonacini's contribution was immediately apparent. He hired Martin Kouprie from Pronto as chef and created a menu of lively, often dazzling Cal-Ital cooking. There was a simplicity to the dishes, an intensity and a clarity of flavour that finally won Peter Oliver unanimous approval from even the toughest critics. Every detail was attended to, from the warm, soft herb bread with fine olive oil for dipping, to the discreet wall of air that kept smoke from the bar out of the dining area. In no time at all, Jump was catering boardroom lunches to the neighbouring towers, and when summer came to Bay

Street, Bonacini brought in Chris McDonald to make Mexican brown-bag lunches out in the courtyard. Occasionally, it is said, Peter Oliver would glance up at the windows of Commerce Court, to the office where he sat sixteen years earlier vowing to make a better sandwich.

In the fullness of time, Peter Oliver and Michael Bonacini merged their talents into a corporate unity. They set about revivifying Oliver's Bistro, turning it into Chapeau, and Brasserie Bofinger, transforming it into Paramount. In 1995 they added another lustrous jewel to their diadem: Canoe, high on the fifty-fourth floor of another downtown bank tower. With Todd Clarmo and Anthony Walsh manning the induction cookers, Canoe became another unqualified triumph, its success compensation for the eventual abandonment of Oliver's Bakery, Chapeau, and Paramount. Peter Oliver had moved on to higher things, cutting his three polished gems, Auberge, Jump, and Canoe, from the matrix of the past. The bistro days, like the recession, were over.

☜ THE YOUNG IDEA ☞

DINING OUT some years ago, at an establishment famous for its tolerance of the young
idea, I was deep in my usual, surreptitious, under-
the-table, nibble-and-scribble note-taking when I
glanced up suddenly and met the calm blue gaze
of my ten-month-old daughter.

"And how is the bisque, my golden girl?"

"Excellent, thank you, Father. May I ask
what you are doing?"

"I'm collecting impressions for a column
about restaurants that put up with children. You
know the sort of thing: places that welcome the
tiny terrorist, where a tantrum won't get you
thrown out, where you can take your crayon to
the walls with impunity."

"I see. Another glimpse through the dimin-
ishing lens of parenthood." She unfastened her
bib and laid it down upon the tray of the high
chair. "Father, it seems to me that yet again you

have grasped the sticky end of the spoon. Why should the restaurant pander to the unruly child? Is it not rather the parents' responsibility to teach their offspring how to behave in public?"

"I couldn't say that! It sounds far too sanctimonious!"

"As you wish, but you know it's true. The polite toddler is well accepted anywhere. The badly brought-up should really be left at home."

"So it's a mark of parental failure when a child trips the busboy or trashes the washroom."

"Usually. Though there are occasions when even the most civil infant will misbehave for tactical reasons. To express boredom, perhaps, or else out of some vague iconoclastic impulse. Or sometimes to deflect attention if the adults are getting too deeply into the Cabernet Sauvignon."

"I see . . ."

"Or it may be nothing more than a healthy curiosity. How is a child to assess the proper limits of social behaviour without experimentation? Do you remember my friend Graham?"

"The one who always asks for plain pasta and parmesan, no matter how interesting the restaurant?"

"That's Graham."

"And who then eats the stuff with his fingers?"

"Even then, his intention is not to embarrass. He merely wishes to test the parameters of adult tolerance. But you look skeptical."

"Well, the boredom I can understand. That's why we bring your crayons and your drawing book, and the little cars."

"Another mistake. Why try to turn a restaurant into a play group? Do adults doodle when they dine out? No. They talk.

If parents talked more to their children, and paid more attention to what was said, the motivation for naughtiness would evaporate."

"Waiters help there too, don't they! I've often read that a chatty waiter makes all the difference when taking children out to eat."

"Ah, but only to the parents. It makes you feel more comfortable. Children are not as susceptible to flattery as adults. Nor are we desolated by nuances of hostility. But don't look so crestfallen, *mon père*. I don't mean to shoot down all your preconceptions."

"So where do you like to eat?"

"I enjoyed the Sultan's Tent."

"You fell asleep on the cushions."

"And Le Continental, before they redesigned it, when it still had the dance band and the huge banquettes and the good linen napkins. Children's lives are full of sterile plastic surfaces. We respond well to a touch of napery."

"And you like Cantonese restaurants, of course."

"Of course. Particularly those with well-stocked fish tanks. And I have fond memories of Tex-Mex finger food."

"Exotic cuisines …"

"Oh, we babies are always game. It's pre-schoolers who are apt to be wary. It takes courage for a tot to put some slippery, brightly coloured mystery into her mouth, not knowing if it will be salt or sweet, if it will burn her tongue or bring tears to her eyes."

"I hadn't thought of that."

"The world is brimming with new experiences. It can wear one down by the end of the day. So if sometimes we fall back upon familiar treats and ask for hot dogs and French fries, do not judge us too harshly."

"We're only thinking of your metabolism. Junk isn't good for you."

"And what makes you think that sweetbreads with cream, cognac and five-peppercorn sauce are any healthier?"

"At least there's dessert. I've seen your eyes widen at many an ornate arrangement of mousses, ice creams, and coulis, all picked out with berries and cocoa dust."

"Yes, I can't help admiring the saccharine landscapes of our better pastry chefs. It's familiar territory for the young, of course: only slightly more bizarre than the confections on the candy counter in the local store, or the Popsicles in the cold cabinet. They remind me of the fruit faces you make me at home. But you were asking for places that I find interesting. Old-fashioned Italian restaurants are generally a safe bet. Good bread, good breadsticks, soft meat. Nice mushy vegetables. Pizza parlours can be amusing if one hankers for the company of one's peers. The service is fast there, too. I insist on that. To an adult the hours are an immutable frame upon which to hang the events of the day, but time is still fluid to people of my age. We experience it subjectively. Ten minutes becomes an eternity when you're waiting for them to bring you a bottle."

"I know the feeling."

She picked up her bib in a tiny fist. "Well, that moussaka should be about ready. Would you tie this back on, please? And next time you need information about diners of my particular era, come to me first. How did Cicero put it? *Percunctare a peritis* – go to the horse's mouth. My memory is not what it was, but I know what I like."

9

THE F WORD

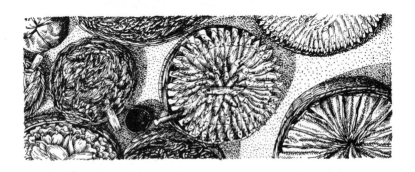

ONE NIGHT I came home with a doggie bag. Normally, of course, I have no need of such things. If the food is good, I eat it; if it isn't, why take it home? That evening, however, professional duty had forced me to roam far and wide across a multifaceted menu, while the portions, in accordance with mid-nineties mode, had been grotesquely large. At school in England, I was trained to leave nothing on the plate ... Dilemma. Anxiety. Doggie bag.

Back in my own kitchen, I was untwisting the scrunched-up seam of the aluminum foil parcel when my daughter, now in Grade Two, appeared beside me. "What's that, Dad?" I spread the foil.

"Gross!" she breathed in a tone that was equal parts awe, disgust, and admiration. The restaurant had put some of the leftovers into individual Styrofoam pots that had split and spilt their contents into the rest of the parcel. Sea bass swam in the jus from five-spice-crusted duck; the duck was caught *in flagrante delictu* with garlic rapini, mashed potato, and mango salsa. "I know what it is," said my daughter. "That's Fusion."

My children's tastes in food have always been subject to sudden, radical changes. As babies they were highly adventurous, eating almost anything that had been turned to a paste in the blender. Toddlerhood polarized the menu into clusters of passionate enthusiasms (the cheese-ball phase, the chicken nugget gold rush) and equally deep aversions (chronic prasinophobia, also known as a morbid fear of green vegetables, and a sudden, short-lived hatred of toast). Oddly enough, they left all these likes and dislikes behind when we took them to a restaurant, slipping out of the backpacks of prejudice and leaving them by the door.

This was particularly obvious when they came face to face with extravagant brunch buffets. Watching adults work a buffet, balancing towers of shrimp on their plates in an effort to eat more than their money's worth, is to have front-row seats at the cabaret of greed. But children prefer to see a buffet as an opportunity for fastidious experimentation. When Joe was seven, he returned to our table from the Olympic-sized smorgasbord at the Inn on the Park with nothing but a spicy Italian sausage and a miniature jar of apricot jam. He ate them together with great concentration and clearly enjoyed the flavour. A logical outcome. He liked jam; he liked sausages. Two plus two equals four.

During the nineties, I came across innumerable menus predicated on the same rudimentary arithmetic. In the name of Fusion, all manner of curiously inappropriate ingredients were pressed together in a haphazard search for new sensations. But you did not have to read very far in your physics textbook to see that Chef had misunderstood the process. Fusion cooking involves a higher math, in which two plus two equals five. For a dish to deserve the name, some new energy must be created, the final product greater than the sum of the parts. Combining the techniques of different cuisines, the raw ingredients of different continents, is fine as theory, but the experiment seems to work with any consistency only when it is conducted in the crucible of a particularly intuitive kind of imagination. Sometimes success leads to a chain reaction, a phenomenon I observed on a trip to Miami in the summer of 1992. It was the first time I ever heard Fusion spelt with a capital F.

Gastronomically speaking, Miami was hot that year. A unique combination of elements had generated a localized culinary explosion, but under controlled and observable conditions. The first of those elements was Florida itself, reaching like America's tasting spoon into the fecund tropics, with exotic produce growing in every backyard. Then there was an immigrant population with its own well-defined cuisines, from sophisticated Cuban traditions to street-corner stalls selling Nicaraguan fritangas. Interspersed among the Hispanic neighbourhoods were areas such as Coconut Grove and South Beach, rejuvenated by Yankee money and eager to party. The only thing missing was somewhere exciting to eat. Detonation occurred when chefs with classical training blew into town and started opening restaurants – A Mano, Mark's Place, Chef Allen's, Yuca, JanJo's – using European-American and Latin techniques with great creativity and a fine sensitivity to local ingredients.

Another example was the Verandah, the indoor-outdoor, pool-side dining room at Turnberry Isle Resort & Club, North Miami's most exclusive and luxurious hotel. Robbin Haas, a self-taught chef from Buffalo, was determined to explore the possibilities presented by Florida when he arrived there in 1989. The idea of incorporating local details into his menu intrigued him, and he dug deep into the historical roots of the region, exploring ingredients and the ways in which they were used.

"I wanted the best South Florida could offer," he explained, "so I put an ad in the local newspaper, inviting people to bring me the fruits, tubers, and vegetables they grew in their own backyards. There's a lady called Edith Elson, for example, who has ten mango trees in her garden. She brings me mangoes at every stage of ripeness that run the gamut of mango flavours from carrot to coconut. I found a fisherman who now calls me directly from his boat on a cellular phone and tells me what he's catching. I get fresh swamp cabbage from a Mikasooki Indian who brings them out of the Everglades."

In Haas's kitchen, that swamp cabbage (a.k.a. heart of palm) was marinated in grapefruit, orange, and lime juice, thyme, and mustard, and served as a salad with asparagus, red and yellow tomatoes, and a chilled passionfruit vinaigrette. It sounds busy, but the freshness of the ingredients made it delightfully vivid, full of sweet, juicy, subtle energies. On Haas's recommendation, we followed it with grilled fallow deer chops, a meat I associate with southern Germany. This was

America and there was no trace of gaminess to the venison, but its flavour was enhanced and amplified by a complex, tropically tart and tangy jus of black truffles, guava, and tamarind.

Not every restaurant I visited during that trip showed such discipline. As Haas put it, "Some of my colleagues bring too much to the party, if you know what I'm saying." But the overall impression of Miami's achievement was tremendously exciting. The U.S. press was equally thrilled. Food writers announced the birth of a new cuisine, something to rival California, but not even the chefs themselves could decide on a name for their revolution. Very late one night in the bar at Turnberry Isle, when most of us had drunk an improbable number of cocktails, I listened to them discussing the titles devised by the pundits: New World Cuisine, New Floribbean, Nuevo Cubano, Miamamerican ... No one term pleased them all. The word that raised the fewest objections was Fusion.

As a process, of course, it is as old as America. The very first Thanksgiving dinner was a Fusion feast, with English cooks using English techniques to prep their own small harvest of European pot herbs and vegetables together with the corn, wild plums, strange birds, and unfamiliar berries provided by their indigenous guests. (By all accounts, incidentally, turkey was not on the menu.) But the pioneers had only two cultures to cope with. In Toronto, in the 1990s, our wild demographic mix created infinite possibilities. A WASP chef in search of inspiration had only to wander down Spadina Avenue on a crowded summer evening to find rooms serving authentic Cantonese, Szechuan, Mandarin, Fukien, Sri Lankan, or Vietnamese cooking. The raw ingredients were there in the stores and emporia; the elderly Chinese ladies crouched by the curb with a bundle of chrysanthemum leaves for sale knew all the best and most traditional ways to use them. This city had become a global culinary resource of staggering plenitude. Indian grocers on Gerrard Street East flew in green mangoes and paan leaves; Polish butchers on Roncesvalles Avenue smoked pork to their grandfathers' recipes. It wasn't surprising that cooks went ingredient-crazy, but so often their experiments ended in disappointment. Loading the menu with fashionable exotica, they borrowed or improvised ideas without any real knowledge of the cultural traditions they were bringing into their kitchens.

The true Fusion engineers were few and far between. Susur Lee, of course. Greg Couillard. And, when they chose to, Barbara Gordon and Bob Bermann. Gordon was chef-owner of La Cachette in Vancouver when Bermann came to apprentice in her kitchen. Romance bloomed; they became partners, moved to Toronto, and opened Beaujolais in January 1986. It was one of those restaurants that deserve to succeed and almost make it, that stick around for three or four years, well reviewed but infrequently attended, and then disappear. Gordon and Bermann, however, weren't about to give up so easily. Instead, they refashioned Beaujolais into something they hoped would appeal more obviously to their Queen Street West locale. The Avocado Club's menu was more multicultural than Fusion – pad thai noodles next to guacamole, but not on the same plate.

"It happened by accident," said Bermann. "We were trying to think what to do, and we started by making a list of the things we liked to eat. We'd go here for Mexican, there for Jamaican jerk pork, to the Indian Rice Factory for curry, or to Spadina for those Vietnamese soups. It was a real hodgepodge, reflective of the city's huge cultural diversity."

It was at their next location that the disparate nuclei fused. Boba opened late in 1994, in the quaint little house opposite Hazelton Lanes that had once been Auberge Gavroche. After waiting politely for a month or so, to allow any dust to settle, Joseph Hoare sent me round to review it. This time, both Gordon and Bermann were cooking, and the menu was knit much more closely. I ordered a starter of tuna. It arrived almost raw with its surface sesame-seared, a way of preparing the fish I had first encountered years before in Santa Cruz, California, but which has now become standard. Beside it were sushi rolls of crunchy vegetables and rice wrapped in pliant nori, while the tuna's red flesh was dabbed with a citrus cream and crowned with enoki mushrooms. Just-cooked rapini was a perfect complement to both, its bitterness sparked by a hint of soy.

Some time later, I asked Bermann where the Japanese influence had come from. "That's where it all started for me," he replied. "With the Franco-Japanese Fusion back in the early eighties. People like Bocuse started opening restaurants in Japan and suddenly chefs were saying, 'Hey, we can do monkfish with wasabe.' You'd find raw fish appetizers in quite staid restaurants in New York and Paris, or a Vietnamese ingredient creeping onto a three-Michelin-star menu through some chef like Georges Blanc – guys of that calibre. Now, of course, it's become so mainstream, and too often it's being done poorly. Throw a little ginger at something and call it Fusion cuisine! But there's no underlying technique."

The technique was always present at Boba. In 1997 I went back and ordered tuna again. This time a hefty slab of the fish, grilled rare, came with noodles in rich coconut sauce, alluding to Southeast Asia. The garnish was a salsa of diced avocado and mango. Bermann and

Gordon are excellent chefs, and they think about food all the time. The elements in their Avenue Road reactor are not chosen at random, and the energies released are discreet and logical. At the same time, they are aware of fashion, and keen to avoid it, where necessary.

"The access here in Toronto to ingredients and to authentic cooking in small ethnic restaurants makes it all very easy to do," mused Bermann. "In fact, it's become so mainstream that I'm reverting to more simple European cooking this summer, and people are responding to the novelty of it all over again."

Another chef who made Fusion flamboyant and fascinating was Renée Foote of Mercer Street Grill. Owner Simon Bower opened his lively place in 1994, in a free-standing, one-storey building hemmed in by parking lots. Richard Eppstadt designed the room, kitting it out in khaki and bronze, embedding cutlery in the sidewalk outside and varnishing a banknote onto the floor by the open kitchen beneath a urethane finish. Customers on their way to the washroom would often bend to retrieve it, to the amusement of the cooks.

The last time Wendy and I went there, Simon Bower came to the table, as he did with most customers, to illuminate the words on the menu with vivid, mouthwatering detail. He proved the consummate salesman, and Renée Foote's work more than lived up to his pitch. Duck livers were sautéed in five-spice dust and lifted on scallion pancakes above subtle passionfruit nectar and savoury pan juices. Swordfish, grilled rare, had a hole drilled through it to hold a plump peg of calamari stuffed with duck, while stout plantain columns supported the fish over a jumble of fiddleheads, baby beets, and other Canadian vegetables. Presentation was unapologetically vertical, while the plate was flecked with dots of nori made with a hole punch, colourful rice cracker balls, and crisp taro noodles that curled like bizarre antennae.

During the comfort food fad, when so many restaurants were mashing their vegetables and using words like "gravy" again, righteously advocating a return to nursery textures, Foote's sense of fun was delightfully refreshing. More important, her dishes tasted like heaven, for all the visual exuberance made marvellous sense in the mouth.

I guess it was inevitable, given this city's demographics, that Asia should have injected such a Fusion infusion into our kitchens. I would challenge anyone, however, to predict the flavours that chef Ismat Jivani creates at Cha Cha Cha, a funky downtown room on the storey above the decidedly unfunky Fillet of Sole. Jivani is Kenyan and grew up with a cuisine that was itself an amalgam of African, East Indian, Portuguese, and British traditions. He worked for years with the Hilton group, toured with Cajun maestro Paul Prudhomme, and learned classic disciplines at L'Escale, a two-Michelin-star restaurant in Marseilles. In all Toronto, his cooking reminds me most strongly of the carefree, reckless energy of Miami.

"I've never been there," he assured me, "though I have travelled quite a bit! And wherever I go, I remember things, play with ingredients, always try to improve. Half the time I dream up ideas, half the time I'm hungry in the kitchen and there's some risotto left in one pot, and a quail in another, and I say, 'Just put that and that on a plate for me, thank you.' And it works. I'll take pasta and add jalapeño peppers and jerk cream sauce just to give it a different life. Or I'll barbecue a duck in the strict Cantonese way, but instead of the traditional glaze I'll use guava juice and Cuban spices."

Jivani made pesto with ancho chilies instead of basil, and he made it hot as hell, offset by shrimp and cool, chewy quinoa. He also invented a uniquely delicious ribeye steak. "That recipe came about because of my grandmother in Kenya. We always had this coffeepot sitting at home, and ten o'clock at night would come by and no one wanted any more coffee, and she'd have to throw half the pot out. One day she said, 'So you want to get into cooking, so tell me, how can we utilize this?' We came up with a coffee marinade for ribeye or flank steak, which goes on to become the sauce, flamed with tequila, garlic, shallots, and a little roux, and reduced to give it more coffee intensity." The world is Jivani's oyster sauce, and he revels in its diversity, laughing at journalists' vain attempts to categorize his creations.

ANDREW CHASE is an author, composer, editor, linguist, and student of art history and philosophy as well as a very fine chef, but he never knew whether to laugh or cuss when his cooking at the late, lamented Café Asia was described by critics as Fusion. On the other hand, he preferred the F-word to the other, much-bandied descriptor of his repertoire: Pacific Rim.

"Ridiculous," was his judgment. "Pacific Rim is not a term I would ever use. I don't do anything Californian. Or Peruvian or Australian, come to that. I remember in Hong Kong watching a Miss Pacific Rim beauty pageant on television, and Miss Israel won. I never could figure it out."

We were sitting on the deck in Chase's backyard – a hot summer's morning – drinking green tea and shooting the breeze. A year had passed since Café Asia closed in 1996, and Chase had been out of the limelight, working on an opera, writing two cookbooks, one of them a collection of Oriental offal recipes. His partner and perennial co-chef, Camilo Costales, had left for work.

"He hates to be unemployed," explained Chase. "He's working as a pasta chef now, until we open our new place."

Unsurprisingly, given his academic past, Chase has the air and some of the mannerisms of an eccentric professor, blinking behind his spectacles. His height and build give him considerable presence, but the effect is tempered by a certain shyness of strangers. If the "new place" were to pan out as expected, he would have to work on that. He and his partners, Costales, Gabriel Bright, and Tom Thai, sushi chef extraordinaire, all of whom cooked together at Café Asia, would be constantly in and out of sight, moving between the kitchen and the open prep stations behind the bar. They wanted to create the informal, sociable mood of an izakaya, a Japanese drinking bar, but with serious Asian food. To this end, they had found a location on Dundonald, a quiet backstreet near Yonge and Wellesley. The menus and wine list were ready and tested. It only remained to think of a name.

"We're awful at it," groaned Chase. "We've sat around evening after evening, the four of us, trying to think of something. We want an Asian name, I suppose, but I don't like those meaningless one- or two-syllable words. A flower name might work, like Lotus or Azalea, but one plant sounds too like another. So we sit and ponder, ruling everything out, then someone suggests Malaria and the whole discussion just collapses into humour."

Whatever their final decision, I was looking forward to the return of Costales and Chase, for together they offered Toronto a different response to multicultural diversity. Their menus reflected many Asian cuisines, but each dish had its own, authentic integrity, an authenticity that had nothing to do with second-hand experiences in Toronto's ethnic restaurants but came from cooking and eating and watching and learning in Asia itself.

Chase was born and raised in Boston, went to Columbia University to study music, but changed his major to the history of Chinese art. In 1976, to improve his Chinese and to gather the background in philosophy necessary for an understanding of his subject, he went to Taiwan to study, took another degree in philosophy, and pursued that interest into graduate work. He lived for a while in Shanghai and then spent some years in Hong Kong, editing an art history magazine. But all the time he was cooking, especially after he joined up with Costales, a Filipino chef who had lived and worked for many years in Thailand and Hong Kong. They came to Toronto in 1988, with a vague idea of opening a restaurant; instead, Chase found a job as an editor at the publishing house Prentice Hall. He had been there only three months when he went to his boss and told her, "Look, what I really want to be is a waiter."

"She thought I was nuts, but by then we actually had a plan. The cooking side of things was fine, but I needed some front-of-house experience. I got a job at the McGill Club for a year, ending up as deputy manager; I took accounting and hospitality courses at George Brown College. I really made an effort! And eventually we found some premises on Berkeley Street, close to Queen East."

The room was tiny, seating no more than twenty-four, and the chefs were forbidden to put any signage on the façade, but the Berkeley Café soon became famous among food lovers who understood what Chase and Costales were doing. The Canadian Opera Company adopted it as their lunchtime hangout, and on Friday and Saturday nights, Chase was turning away twice as many reservations as he could accommodate. A good many Thai dishes found their way onto the menu, dishes that astonished customers used to the sweet, timid, Westernized Thai food that Toronto then found so palatable.

"Real Thai food," Chase explained, "isn't like that at all. Thais love things that are very bitter, very sour, and very, very hot. Canadians probably wouldn't like half the things people eat in Thailand. But to be authentic is very costly, because you have to use the proper ingredients. We can get them – there are a couple of stores in the city that fly them in – but your food costs soar. We were so small, it was all we could do to break even."

Size had its advantages, however. It allowed Chase and Costales to cook the complex and obscure dishes they loved. Often they had to eat them, too.

"That's one thing about Toronto that amazes me: when people go to a restaurant and then say, 'Oh, I've never tried that, so I won't order it.' I call things by their English names on the menu, and that produces other strange comments: 'Well, I'll eat calamari, but I won't eat squid.' We heard that a lot. Or pig face salad. It's a Filipino specialty made from a pig's ears and face, with mashed-up brains instead of mayonnaise. No one would order it! Even when we called it pig head salad, it didn't go. But it's delicious and we were always happy to have it ourselves for Sunday lunch."

In 1993 the Berkeley Café's landlord declared a monumental rent hike, and Chase and Costales decided to move. They found a location on a stretch of Yonge between Bloor and Rosedale that was devoid of fine-dining rivals. They opened Pine and Bamboo. This time, the name virtually suggested itself: a style of classical Chinese porcelain that also reflected their bipartite menu, half Western, half Asian. It was a plain but pretty room, the one visual gimmick an aquarium fitted into the service window between kitchen and dining room so that the chefs appeared to be working in a blue submarine environment. They never got their heads above water. The location was bad, and while their Thai salads and fascinating Filipino curries were fabulous, European-style dishes were not a house forte.

Chase and Costales moved on, ending up in the vast, labyrinthine reaches of Matsuri, a doomed Japanese teppanyaki restaurant in the basement of the King Street Holiday Inn. How long they might have languished there is a mystery, had it not been for a chance meeting with Jurg and Ingrid Sommers, a glamorous couple involved with a Swiss investment group. Chase and Costales cooked them a meal, and the Sommerses were so impressed they persuaded their group to finance a gorgeous new restaurant for the two chefs in Matsuri's space.

They called the place Café Asia. Its walls were cunningly painted in a rainbow of colours and metals, so finely that the finished effect was of shimmering golden silk. A faint aroma of incense hung in the air, sandalwood or shalamar, and a massive, dark bronze statue of a prowling tiger, borrowed from the Sommerses' cottage, stood guard at the door. There was a sushi bar and a room devoted to Korean table-top barbecue; another area housed the teppan tables. Close to the entrance, a vestibule led into a bar for billiards and cigars, panelled in mahogany and furnished with deep, soft sofas. The wine list was long and laden with expensive treats – a Condrieu, for example, that proved a superb match for the cooking.

But it was the food in the main dining area that brought in the customers. The team in the kitchen offered a menu that was dazzlingly new, simultaneously traditional and avant-garde. There were dishes from Thailand, Vietnam, different regions of China, Korea, Japan, and the Philippines, all interpreted by the Chase and Costales imagination. Like the shape of the café itself, the approach was more pluralistic than Fusion. It was most important to Chase that each dish, even the sushi, retained the integrity of its particular culture, whatever changes were made to the actual ingredients.

"I suppose when I cook sweetbreads with taro leaf in an Asian way, that is Fusion, if only because Asian people don't kill their cattle young and so don't have sweetbreads. And yes, I might add sage, which is European. But I've always seen my cooking as purely Asian – pan-Asian, maybe, if you must search for an adjective. I learned it in people's homes when I was living there. Asian cooks improvise all the time, and I like to think this is how they might respond to something like sweetbreads. Don't forget, Southeast Asian cooking is already full of Chinese and Indian influences, while the Filipino urban cuisine reflects four hundred years of Spanish rule. You'll find brandy and olive oil in many of their recipes."

I guess a chef can call his food what he wishes, especially when the food is as marvellous as it was at Café Asia. First there was the sushi, of a freshness and imagination that made most other Toronto attempts at the art taste like dead fish. Tom Thai is a graceful young Vietnamese guy with a wife who is Japanese and a temperament designed to push the envelope of any tradition. He learned sushi from Hiro Yoshida and from his father-in-law, a sushi chef in Osaka, mastered both Kansai and Kanto styles, and then let rip at Café Asia. "Use Arctic char," Chase told him. "Just be sure you use it with respect!" So he did. And horsemeat. And living shrimps. He also cut blue marlin sashimi and touched it with sesame, sliced a roll of salmon and sea-urchin roe and served it with a piquant oba leaf, mixed gooey white yamaimo with tiny cubes of raw tuna.

Every evening, the kitchen rose to such brilliant beginnings. Here was a Korean salad of raw shark, garlic shoots, and chili, and there a fantasy of steamed kingfish, flavoured with coconut, garlic, and lemongrass, wrapped in banana leaf. Those Filipino sweetbreads were supple and soft as butter in a tangy green coconut sauce, the chopped taro leaves tasting like a delicate hybrid of spinach and mint. Desserts were no disappointment in this pan-Asian haven: pungent ginger and caramel ice cream, perhaps, or a sort of white lemongrass mousse with sour apricot sauce and a hank of spun grape sugar.

If everything was so magnificent, you may ask, why is Café Asia no more than a memory? Partly because of its location. King Street West is one of the busiest restaurant strips in the city, but with all respect to the Holiday Inn, hotels of that name are not generally associated with innovative, expensive fine dining. What is more, the restaurant was in the basement. Passers-by could not see in and had no idea what they were missing. Above all, the place was too big. Two hundred and thirty seats were too many to fill and caused too much waste in the kitchen. Often, days would go by with no call for Korean barbecue or steak teppanyaki, but the necessary ingredients had to be purchased and prepped. And there were other reasons. The billiards and cigar bar remained terra incognita to Toronto's élite – a tragic waste of a spectacular room. More alcohol was consumed in the kitchen and front of house than was sold across the mahogany. The whole enterprise was beautiful, clever, sophisticated, and fascinating, but the numbers never quite clambered out of the red. Almost making a profit was not good enough for the distant investors. The plug was pulled. The lights went out on Costales and Chase's multicultural collective, and Fusion's most significant philosophical challenge was snuffed.

In the end, Chase, Costales, Thai, and Bright came up with a name for their new enterprise. Youki (named after Tom Thai's five-year-old son) opened in the autumn of 1997 and was packed from the outset. A good many critics and customers referred to the cooking as Fusion. It remains a vague enough term to cover almost any gastronomy that is not strictly ethnic, it still carries some of the gravitas of OAC Physics, and (from a purely professional point of view) it offers energy-conscious journalists a useful bounty of puns and wordplays for titles and closing paragraphs.

Will the term ever be endorsed by a quorum of Toronto's chefs and restaurateurs, as it was in Miami? Not officially. Miami's chefs started with a clean slate, in a city devoid of postwar American cooking. Here, there is already far too much going on. Our individualistic chefs have no time to draw up a manifesto and no inclination to bond into a single stylistic unit. Their attitude is, Just do it. There are no rules. Put taro with foie gras, grab a handful of beef Stroganoff, stir in galingale and salted lemons, then you can take your taco and stuff it. Sausages and jam ... Andrew Chase compared it to children playing with food, but for now Toronto is happy to call it Fusion, and until we come up with a better word, Fusion is what it must be.

THE RULES OF THE GAME

PEOPLE WHO EAT professionally are superstitious folk. Somewhere within their souls there hovers a dim awareness of an obligation to destiny, a sense that they are lucky to have such a lovely job. The notion is constantly reinforced by the opinion of others. I once met a man at a party who spent an hour telling me how he had inherited millions at the age of twenty and now divided his time between homes in London, Aspen, and Mauritius. Then he asked what I did for a living. "Lucky you," he sighed when I told him.

When restaurant critics write books, they invariably stir an apology for their good fortune into the text. The three-headed hound of envy demands such honey cakes. But read on and the winsome acknowledgment is soon mitigated by provisos. We hear of the heartbreak of having to go out to dinner again, when all one longs for is bed. We share the agonizing duty of tasting a chocolate dessert when one is trying to diet. Yes, it's nice to be known as a gourmet, the writer concedes, but the tragic flip side of the coin is that all of his friends feel too nervous to ask him for dinner. As a reader, I can't help but wonder if that is really the reason. Maybe they just dislike the guy.

We all carry preconceptions about the jobs other people do. In my experience, the public image of the restaurant reviewer is of a composite figure, part spy, part sensualist, part prosecuting attorney. I share such prejudices. Whenever I go out to dinner, I keep an eye open for critics – men with false noses who ask too many questions about herbs in the soup, women in unsuitable wigs. Some reviewers are obsessive about their own anonymity, but Toronto is a small town and career waiters know the face of the enemy. The good ones even know their regular aliases and the licence plates of their cars. But they make it a point of pride to carry on regardless, showing no special favours, resisting the temptation to indulge in messy acts of revenge.

In the early days of my work, I went to great lengths to keep my mission covert. One evening, Joseph Hoare sent me down to the Beach to eat at Loon's, a fine little bistro owned by its chefs, Charles and Jennifer Part. I had hit on a brilliant way of taking notes about the food: a miniature tape recorder hidden in my jacket with a wire running down the inside of my sleeve to a cufflink microphone. When I wanted to record an impression I had only to rub my cheek or finger my chin while murmuring into my wrist. Back home, jubilant as a bank robber counting his money, I played back the tape. The whispered words were inaudible under the rustle of fabric and the rhythmic boom of my pulse. I had to go back to Loon's. For the next job, I took a pad of paper and a pencil and pretended to be interviewing my dinner companion whenever a waiter passed by. The questions became too personal and I forgot to take notes on the meal. Some of my colleagues rely on their memories and dash to the washroom four or five times in an evening to jot down impressions. Soon everyone in the restaurant is staring, either in annoyance at the disturbance or in sympathy. These days I rely on a notebook, hidden under the table.

In 1995 *Toronto Life*, in its wisdom, put my photograph on the cover. I have no proof that anyone in the restaurant industry ever saw it – perhaps they were too polite to mention the fact – and I do not believe it compromised my position. Soon after I started reviewing for the magazine, Joseph began assigning me columns, and in the interests of thorough research, I met and interviewed many chefs and sommeliers, waiters and restaurateurs. Matching a face and a personality to a menu gave me far more insight into what was happening on the plate than a telephone call ever could. Getting to know them did not cloud my objectivity. Work is work, and keeping the critical faculty ungummed by sentimentality scarcely ranks with rocket science. Obviously, when reviewing restaurants, I made reservations under an alias and had credit cards in other names than my own to cover my exit. If I was occasionally recognized, it did not mean that portions got suddenly larger or that surprising side orders of caviar appeared unexpectedly with the butternut soup. Even if that had been the case, such tricks would have been easily spotted and just as easily ignored. A chef can't suddenly whip up a better stock or buy better meat; most of them have such well-developed egos that they wouldn't want to.

Very rarely, a problem arose at the end of a working night when an owner or chef tried to pay for my meal. I never knew quite what to say, how to refuse the generous offer without seeming gauche and rude. But there was no question of accepting. *Toronto Life*'s policy forbidding all freebies was carved in stone long ago. I would much rather have offended a kitchen brigade of a thousand fully armed chefs than have faced Joseph the next day, stammering my explanation into the antarctic silence of his disapproval.

My godfather handled such situations with far more aplomb. He once took my whole family, and most of his, out to dinner at the carpet-hushed, chandelier-glittering restaurant of the Ritz Casino on Piccadilly. He had been there the evening before and had lost a great deal of money at roulette, a game he took very seriously. That night he intended to try to win it all back, but first there was time for Champagne, artichokes or smoked salmon, sole meunière or roast grouse, croquembouche ... It was a long and delightful meal and Robert was on the best possible form, his mischievous sense of humour sharpened by anticipation of the wheel. The waiter brought the bill. Robert looked at the dark leather folder. His lips were twitching with wickedness.

"What's this, dear?" he asked.

The waiter looked nonplussed. "The bill, sir." Robert turned to face him, his expression now one of blue-eyed innocence.

"Really, darling, you don't expect me to *pay* for all this, do you? Perhaps I should speak to the manager."

The waiter beat a retreat while we gaped at my godfather, astounded by his nerve. "Oh dear," laughed his wife. Some time passed before I caught sight of the manager, an elegant figure in a dark grey suit, gliding slowly towards us across the room. He was holding the bill in his hand. It seemed to me he took half an hour to reach the table. Just as he loomed, Robert turned and looked up at him; their eyes met for a nanosecond. With superb dignity, the manager gave an infinitesimal bow. "Of course, it has been our pleasure to host you tonight, Mr. Morley," he murmured, folding the bill and slipping it carefully into his pocket.

"Quite right, dear. Thank you," beamed Robert. The manager moved on. I finally felt able to exhale.

That night, my godfather left an enormous tip by his coffee cup before he and my father headed off for the salon des jeux. "If I'd thought for a moment I was going to get away with it," Robert was saying, "I would have ordered another bottle of Champagne."

10

FRENCH WITHOUT TEARS

I N MY TWENTIES, I went often to France, looking for the gastronomic epiphanies that so many food writers had described. Paris was perpetually disappointing. In a promisingly shabby little boîte in Montmartre, I was dismayed to find canned vegetables and sauces that were as stolidly glum as the service. A goulash in the cheerful vastness of La Coupole was just awful, gooey beef stew with a stir of paprika. Of a dinner at Le Chamarais, I remember only the superb

Armagnac that we ordered as consolation for the lacklustre food. The most exciting meal was a couscous in one of the Algerian dives in the student quarter. Leaving the restaurant, we found ourselves in a mob, sweeping swiftly through the streets, ending up in a surge tide of youth on the Boulevard Saint-Michel. A car was upturned to predatory cries. When the riot police appeared, marching forward behind helmets, batons, and Plexiglas shields, they were greeted by volleys of coat-hangers and cobblestones. My friend and I found ourselves alarmingly close to the vanguard of protest. Sudden panic turned the mob. We fled with them, saw an alley, dodged up it, hid behind trash cans, and watched the armoured phalanx of law and order pass by.

Over the years, I have encountered fewer distractions and better cooking outside Paris, in the diverse, bourgeois vastness of France. The most memorable meals were always lunches that lasted for most of a brilliantly sunny afternoon. And the bill was never a surprise, always substantially more than I could really afford. The French know the value of quality to the nearest centime.

In the early 1990s, there was a lunch at a country restaurant called Le Belvédère, near Crançot, a plain, unpretentious building perched on the edge of a spectacular gorge in Jura. A well-known local chef, Michel Noir, had recently acquired the place, but he was away that afternoon on a publicity drive for the cuisine of the region, an activity that seems to preoccupy French chefs once they reach a certain eminence within their profession. Word of his absence had spread and the room was empty, but my host, Alain de Laguiche of Château d'Arlay wines, did not seem to care. A boy came out of the kitchen: Noir's self-possessed nineteen-year-old protégé, Dominique Bouvier. He hadn't expected customers; there wasn't much in the kitchen, would we permit him to choose the menu? De Laguiche nodded his head.

I had expected local specialties – cured meats, wild mushrooms, pike, trout, or crayfish from the cold mountain streams – but Bouvier was out to impress. As an exercise that morning he had finished preparing a firm, delicately flavoured terrine of skate and salmon; we began with thick slices of that, after a tiny cup of light, tangy sorrel soup, as green and pure as an emerald. The main course was a magret of duck in a sauce of cream and vin jaune, the great wine of the region, a bone-dry, sherrylike fermentation of the Savagnin grape. Some cheeses: Comté, like a nutty, fudge-textured Gruyère, thick, creamy Morbier, with a horizontal line of blue-black mould through its heart, a wedge of big, rugged Bleu de Gex. To finish, sorbets of green apple and cassis, with crumpled, sugar-dredged pastry crisps that Bouvier made while we ate the duck.

"*Pas mal*," grunted de Laguiche, lighting up a Disque Bleu. "The boy's coming along."

Le Belvédère illustrated one of the strengths of French gastronomy: the depth of talent and energy that continuously wells up from the next generation, and the dedication of kids who are willing to pay their dues. But there's more to it than that. Some years earlier, I was staying at Les Paulands, a small hotel outside Beaune, where the vineyards of Pinot Noir begin under the bedroom windows and rise away to the distant castle of Aloxe-Corton, its steep roofs tiled in patterned Burgundian colours. In those days, the food in the hotel dining room was good enough to keep me curious, but not so marvellous that my senses swam, and I found myself distracted by the heavy-set, elderly gentleman at the table next to mine. It was not his conversation that intrigued me (he said nothing to his wife after ordering their meal, and only muttered occasionally at the waitress). It was the intensity of his devotion to the act of eating. I had never heard anyone tuck in with such dedication and brio, and sustain the concentration for almost two hours of near-continuous ingestion. I felt as if we were sharing his dozen escargots, sucking together at each buttery shell. When our plates of grated crudités (raw carrot, beetroot, and celeriac in three pungently dressed mounds) arrived simultaneously, it seemed to be me uttering those equine grunts of satisfaction at each crunch. As he savoured the warm and sticky flesh of a noble duck confit, mopping up the last smears of sauce with a slice of bread and popping it into his mouth, I experienced the eerie sensation that his dentures were somehow my own.

By the time he summoned the cheese board, with a debonair flourish of his napkin, I was lost in admiration of his technique. For a full minute he stared at it, scowled at it, took its measure. Finally, smacking his lips, he called to it out loud: "Oui, oui ... Oui!"

While the waitress held the tray within range, my gentleman reached forward. From the fifteen fresh and aromatic forms presented he carved himself first a hunk of the *blanc* and then a wedge of Chaource, a fat, supple cheese with the downy white rind of Camembert and a heart as sweet as fresh milk. Lest the local dairymen should feel neglected, he completed his selection with a slice of Nuits-St-Georges, an orange cheese with the texture of Plasticine and the alkaline tang of oak-aged Marc de Bourgogne. He ate all three with his knife and fork, unadulterated by bread or biscuit, while his wife (who was saving her own considerable appetite for the ice cream with meringue and crème de cassis) gazed fixedly at the movements of his jaw, like a trainer scrutinizing an athlete's form.

With a nation of such devoted gourmands as their audience, it's no wonder French chefs take themselves so seriously. One suddenly understands why the recent debate between such culinary giants as Ducasse and Robuchon promoting regional integrity and simplicity, and Bras, Veyrat, and Bocuse advocating the liberty of Fusion cuisine, became a matter of the utmost national importance. International importance! For months, newspapers and magazines across Europe, in America, England, and even Japan followed the passionate arguments. In all those places, modern French cooking is treated with the highest respect. In Toronto, nobody gave a damn.

Our French restaurants hit an all-time low in the winter of 1996. Two stalwart veterans had recently closed, without any warning: Le Rendez-vous, on Prince Arthur, after sixteen years, and La Grenouille, on Yonge north of Eglinton. Auberge du Pommier had just divested itself of its recently acquired French personality, to wit, chef Jean Pierre Challet. Chef Eric Vernice had left Chez Max for the slopes of Whistler, hard on the heels of Zola's Olivier Boels, who had already hightailed it out to B.C. Philippe Coeurdassier, after taking over at Zola, had moved to Montreal. The stars of yesteryear were still in town, but many were treading water. Marcel Réthoré was waiting table at Cibi. Claude Bouillet had emerged from two lean years to take over the tiny kitchen at Provence, a Cabbagetown bistro. Adding up what was left, I counted one exceptional French restaurant (Truffles), another that was sometimes good and sometimes flawed (Azalea), and perhaps fifteen bona fide bistros, ranging from pride of the neighbourhood to purgatory.

Well into the seventies, it was a given that French cuisine was the ultimate expression of culinary art; now it seemed little more than an ethnic curiosity. Hoping to find out why, I decided to conduct an informal survey among a group of well-heeled, relatively sophisticated diners. Their testimony was a veritable pot-au-feu of contradictory prejudices. Some said French food was too rich and heavy; others found portions too small and insubstantial. Some were put off by "Nouvelle notions like chicken with kiwifruit sauce," while others criticized the changeless clichés of onion soup, escargots, and pepper steak. Like the broken watch on the murder victim in a cheesy thriller, these prejudices were a telltale indication of the last French meal the person ate: something indigestibly heavy in a hotel, something whimsical, bizarre, and unsatisfying when Nouvelle Cuisine was chic, something grim and garlicky in a bad local bistro, washed down with cheap Bordeaux. It infuriates French chefs and restaurateurs that such antique images should linger in the public mind. Then again, the experiences that generated them were real enough. The city has certainly seen its share of lousy French restaurants.

"You want to know the problem?" asked Didier Leroy, one afternoon. We were having a glass of wine in Azalea, the Rosedale restaurant where he cooked. "French food is art. *L'art culinaire*. It is not a business. Many years ago, some French chefs came to Toronto. They said they had come to show the art of classical French cooking, but in fact they just came to make money. They cooked soupe à l'oignon, French fries, steak. Then they bought themselves big cars and drove around the city. As people here learned more, they remembered those guys, and it left a bad taste in their mouths.

"Another problem: the kids here. They don't have the basic training. They come out of George Brown thinking they're stars. In Paris, Joël Robuchon has twenty cooks. He doesn't pay them, because they're kids. They don't care, they just want to learn. In France, everyone goes to school to learn to be a pastry chef, a baker, a butcher ... Everybody has his own job, because you can't do everything.

"Money. Also a problem. To create a great French restaurant takes a lot of money, and time, and patience. You could do it here, because people in Toronto do recognize quality and beauty, but it's hard to find backing. You must understand business, in the way Mark McEwan and Franco Prevedello do. I admire Franco's strength. I wish he was French. In Tokyo, they spent $75 million building a restaurant that looks like a French château, then they gave Joël Robuchon a ten-year contract. Seventy-five million! When I saw the place, Le Château, I felt such pride in my country, my culture. A restaurant dedicated to *l'art culinaire*, where every customer can feel like a king."

If making the clientele feel like royalty is part of the deal, I reminded him, how come your own customers sometimes find them-selves at the mercy of your temper? In my informal survey, everyone had agreed that their enjoyment of dining à la française had too often been poisoned by the arrogant, condescending attitude of French chefs and waiters: maître d's with their noses in the air, failing to recognize that their clientele no longer found them awe-inspiring; chefs who threw a hissy fit if we asked for lamb that wasn't bloody or refused to eat our vegetables.

Leroy shrugged, looking at me as if the answer were obvious.

"Cooking is an expression of the self. The chef is like a painter, an artist. You do what you must do and people either like it or they don't. If I don't like someone, it's hard for me to cook for them. I ask my sous-chef to do it instead. But I don't have an attitude. When I refuse to cook pasta, what I'm really saying is, 'Think twice before you ask!' I do a seared foie gras with a salad of purslane flown in from Nice, and I do a port sauce with it, and I charge $14.50. I don't make any money on it. My foie gras is from Quebec, better than anything they have in the States, but it costs me $87 a kilo. An Italian restaurant asks $15 for a dish of pasta that costs them 99 cents a kilo. So I'm giving the customer good advice."

Slim, forty, handsome, with dark southern colouring and wavy black hair worn down to his shoulders, Leroy looks more like a gypsy than a chef. Give him a rapier and he could pass as a haughty Gascon swashbuckler.

"We have another big problem in Toronto," he said, raising his eyebrows. "Chefs do not work together. In New York, in Los Angeles, in Montreal, in Quebec, the chefs work together. If one guy has problems buying fish, then the other chefs unite and tell the suppliers that none of them will pay $14 a pound. They say they'll pay $10. But here, everyone keeps to themselves. There is no unity. Paul Bocuse knows five thousand chefs and shares everything with them. There are a lot of very good chefs here, but there is not enough support for each other. If there was, Toronto could be the second city in North America for food."

Leroy was right, of course. No restaurant is an island. Unless you happen to work in one. Then it's worse than an island: a storm-tossed ship alone on benighted seas. Nevertheless, even a busy chef gets to go out to eat occasionally. Leroy advocated a system of mutual support among this city's French chefs. Where did he like to eat on his evenings off? North 44° or Lotus. Not exactly bastions of French cuisine. And also, once a year maybe, he went back to France, to drink deep from the cultural source.

A few months later, he was in Lyon, an observer at that city's own culinary eisteddfod, its gathering of the clan gastronomique, the Bocuse d'Or competition. Newly inspired, he returned to Toronto and went in to work as usual on Monday morning. There was a notice in Azalea's window. In his absence, the restaurant had closed, a victim of long-accumulating but unsuspected debts and a sudden rise in rent imposed by the new landlord, Franco Prevedello. A few days later, Leroy broke his leg. Not a good month for Chef. Talking to him on the phone that week, I found him understandably disillusioned. He thought he might go down to the States, where people appreciated French cuisine.

AZALEA'S CLOSING was a blow to the city's beleaguered Gallic contingent, but down in the trenches, in the neighbourhood bistros, the veterans soldiered on. Philip Wharton, the friendly, English-born owner of La Bodega on Baldwin Street, was pleased to see that his clientele was getting younger and now included a substantial number of Asian customers. "We missed part of a generation," he told me, "the ones who thought all French places were stuffy and expensive and who spent the last ten years exploring Italian food. It's a matter of public perception. Unlike the Italians, we have had very little support from the French trade commission in terms of publicity or wine and food tastings. Nevertheless, there is a revival."

And reinforcements, too – a steady trickle of talent from, of all places, the north.

A few years ago, when Wendy and I stayed at the Inn at Manitou, near McKellar, we borrowed mountain bikes, cycled up the sandy track beside the tennis courts, and found ourselves unexpectedly entering a small but vivid scene from Wendy's youth.

"I recognize this! This is where I came to theatre camp when I was seventeen!"

Judging by the sound of tap shoes and tubas coming from a hut, the camp was much as it had been, but the inn, which owners Ben and Sheila Wise originally created as a place where the parents of campers might stay, had changed out of all recognition: a spa, a tennis club, sinfully comfortable rooms, luxury's irresistible lap.

Finding talented chefs who don't mind seeking other work for half the year has always been a problem for Ontario's seasonal resorts. The Wises' solution was to use the inn's connections as a member of the Relais & Châteaux hotel group. Each November they placed an advertisement in *L'Hôtellerie*, a Paris trade paper. Then they flew to Paris, took a suite at the Hôtel de Crillon, and spent a week choosing a kitchen team from the hundreds of young cooks who had responded to it.

"We only want people who have worked at other Relais & Châteaux properties or at two- or three-Michelin-star restaurants," insisted Ben Wise, "and we have the luxury of being able to turn down any smart-alecs or any characters who are going to miss city life after six weeks. They long to come to Canada. They see it as the land of opportunity, compared with the stultified pecking order in France. So they come to us for a season. Some return the following year; some move on to Toronto if they can get their work visas extended. We have infused the top echelon of the food service industry with dozens of young French talents," including the aforementioned Challet, Vernice, Boels, and Coeurdassier.

For years, the Inn at Manitou was a conduit into Canada for modern French cooking prepared by chef Eric Samson and a hand-picked group of young bloods from France's top hotels and restaurants, but I wonder how many of its guests even recognized the cuisine as French. No pommes frites. No onion soup ... When we were there in 1997, the three-course prix fixe began with tomato consommé, clear, pure, sweet, its flavour delicate enough to pick up tones from slivered morels, julienne of crunchy green beans, asparagus, and chervil. Or else seared foie gras, conserved as a confit before being sliced and warmed, a technique that gave it a texture approaching smooth pâté. Proud of his new wood-burning grill, Samson used it to cook a fresh fillet of arctic char, which he served with wonderful buttery spinach and a light hazelnut sauce. Some little touches brought Provence to mind: a globe artichoke heart, for instance, stuffed with a pungent concassé of tomato, thyme, olive oil, and a dab of bitter tapenade; the juices that seeped onto the plate became the sauce for a flaky fillet of broiled red snapper. Other treats were more classical, such as a faultless passionfruit soufflé, served with an intensely flavourful passionfruit sorbet, the seeds of the fruit providing delightfully unexpected crunch. Little extra courses were slipped in, extending the meal into an evening framed by the pleasant rituals of canapés and petits fours ...

You get the picture. Far from the crass Gallic stereotype, the inn offered fine, imaginative, modern French cooking. For a good few years in the nineties, only one other French restaurant surpassed it.

Truffles, in the Four Seasons on Yorkville, has always stood above the sweaty cut and thrust of the industry, largely because it is the signature restaurant of the flagship hotel of a major international chain. It draws its senior personnel from outside Toronto; it bankrolls its kitchens and wine cellar with an eye on global rather than local recognition. Its service, however, has the sophistication of warm, personal concern. Show an interest in wine and a ten-minute conversation with the sommelier ensues; ask for advice about what food to order, and restaurant chef Xavier Deshayes appears from the kitchen to discuss an individual menu for the evening.

Born in the Roussillon region, Deshayes came to Canada in 1994. He had worked for a while with Marcel Richard at Citron in Los Angeles, and at Le Manoir aux Quat' Saisons outside Oxford, honing his techniques in Raymond Blanc's kitchen. Soon after his arrival at Truffles, he and executive chef Denis Jaricot created a program for the second half of the year, a Tour de France featuring regional menus in the styles of Bordeaux, Brittany, Burgundy, Provence, Périgord, Alsace, and Champagne. The restaurant was full nightly, and well over half the customers were local gourmets, a repeat clientele dazzled by his expertise.

On one October evening, Deshayes sent out a menu de dégustation of ten courses, but the initial offering was enough to convince me that Truffles' new chef was for real: a tiny cup of green lentil broth, tasting like the intense Platonic ideal of the lentil. Hidden in its depths lay little dice of foie gras, piping hot, molten at heart, but by some cunning coup de cuisine, still crisp on their surface. Like Jaricot, Deshayes is a master of the soup. On another occasion, he sent out a bowl containing three plump, creamy Malpeque oysters on a miniature nest of carrot threads and finely minced shallots. The waiter poured in the broth: a thin cream spiked with Champagne and a hint of lemon juice, perfectly judged to amplify the flavours of oyster and allium. Sommelier Norman Hardie paired it with a glass of Cloudy Bay Sauvignon Blanc, and the choir of angels sang.

I don't know whether it reflected some policy decision on the part of Jaricot or whether North America was exerting a subtle influence on Deshayes, but as the years went by, his cooking grew less specifically French. His forthright, almost challenging use of salt and dairy in the early days mellowed in favour of natural flavours, enhanced by reduction or juxtaposition. Textures seemed lighter, the treatment of big-ticket ingredients more creative. The last time I ate at Truffles, he served Osetra caviar in a sorbet glass, mixed with iced lemon granita, vodka, minced tomato, and a sprinkling of chives. The flavours were impeccably balanced, the little joke of a savoury ice completed by a deck of translucent wafers that turned out to be sweet fruit crisps. Rack of lamb and pissaladière were still on the menu, the sauces still had a classic, Gallic refinement, but desserts had left the land of crème brûlée and feather-light lemon pastries in favour of elegant Americana: pumpkin tart and whiskey parfait, soft gingerbread layering vanilla ice cream with fresh mint to cut the sweetness.

In a different city, Truffles could have become the standard-bearer of the genre, but the distance between it and the rest of the industry showed no sign of narrowing while Deshayes was in charge of the kitchen. Other French chefs have hinted to me that his attitude towards them is one of indifference, even disdain. If so, the emotion seems to be mutual – more little barriers of arrogance to thwart potential cooperation.

In the winter of 1996, just as darkness seemed about to settle upon the French, I began to notice other glimmers of hope. One cold night, I schlepped out to Bloor West to check on a new French restaurant called Le Nouveau Parigo. For years, it had been just Le Parigo, a decent, unspectacular neighbourhood bistro; now it was in new hands, with two young women in the kitchen, neither of them French. The chef was Toronto-born Elaina Asselin, whose impressive dossier included stints at King Ranch, Scaramouche, Toqué in Montreal, and most recently Avalon, where she was Chris McDonald's pastry chef. Her sous, Kathryn Russack, had worked in several restaurants in her native Australia before enrolling at the Stratford Chefs School. From there, she joined Mildred Pierce, the eccentrically decorated restaurant in the King-Dufferin artist-warehouse colony that chef Anne Yarymowich had put on the map. I had written about Russack when Yarymowich promoted her to sous-chef; I was interested to see what she was doing now.

Le Nouveau Parigo turned out to be a pretty little room, flatteringly lit, neat and tidy in the flush of redecoration, and Asselin's cooking was a delight. Her plate presentation was simple, elegant, but the flavours of fresh, seasonal ingredients fairly glowed on the tongue. Was it French? Classically so. Meats and offal had been restored to their traditional pre-eminence, while half a dozen classical stocks had been bubbling away all day to be used as the base for various sauces and soups, most notably a lightweight but wonderfully intense herb and wine broth for mussels. Instead of dumping jam on her foie gras, Asselin had turned it into a terrine, discreetly quickened with a vein of minced prunes that had been soaked in Armagnac.

I had asked Didier Leroy if he thought you had to be French to cook French. "Oh yes, I think so," he said. "I mean, do I cook Chinese?" Asselin proved him wrong. Even her cheeses were well cared for, prompting me to mutter Oui, oui, oui, and persuading me to linger a little longer at the table.

"That's the trouble with this city," she exclaimed. "If only the rat-racers would calm down for a bit! When I worked at Toqué, people dined. They gave it the whole evening. In France, it's the same. They relax, they have a nice wine, enjoy the conversation, the surroundings. That's what French restaurants are really about."

By 1997 there were other signs of recovery. Marcel Réthoré stopped waiting table at Cibi in order to open a new place of his own, a promising little bistro called Quartier, on Yonge, south of Eglinton. Georges Gurnon made an amicable departure from his post at Avalon and quietly opened Pastis in the premises that had recently been Azalea. He invited Claude Bouillet, his former partner at Le Bistingo, to join him as chef. Taking over from Bouillet as chef at Provence, in a neat little tit-for-tat, was Azalea's Didier Leroy, who had decided to stay in Toronto after all.

Walking into Pastis for dinner, a week after its début, I found myself praying that it would be wonderful. Bouillet had been miserable since Le Bistingo had closed. Looking for work at bistros around town, he was told he was overqualified (a peculiarly Torontonian response to talent and experience). After he finally found a job at Provence, cooking on his own in a tiny kitchen with a miniature budget, he was dismayed when the *Globe and Mail* asked him to pose for a photograph, then ran it beside a condemnatory review by Joanne Kates, taking the restaurant to task for not being Le Bistingo.

Gurnon fared better in what he calls "the years of shadow," his work at Avalon keeping him in the public eye. As he showed us to our table, however, he was positively twinkling. Business had been strong as word spread among Le Bistingo's former devotees. Many were greeted by name, for Gurnon had been able to reassemble a front-of-house crew from Queen Street days. Wendy and I asked the waiter to let Bouillet choose our menu, then we waited to see what might transpire.

The first thing to appear before us was a dish of radishes and a small pat of butter, a classically simple hors d'oeuvre that served as an eloquent statement of intent. Next came a salad of bright, sweetly sapid wild greens tossed with fresh chervil, slivers of tomato, and a dressing of oil, lemon juice, and salt. Strewn over it were coins of thinly sliced smoked monkfish, firm and moist. And so we began our exploration of the menu. Minced wild mushroom and shrimp filled small, soft buckwheat crêpes, bathing in a subtle, silken Sauternes sauce as smooth as butter. Tender scallops, oysters, and clams shared a vermouth-scented broth with chanterelles, julienne of leek, and a tangle of juicy, crunchy green rock rose stems. The final splendour was Bouillet's perfect apple tarte tatin, cooked to order and served as it was in the pre-recession glory days of Le Bistingo, with a separate bowl of warm, foamy Calvados sabayon. It was a stunningly good meal. Suave. *Sérieux.*

So Gurnon and Bouillet were back, not as partners this time (the business belonged to Georges), not even as great friends (by all accounts, they have never been particularly close), but as colleagues who understood how to make a restaurant work. Did the set-up cost a fortune? Of course not, said Gurnon. Did Bouillet have trouble finding help in the kitchen? Far from it. He was happy with his team of three: David Jones, who had been Michael Stadtländer's assistant at Eigensinn Farm, Michel Jonquet from Lovelock's, and Stratford Chefs School alumna Camilla Graziani, who came to Pastis from Scaramouche. Their landlord, Franco Prevedello, was happy, too. Having once employed Gurnon and Bouillet in a brief attempt to revivify Acrobat, he knew their strengths. When Azalea closed, he received several other proposals from restaurateurs who might have paid him more rent, but Pastis was the idea that appealed. Now Rosedale had its neighbourhood rendezvous restored, and Toronto once again had a good French restaurant that nobody could mistake for a bistro or a brasserie or a hotel dining room.

In the past, I might have hailed the success of Pastis as a sign of a rekindling love affair between Toronto and French cuisine. It is in the journalist's nature to look for patterns, to see the birth of a movement in unconnected events, finding foreshadowings of the general in the explicit, and basically grasping the wrong end of the stick. The restaurant business doesn't stay still for long. Looking at it closely is like looking down a kaleidoscope. The tiny, colourful fragments are always the same, but the pictures they form are forever changing. Xavier Deshayes left Truffles, quietly planning to open a place of his own. Elaina Asselin left Le Nouveau Parigo and is no longer cooking French food. Didier Leroy left Provence for the Fifth, a downtown supper club where he finally has carte blanche to pursue his own *art culinaire. Plus ça change …*

Someday, perhaps, all the French chefs and restaurateurs in town will work together to win back the interest of the public. They will lure the next generation of apprentices into working for nothing and shine so brightly that bank managers will race to subsidize their dreams. Once more, French cuisine will dominate Toronto. And pigs will fly.

SILVARADO

MARCH 1997. Another evening comes to an end at Chiado. The customers have long since left, and the open kitchen at the rear of the restaurant is dark and empty. One by one, the cooks and waiters pass our table, bidding good-night to the boss, hurrying home along College Street. The last to go turns off the music, a tape of traditional Portuguese fados, songs of passion and lament that sound like a man two streets away shouting his sorrows above the throbbing of many guitars. Background music has a way of intruding disastrously into my tape recorder when I try to interview late at night, so I am grateful for its extinction. In that instant of abrupt silence, Chiado ceases to be a restaurant and becomes merely a large, elegant, dimly lit room where Albino Silva and I sit into the small hours, retracing meanders and turning points in the road that has led him here.

He is undoubtedly Toronto's most handsome restaurateur, over six feet tall with black hair, a dancer's slim build, and the fine features of a matinée idol. He is in his forties now, though you'd never guess it, and he has a boyish way of smiling with half his mouth that leaves female customers at Chiado weak at the knees. The smile is so effective because it appears unexpectedly out of a context of impeccably formal manners, a sort of sombre Iberian seriousness that contains a hint of melancholy. To the ladies who watch his weekly cooking segment on CFMT's *Comunicoisas* television show, he is the dream son, simultaneously self-confident and respectful. He is also highly intelligent and prone to self-analysis, a man who has recognized his own ego and evaluated its uses and its dangers.

"A chef must have an ego in order to perform," he tells me later, "but it can't be an end in itself. You need self-esteem and passion and force in order to go forward, but you must also realize your own faults and limitations."

Tonight, Silva is not performing. He speaks quickly, with a quiet intensity. From time to time, emotions well up to colour his words: pride and merriment when he mentions his sixteen-year-old son (an occasional waiter at Chiado) and the friends of his own boyhood, all of them fellow alumni at Central Technical School and still a tight-knit group at the high end of the restaurant industry; regret and sorrow as he talks of friends and relatives who have passed away, and of the fooling around that brought his marriage to an end; passionate enthusiasm when the subject turns to the loyalty of his team at Chiado or to his long-term plans for the vineyards on the family farm in Portugal's Trás-os-Montes region.

He was born on that farm. His parents were living in Lisbon, where his father, Antonio, was a pastry chef, but they wanted to give their children a more defined sense of place, a feeling of entitlement to their rural birthright. When Albino was four, his mother took the children back to the farm to live.

"That's where I learned to cook," he explains, "with cast-iron pans on an open fire. We had no electricity, no refrigeration, so everything was marinated to preserve it. We ate what we grew, baked huge crusty loaves of cornbread twice a week, and sold corn and potatoes and wine to buy anything else we needed. It was very frugal, very rustic, and one of the truly great experiences of my life. The sort of cooking I do here is based entirely on that style – simple techniques that bring out the flavour of exceptional ingredients. For example, we used to keep ducks on the farm. Whenever we killed one, we would use its blood to make a risotto. An amazing dish. I still make that here sometimes, as a special."

When Chiado opened in 1991, it was immediately clear that this was no ordinary Portuguese restaurant serving the heavy, well-oiled rustic dishes that Toronto had learned to expect, washed down with the same old half-dozen plonks that the LCBO had been selling for decades. Instead, it was a cultured embassy of the most refined Portuguese cuisine most of us had ever tasted. The fish was the freshest in the city, flown directly from the Azores, twenty-four hours from ocean to plate. The wines were also a revelation, from bone-dry single-varietal vinhos verdes to bottles such as the one Silva has opened for me tonight, a superb Verdelho Solera 1887 Madeira. There were vases of orchids on the snowy tablecloths, marble on the floor, handsome oil paintings on the walls ... Discovering such finesse on this dusty, blue-collar stretch of College near Ossington was like finding a sapphire on the sidewalk.

Since then, Silva's fiefdom has grown. He helped to create Boémia, a small, sophisticated spot in Bloor West Village, and Circo, a colourful restaurant on Eglinton East's mercurial strip, casting both kitchens in his own image. In 1996 he opened Adega, downtown on Elm Street. At a time when Toronto was awash with restaurants that offered a vague, undefined Mediterranean menu, the diluted legacy of the Cal-Ital eighties, Adega defied the generic through the strength and focus of its authentic Portuguese soul.

THE STORY of how the farm boy from Trás-os-Montes came to power in Toronto begins in 1967, when Silva, aged ten, moved back to Lisbon. Just as Toronto has a bank at every intersection, so Lisbon boasts a bakery on every street corner (a telling comparison), and one of them belonged to his father. So the young Albino went to work as an apprentice, putting in the hours after school, and working three nights a week in a civil engineer's office to make some contribution to the family's minuscule budget. By the time he was fourteen, he had obtained the necessary diplomas to become a pastry chef. "But I was a rebel. I couldn't wait till my sixteenth birthday, when I would have gone into the army."

Instead he came to Toronto. The owner of the Barrica bakery, on Augusta Avenue in Kensington Market, had gone to Lisbon to find a pastry chef and he liked what he saw of Silva's father. It was an opportunity to move up in the world, and the family seized it.

Augusta was the heart of Toronto's Portuguese community in the early seventies. Immigrant families moved into the streets around Kensington Market, up to College, down to Dundas, west of Spadina, and east of Ossington, replacing the Hungarians who had come to the city in 1956 and had then moved on. They shared the area with the dwindling Jewish community, the College Street Italians, and the Chinese, who had been pushed a block or two west by the development of the original Chinatown around Dundas and Bay. The Portuguese painted their houses Lisbon-fashion, in bright colours that seemed outlandish to Anglo-Saxon Toronto. They opened bakeries and fish or fruit stores in the market, cafés and restaurants, and they stuck together, maintaining an enclave within the strange, rather reserved city that surrounded them.

Outside school, the boys played hard, cycling through the backstreets or sitting on someone's front porch, watching the CN Tower grow, sucking back Red Cap beer. They all had jobs. Tony and Mario Amaro worked for their brother, Joe, at his fruit and vegetable store on Augusta; so did their friends Tony and Roger Vieira. Silva worked with his father in the bakery, cleaning sheet pans and forms, the same jobs he had been doing when he started his apprenticeship. For all of them, the restaurant industry seemed a natural next step.

"There were many good Portuguese restaurants in those days," says Silva. "They were run with pride and passion, and they were well patronized. Imperio seemed very grand, though it had a smaller side that catered to a blue-collar clientele, Lisbon Plate, Ottavio, the Boat – and it seems to me they did a better job then than they do now. As for me, I was ambitious. I could already cook, but I wanted to learn how to be a maître d'. Toronto was a strong hospitality centre in those days, a perfect place to learn table service, with very good waiters and maître d's everywhere, all from Europe, of course, working strictly by the book.

"So I went to work as a busboy at the Cossacks, a new place on

Queen West at Duncan. I think it was the city's first upscale Russian restaurant, and it was fabulous, all Russian service with lots of table-side cooking. There was no stainless steel, only silver dishes; no glass, only crystal; huge, beautiful Wedgwood bone china plates and fifteen cooks on the line. It was expensive, but deservedly so, with two kinds of caviar, four kinds of oysters, zakuski served on a raised silver platter. Outstanding.

"At first, I was terrible. What a loser! The waiters would all say, 'I don't want this kid on my station.' Then after a little while, they were saying, 'Albino is mine' – 'No, Albino is mine.'

"The owner, Tom Zimonjic, was an outstanding restaurateur and an exceptional maître d', but he began to lose his grip. He person-ally drank two bottles of Bacardi a day, with a splash of Coke – I know, because I would carry them up to his room – and one day, the kitchen staff all walked out. I had told him once that I wanted to work in the kitchen. Now he said to me, 'Kazachok' – that's what they called me: it means a pageboy in the court of the czar – 'here is your opportunity. You do the garde-manger and I'll cook the hot food.' A couple of weeks later, I saw him looking at me. 'Kazachok,' he said, 'you're better at this than I am. Hire someone else for the garde-manger and you take over the hot station.' So there I was, seventeen years old, still in Grade Eleven, scared shitless, cooking for 120 people a night, working as chef in the best restaurant I had ever seen. I never told anyone at school. It was my kitchen for the next eight months, until I realized I was much too young for the job."

Still hoping to master the skills of a maître d', Silva left the Cossacks and moved into the dining room of Whaler's Wharf, the popular seafood restaurant owned by Walter Oster. By the time he was twenty, he had risen to the rank of manager. One day a Russian lawyer came to visit him.

"He told me that Tom was finally on the verge of bankruptcy. He said, 'It's time for you to go back and buy the Cossacks. Go and offer him $75,000 for the whole thing.' So I did, but Tom was proud. He couldn't bear to lose it all. He offered to sell me 50 percent. I said no. In the end, the receivers went in. Everything was auctioned off. Six-hundred-dollar chairs going for $20 each. It was heartbreaking. They made a total of $32,000. Today $2 million would not set it up."

Silva stayed within the Whaler's Wharf empire for almost ten years, rising through the ranks, aware that he was being groomed by Oster for an important destiny. Meanwhile, the rest of the Central Tech group were also moving up in the world, finding jobs as waiters and managers in top dining rooms – Noodles, Fenton's, the Millcroft Inn – sticking together, helping one another out. It was Silva who took the next step. In 1980, he and a group of six friends opened a restaurant called Eurosol on College Street. Silva was still at Whaler's Wharf, but as the only partner with serious restaurant experience, he set up the dining room and kitchen. On Sundays he tended the bar in the basement pub, a space that became the arena of cool for young Portuguese on Sunday afternoons, so much so that a local radio station took to broadcasting live from the premises. It all sounded more like an excuse for a party than a serious business venture, and eventually the young partners started to wrangle. After a year and a half, the place closed.

Perhaps it was that experience that convinced Silva that he needed to find out more about the business side of the industry. In 1985 he gave three months' notice to a disappointed Walter Oster and went down to the States, working as a restaurant troubleshooter for a consulting company, and finally joining the prestigious Culinary Institute of America outside New York City at Hyde Park. He was the youngest faculty member ever, teaching table service and his own course in restaurant etiquette, protocol, and manners. In 1989 he returned to Toronto for good. By then, Tony Vieira was working as a floor manager at Centro. With a little help from him and his own CIA credentials, Silva was taken on as a cook in Raffaello Ferrari's kitchen.

"It was actually on my very first day," says Silva with a gleeful smile, "that I got into a shouting match with Franco Prevedello. I was writing notes in the kitchen while Raffaello was explaining what he wanted me to do that evening, and out of habit I put the pencil in my mouth. I heard this voice: 'Take that fucking pencil out of your mouth!' I wasn't used to being talked to like that. It wasn't how we communicated at the CIA. I looked up. There was this guy, not wearing whites, glaring at me. I said, 'Excuse me? Are you cooking? You don't seem to be cooking, but this is the kitchen and unless you're cooking you can get the fuck out of here!' Raffaello, may he be at peace, hurried up and told me who he was. After that, Mr. Prevedello barely spoke to me again, except once, after I'd moved out of the kitchen into the dining room. I felt his eyes on me. 'You're stealing from me,' he said. I said, 'No, Franco, I'm not stealing!' He said, 'Yes, you are. You're stealing my ideas. You're seeing how it all works.'

Prevedello was right. All the while he was at Centro, Silva was watching and learning, thinking about a restaurant of his own. Since then, he has grown accustomed to people referring to him as the Portuguese Prevedello, and he concedes his long-term business plan is a conscious copy of his old employer's, albeit on a smaller scale.

Going fifty-fifty with a financial backer, Silva bought the building on College near Ossington that would soon be Chiado. His idea was to give the Portuguese community a Portuguese restaurant that would set a new standard for quality, and that might at last show the city why his countrymen take such pride in their gastronomy. Both ambitions came to pass, but slowly. The local community gave the new restaurant their approval and their respect and enjoyed its celebrity; at the same time, they stayed away in droves.

"It's true," he sighs. "My Portuguese clientele is only about five percent of total business. Maybe it's a little too much for them. We are still simple people."

But the rest of the city loved it, and with good reason. The cooking was a revelation for anyone who thought Portuguese cuisine was necessarily crude and heavy. The menu was a direct reference back to the food Silva grew up with, full of clear flavours, making much use of marinades and the grill, but leavened, refined, and enhanced by his twenty years in North America. When Silva marinated a superbly fresh piece of swordfish with a touch of ginger and a hint of soy, we tasted the influence of Toronto; when he added shrimp and monkfish to the traditional açorda, a poor man's dish of bread, coriander, olive oil, and egg, he changed its status but not its soul. Smoked alheira sausages, made with chicken, rabbit, and veal by the mother of one of his waiters, looked dauntingly sturdy on the plate but turned out to be soft as clouds and delicately spiced, their smokiness harmonizing beautifully with the bitterness of the little heap of rapini beside them.

I have never seen Albino Silva actually cooking, though he does take the odd evening at one or another of his restaurants. He prefers to develop recipes in the kitchen when Chiado is closed, working closely with his team. During the evening, Manuel Vilela is actually at the stove.

"Manny is as good a cook as Toronto has right now," he says. "He was brought up in the same way that I was; we share the same points of reference. But my whole staff are just as close. We trust each other absolutely. We all feel a sort of sacred obligation not to spoil this particular energy that we have."

"Albino was the first to offer the best of Portuguese food and wine to Canadians, with pride and with joy," says Tony Vieira. "He brought it out of the Stone Age and into a bright new light. He might have achieved the same success faster if he had done what Tony and Mario Amaro did with Opus, creating a top restaurant with a more conventional style in a more fashionable part of the city, but he went his own way. It was courageous, but it was also smart, because there was no one else to challenge him."

IN 1996 SILVA DECIDED the time was right for another venture, this time in the heart of the city. Not for the first time, he took a leaf out of Franco Prevedello's journal: set up a place to your own precise specifications, find a chef and a manager you can trust to be on form every night and give them a minor partnership as an added incentive, be there yourself as often as possible, and keep a close eye on every detail.

The week Adega opened, Joseph Hoare and I went there for lunch. The room was attractive – bright, energetic – and the service was first-class, but the menu seemed vague. We were hoping, I suppose, for another Chiado, but found no anchoring ethnic authenticity. The

Portuguese elements were muted or camouflaged altogether beneath the over-familiar standards of generic Mediterraneana.

"I was nervous," admits Silva with a shrug. "Our first menu was a mistake. I should not have compromised, but we sat down and tried to work out what the downtown customer wants. We did all right, but I wasn't happy with it."

Silva's decision to boost the Portuguese content was a brave one. To me, it set him above most of the restaurateurs in the city, in the same way that a single act can turn a politician into a statesman. Suddenly the restaurant discovered a strong personality, and the excellent staff found a new sense of purpose as evangelists of Lusitania. The olives that appeared with the menu were Portuguese; so was the heavy, fresh cornbread and the excellent olive oil in which it must be dipped. Piripiri added subtle heat to grilled tiger shrimp, the fish specials were species that have no name outside Portuguese waters, and the braised rabbit had passed through a marinade that would be instantly recognizable on the Silva family farm, where Albino's father had retired to perfect his winemaking techniques. Chef Jamie Cordova, once a pupil of Silva's at the CIA, and a former sous of that other educational establishment, Chiado, executed his mentor's wishes impeccably. The Silva hallmark was unmistakable. If Cordova came up with so much as an aïoli that departed from that ethos, it was tested, found wanting, and removed. There are shades of autocracy about such a system, but one artist's vision is always more interesting than the generic alternative.

Tonight, at Chiado, that vision is growing blurred. Albino Silva seems tired, and he's flying to Portugal tomorrow to look for new wines for his restaurants. Then again, he is used to late nights, to unwinding with the Amaro brothers down at Opus, or with Tony and

Roger Vieira at Circo when the last customers have gone home. I once asked Tony Vieira what the old Central Tech crowd talk about when they get together, shooting the breeze in the wee small hours. Old times are only a part of it.

"We have often said," Vieira replied, "that maybe, with luck, and if the right wheels are set in motion, we could be the next phase of top restaurateurs in this city. It's a long learning process, but why not?"

RELATIVE VALUES

W HEN ONE of my mother's clients comes to Toronto to make a film or act in a play, I think they half expect to find my house a replica of hers, with armchairs pulled up to the fire and magnificent meals appearing by magic. Rather than disappoint them, Wendy and I take them out on the town, which tends to set all sorts of distant gongs, chimes, and bells ringing in my memory. Twenty years vanished when Alan Bates arrived for a month in 1997 to play Ibsen's *The Master*

Builder. He was staying at the Royal York and performing at the Royal Alex (the star dressing-room looked every bit as shabby as I remembered); he was even invited to the ritual cast banquet down the street at one of Honest Ed's restaurants. "They say steak is the big thing in Toronto," he remarked. "Is there any escaping it?"

Squiring a stranger around Toronto helps me look at the city's restaurants from an unaccustomed angle, especially when the stranger has a European sensibility. Bates loved Borgo Antico and was flattered when the owner-chef, Pino Posteraro, sent out extra treats from the kitchen, but he remained unimpressed by Sequoia Grove's messy Fusion. He delighted in Acqua's energy, but not Bistro 990's lazy service and crude, careless cooking. He and the company made a habit of weekend brunch at the King Edward Hotel, and he found Café Asia fascinating, unlike anything he had ever encountered. When his month was up, I asked him if he had decided on a favourite. Out of all the restaurants he had visited, he named Kit Kat on King Street West, because it was witty and comfortable, with good, reliable, sustaining cooking, and because he enjoyed owner Al Carbone's warmth and soft-spoken, beneficent gravity. The mood of the room reminded him of some of the small, long-established, family-run Italian restaurants in the Soho backstreets behind London's Shaftesbury Avenue, graciously Bohemian places that have evolved organically over the decades, acquiring a natural patina.

I envied Bates the luxury of his prejudices. For years I have suppressed my own. As a reporter, my obligation has always been to report, to analyse and describe, taking every restaurant on its own terms. Recently, however, I have noticed other values insinuating themselves into the objective critical process. I look at Toronto differently these days. I can no longer walk its streets and dine in its restaurants with the detachment of a travel writer in somebody else's town. To my surprise, I find that I have started to care about the city as if it were my own.

There are two main reasons for this change. The first has to do with Mike Harris. Like so many Torontonians, I have been politicized by the astonishing insensitivity of his methods. The socially divisive side effects of his policies seem too great a price to pay for accelerated economic regrowth. The second reason is more or less connected to the first: a dismaying shift in the basic values of a significant section of the restaurant industry.

What do you see if you split open a restaurant and peel back the show? At the core is a moving part, an energy source, two opposing forces that spin continually, each striving for domination. One is artistic creativity; the other is commercial efficiency. Their competitive dynamic drives the whole machine: the artist duking it out with the accountant, ambition wrestling with compromise. Without that struggle, restaurant life as we know it would cease to exist. If the values of commercial efficiency were uncontested, we would have nowhere to eat but chains and franchises. If artistic individualism went unchallenged by practicality we would have nowhere to eat at all.

These are the innate values of the traditional restaurant, regardless of its budget and size. What concerns me about Toronto today is the growing number of establishments that deliberately fix the fight. The team in the red corner is the same: accountants, investors, controllers, food and beverage managers, owners striving to turn a profit. But the blue corner is empty. No creative types in the kitchen, no dedicated front-of-house personnel. In their place there is merely the show, the set dressing, the ambience and décor. These are not just lousy restaurants that lack talent, these are anti-restaurants, and they exist at every level of the industry.

On the lower echelons are the huge, themed barns that are such a feature of the suburbs and that cluster within staggering distance of SkyDome. They call themselves restaurants but their roots lie in a different demi-monde: the world of the bar and the nightclub. Of course, bars and nightclubs have their own legitimate system of values. Because the products they sell are the same the world over, they rely on looks and atmosphere and themed gimmickry to bring in the crowds. That's fine. To each his own. But it is a philosophy that has no place in the world of restaurants.

The proliferation of these places alarms me. I watch the crowds at the tables tucking into pretentious canteen food, stuff that has arrived in the kitchen half-cooked from a factory, rubber seafood, extruded fries, pre-cut vegetables that travel in huge white plastic tubs of brine. These ingredients are deliberately insipid: flavour is added later in the form of garlic salt, ersatz Cajun powder, sour frying oil, and the inevitable twist of the waiter's peppermill. As a rule, I refuse the offer of freshly ground pepper. To offer it before the customer has even tasted the food is absurd; to offer it at all is a clear admission on the part of the restaurant that the chef doesn't know how to season his cooking. In the bar-barns, however, I have learned to say yes to the mill.

The owners of these establishments have their own gastronomic philosophy. With a certain degree of pride, they explain that cooking with so little character offends no one. They boast of the numbers they serve and remind me that this clientele prizes speed of service, large portions, and familiar fare. They find my position élitist, reactionary, and hypocritical. How can I keep on celebrating the extraordinary variety of restaurants available in Toronto, and then exclude places like theirs from my otherwise catholic list? My only response is that these enterprises dilute the overall quality of the restaurant industry. They threaten the still vulnerable accomplishments of a local fine-dining tradition that is barely thirty years old. They act like a brake on its progress and soak up millions of dollars that could be better spent. In other words, their values are not my own.

I guess it all boils down to the age-old clash between art and popular culture. Toronto has a taste for the latter, which is why we end up with Shakespeare performed on a patch of wasteland under the Gardiner Expressway while our beautiful old theatres are wasted for years at a time on Andrew Lloyd Warblings.

More dangerous than the barns because they are less easy to recognize are the anti-restaurants further up the food chain. A hypothetical composite of these places would be large and sumptuously decorated. Mannequins wait by the door to greet the customers; managers dressed in clothes I could never afford prowl between the tables, interrupting conversations to ask often if all is well but never listening to the answer. The waiters have no knowledge of the menu, and half the items on the overpriced wine list are out of stock. Everything is a feast for the eyes but not for the appetite, for the food seems an afterthought. It's Fusion, of course, and laden with the trendy ingredients of the hour, notions copied from other imaginations but without any grasp of purpose. Big impact, big glamour, the attraction of artifice: these rooms are the bastard children of nightclubs, manufactured to take advantage of a moment in fashion. The sensibility of the investment groups that create them is 90 percent visual. In the planning stage, I am certain they spend far more time with interior designers and accountants than with their chefs.

Who eats at these dazzling locations? Everyone visits once, to see what the fuss is about and to enjoy the surroundings. I sit in their midst, behaving myself, watching the cards fall, letting the other guy play his hand. But I think about the size of the coming bill and weigh it against the waiter's indifference, the tepid mediocrity on the plate, and I find myself growing resentful. By eating here, I am buying into the values of the team that assembled the place. My money is helping to pay for the million-dollar décor and supporting the philosophy that high ceilings and marble fountains mean more in a restaurant than the hands and mind of a chef.

THE RISE of the anti-restaurants marks one change in values as the nineties draw to a close. The other most active movement in the industry also springs from a shift in standards: the growth of restaurants that only the rich can afford. The wealthy want their treats again, and our restaurateurs are happy to provide them. It isn't that the eighties have returned. Ten years ago, the booming economy subsidized a quest for novelty, flamboyance, and exotica. This time around, the reappearance of spending money coincides with a different spectrum of tastes. There is nothing novel about steak and cigars, sushi and caviar, fine Burgundy and classical French cuisine. These are deeply conventional, old-fashioned status objects. To me it seems an alarming example of creative exhaustion that the inspiration for our latest restaurants should come from the 1970s, a decade we spent the last eighteen years trying to forget.

Michael Carlevale's Black and Blue was the prototype of the

plutocratic cigar-culture hangout. On that grey March morning in 1996 when he walked me through the construction site, his intentions were clearly defined. "This place," he explained, "will be bloody civilized, not at all derivative, which is very important to me, and, let's face it, expensive. It's not for everybody, but fine and elaborated gastronomy is not for everybody. I'm going to charge a lot of money to sit in it because the reality of what these things cost me is going to be there on the menu ticket."

His candour was startling in a city that still paid lip service to a warm and woolly political correctness. But within a year, cigar-culture temples were blossoming all over the downtown core. The manifesto accompanying each opening was the same: the offer of old-fashioned quality at a price, a celebration of money and the good things it can buy. And beneath the big words lay a subtext, the cigar culture's raison d'être: the quest for status.

It was interesting to see how the restaurateurs each made their bid for that elusive prize. At Black and Blue, and later at the Boston Club, Carlevale merely gave full rein to his own sophisticated taste. At Rosewater Supper Club and then at the Courthouse, Nick di Donato borrowed the gravitas of magnificent old buildings to give his ambitions stature. A project such as the Fifth, a true supper club with an annual $1,000 membership, used money and a double-secret entrance through a service elevator to convince its clientele of their exclusivity. Inside every one, the trappings of status were displayed in their glory: pampering service, fine food and deluxe décor, high prices, a fabulous wine list, a noble humidor. The customers lapped it up, but the owners soon saw the paradox in the game. There is only one way in which a restaurant acquires legitimate status. It happens when people of status eat there. The restaurateurs laid their bait for the bona fide VIPs only to find that it also drew mere status-seekers, and tables crowded with status-seekers bring a restaurant no status at all.

No one understood this better than John Arena. When he bought Winston's in 1966, he knew he was buying a potent name, and through hard work and the force of his personality he turned it into the clubhouse of the élite, sustaining its power through the 1970s and beyond. By late 1997, the values his restaurant stood for were once again current, so it came as no surprise when I heard in November that Winston's was reopening. The property had been purchased by Zisi Konstantinou, proprietor of a nightclub called Limelight. His managing partner in the new venture was Rony Hitti, lord of Bouffe, a small Yorkville bistro, and also of Zola, the stylish French brasserie in the same neighbourhood. They had engaged Hitti's cousins, the Gatserelia brothers, to redecorate, and I wondered how that would play. The Gatserelias had designed Terra and Acrobat, extravagant, glittering post-modern rooms; they had also created Zola's look, a witty pastiche of Parisian Art Nouveau décor. As for the chef: Hitti had chosen Michael Potters, a young talent who had wowed the critics at the short-lived Ivory, but whose over-ambitious Fusion cooking was less impressive at Rosewater Supper Club.

One night, driven by curiosity, I pushed open the famous old door on Adelaide Street West and climbed the stairs to the dining room. Any doubts I had that the new Winston's might turn out to be an anti-restaurant were quickly dispelled. The Gatserelias had exercised restraint in their redecoration. Kerenyi's carved wooden ceiling partitions were still in place, but the central lines of banquettes had gone and on the columns that replaced them were glass light fixtures like many-winged insects, faithfully copied from Maxim's in Paris. The canvasses had vanished from the walls, which now glowed turquoise and gold. Instead of the gawdy Tiffany lamps of the old days, discreet yellow glass shades hung from the ceiling like upside-down limpets. There was no carpet, which made the room look spare, and the missing banquettes had reduced the seating from about seventy to forty-eight, which illogically made it feel smaller. Winston's had never had windows but somehow the lack now seemed more obvious. The overall effect was subdued and European rather than ostentatiously lavish. Could it be that Hitti was more concerned with substance than style?

I began to suspect that the answer might be yes when I noticed familiar faces above the management's tuxedos. In the spot where Arena used to meet and greet the people that mattered stood Lebert Williams, an accomplished manager who learned his trade at La Scala and was at one time a Splendido mainstay. At the back of the room, I saw maître d' Jean-Christophe Morlière, another strong presence who had worked for the Roux brothers at the Waterside Inn in Bray-on-Thames, England, and had then given Zola its well-deserved reputation for customer coddling. The sommelier was Andrew Laliberte, a familiar figure from Fenton's, Nekah, and Chiaro's at the King Edward Hotel. That Hitti had brought all three together suggested a major commitment to traditional standards of service. And along with the personnel came an emphatically Old World style. I watched plates of food borne in on trays, as they always used to be in formal restaurants until Fenton's broke the tradition and the rest of Toronto gratefully followed suit. Silver cloches covered the plates, to be simultaneously whipped away by the waiters after a second's pause to build tension. Even the butter dish had its own tiny dome, its own miniature flourish, a detail that came perilously close to theatre of the absurd.

But it was the menu that set everything in perspective, proposing dishes not heard of in this part of the world for decades – mosaique of game with Madeira aspic; sauce Albufera with the saddle of arctic hare – and at prices that caused the jaw to drop. Few restaurants in the nineties had dared to break the established ceiling of $30 for a main course; here the average price was $53. The "Artic hare" came in at $62, a "Tournedos of Beef Perigueax" at $60. For that sort of money, they might have got the spelling right. It seemed that Hitti had shifted the burden of his dreams squarely onto the shoulders of his chef. The food was going to have to be stratospherically good to justify not only the prices but the whole opulent package. Mediocrity in such a setting would bring the evening crashing to earth in a dust cloud of pretentiousness and vulgarity.

The first offering from the kitchen was an amuse-gueule to pique the appetite: a tender scallop, sautéed rare, crowned with a hefty slice of black truffle, with a subtle red wine sauce. It was a delicious little mouthful, and the truffle made a clear statement that Potters intended to give his customers plenty of bang for their buck. As an appetizer, I had ordered the mosaique of game, an antique item like a terrine composed of various meats held in a matrix of mousse. Making one is a time-consuming business, and expensive if you use the sort of ingredients Potters favoured: fillet of fallow deer, fillet of lamb for its perfume and contrast, breast of guinea fowl, partridge, and squab, and for the mousse, trimmings from the birds, cream, egg yolks, truffle essence, and black trumpet mushrooms. Some terrines end up pretty but numbingly bland. This one was marvellous. Each of the meats had retained its own sapid identity; every taste was a new experience, harmonized by the tiny cubes of firm, transparent Madeira aspic. I was warming to the new old Winston's.

"I've never had a chance to work with ingredients like this before," Potters told me the following day. "Coming into the kitchen is like walking into Tiffany's. The diamonds are here, the gold there, the platinum there. The green bass comes in alive, we have turbot caught in the English Channel – the real thing – the best venison, U.S. sterling silver beef. Rony explained what he wanted: research the menus from three-star Michelin restaurants, no Fusion – and to tell you the truth I feel more comfortable with this food. It's what I was trained to do, long ago at Les Copains on Wellington Street, at Le Bistingo and Auberge Gavroche. After I left Rosewater, I was feeling really fed up with the restaurants in this town. Now I've fallen in love with cooking again. I wish we had a Michelin star rating in Canada, because I'd really like to take a shot at one."

The main course might just have qualified: a sweetbread imbued with the flavour of truffles, perched on a tender medallion of veal, like the eye of a chop, cut with a good fringe of fat. Baby golden chanterelles lay seductively beside it, with a scattering of whole hazelnuts. A little spinach and a soft potato galette lurked beneath. The vegetables were served as a separate garniture: a timbale of pure beetroot mousse, baby carrots, braised fennel hearts, so simple, so effective. Andrew Laliberte poured me a glass of Savigny Vergelesses La Bataillère 1993, a wine that fell perfectly into place.

The wine list offered few wines that cost less than $60, but the prices were fair for its Burgundies, Rhônes, and Bordeaux. "Yes, we start at a higher level than anywhere else in Toronto," said Hitti when he joined me at my table, "but that is because I want to do it right. If I were to serve a $25 bottle of wine it would be an injustice to the food. The same with the menu. I want a menu that stands on its own in the city, that you can't find anywhere else. We don't decide what our price point will be and then plan dishes around it. We cook what we want, regardless of what it costs in labour and fabulous ingredients, and then charge accordingly."

Hitti was high on his new endeavour, energized, buzzing. He had opened restaurants before, but never on such a scale. He came to Canada with his parents from Lebanon in 1980, and while they resumed their careers as restaurateurs, he tried everything he could think of to stay out of the business. With an MBA in finance, he entered the world of banking but quit after five days. "I realized I hated it. This was in 1986. I went to my father and said, 'Dad, I'm ready to manage your business.' He said, 'That's perfect! Here, you're manager of dishwashing from now on.' I started from the bottom, worked my way up, worked in hotels, did a *stage* in Europe. I ended up managing my father's restaurant, Roussalka at College Park, for a year, then opened my own place, Boa Café on Bellair. It did fairly well." In 1993, against all advice, he opened Zola and soon bought out his partners. "I remember a very interesting comment from one of my regulars there, a wealthy lady. She said, 'What we really need in Toronto is a restaurant where even the very wealthy can feel it's an evening out rather than just another dinner.'"

Pain in the pocketbook is a jaded way to evaluate quality, but the remark clearly impressed Hitti. His large, dark eyes were shining. There was a look of wonder on his handsome face. "Everyone says this city does not support expensive restaurants. Every owner would like to do what I'm doing here, but they think I'm a lunatic. Toronto has always been willing to pay the price of dinner, but not of gastronomy. There's a difference. So, yes, it's a gamble. But if there's ever been a time since the mid-eighties when the economy permits something like Winston's, it's now. Our aim is to win back the big power executive lunch, the old boys' network. I think they will respond to the feeling of exclusivity. And we will be the city's great evening out. When wealthy tourists ask for *the* restaurant in Toronto, this is where the hotels will send them."

Status ... I applauded Hitti's quest for quality; I was less attracted by his all-out pursuit of an élite clientele. Whether Winston's will again become the city's signature restaurant remains to be seen. Given Toronto's neo-conservative mood, anything's possible. A few weeks after my visit, Hitti lowered the tab a little, which focused people's attention onto product rather than price. Dining there still costs the earth. Money is the latest fashionable ingredient in our restaurant kitchens, ostentatiously over-used. However good the cooking, I find it leaves the taste of metal in my mouth.

THE RICH have new playgrounds in which to revel; the poor and the dispossessed, under the present provincial administration, have come to rely increasingly on volunteer groups for their welfare. Our top chefs, restaurateurs, and suppliers pitch in with time and talent, at auctions and charity events and through the work of Second Harvest, a not-for-profit organization that benefits Toronto's hungry and homeless. Its drivers pick up unwanted fresh food from restaurants, cafeterias and caterers, grocery stores, manufacturers, and specialty retailers and deliver it to some eighty social service agencies around the city – a satisfyingly logical way to do a power of good. Its annual fundraiser is a culinary gala called Toronto Taste that gathers together more than fifty of our finest chefs. They set up stations in the house and gardens of Vaughan Estate, a handsome old party venue on Bayview Avenue, and cook for the paying public.

In 1996 torrential rain had turned the event into a submarine party. A year later, everyone prayed that Sunday, June 8, would be blessed with something approaching clement weather, and the prayers were answered. All morning, the sun shone down on the black-clad volunteers as they set up trestles and tablecloths under the great white canopy that covered the lawn. By mid-afternoon, the chefs and their minions had worked up a sweat carrying apparatus, decorations, and trays of food from the driveway where their vans were parked to their allotted stations. Barbecues and Calor gas stoves were in place, coolers tucked away out of sight. Restaurateurs and chefs wandered about, renewing old acquaintance, introducing their assistants, discreetly checking what everyone else intended to serve.

Almost every high-profile chef in the city seemed to be present – even Susur Lee, who always manages to be the last to arrive. The Stadtländers had driven down from Eigensinn Farm; Jamie Kennedy had left his kitchen at the Royal Ontario Museum. Michael Olson came up from On the Twenty in Niagara, bringing a portable oven to roast juicy loins of pork. Hiro Yoshida stood behind his portable wooden sushi bar, mentally preparing to cut and press three thousand pieces of sushi. Keith Froggett of Scaramouche was taking a nap on the grass. Chef Brad Long of 360, the restaurant on top of the CN Tower, spoke of his trip to the Baltic, scouting the cuisines of other sub-Arctic countries. Marc Thuet, the extraordinarily talented chef and part owner of

Centro, looked exuberant but a little dazed. Forty-eight hours earlier, he and Centro's manager, Tony Longo, had bought Franco Prevedello's half share in the restaurant for something in the region of a million dollars. I noticed Albino Silva. My column in that month's *Toronto Life* was a detailed piece on his life and work and I had no idea how he felt about the story, but he smiled as he shook my hand.

"I feel naked now," he murmured.

"Half of Toronto would like to see that," laughed Arpi Magyar of Splendido, slapping each of us on the back.

While the chefs hobnobbed, the ladies and gentlemen of the press were hard at work sampling cocktails in a roped-off area in the woods, prepping their appetites for the serious eating that lay ahead. Musicians played, the volunteers on the lawn handed out napkins and wineglasses as the public began to arrive. Now the cooks buttoned their whites and set to work. And the weather held. A badly bruised cloud mass heading in from the south produced a single admonitory thunderclap, but the rain stayed away.

By eight that evening, when a thousand sated gourmets staggered home with their Body Shop loot bags, $300,000 had been raised to keep Second Harvest's trucks running. For the chefs and their teams, it was a rare opportunity to mingle and meet, to feel part of a single profession and to reacquaint themselves with its fundamentals: notions of hospitality, sustenance, the shared breaking of bread. Removed from the purdah of the kitchen, lacking the ramparts of décor, the barrier of the table, the distancing intermediary of service, their work that day came closer than usual to these truths. For me, the event provided invaluable gossip, inside information I could share with Joseph during our regular, first-thing-in-the-morning telephone conversation. He would want to know what had been the strangest sight. Was it the smoked salmon ice cream served on a pappadum by Christopher Klugman of Oro, or that tall waiter from Southern Comfort cross-dressed in a Day-Glo green frock with a colour-coordinated colander on his head? And the most delicious creation? Was it Mark McEwan's grilled rabbit on toast with crispy onions? Jamie Kennedy's morels stuffed with chicken and peas? Borgo Antico's eel or Canoe's tender sweetbreads, which spurted scarlet sauce all over my shirt as I bit into them?

For the best part of nine years, every working day began with a call to Joseph. After certain ritual preliminaries, enquiries about the well-being of friends and relatives, we moved on to news of the restaurant business. His vast knowledge and erudition always put matters into an agreeable perspective; there were long, comfortable pauses and a good many jokes. During the summer of 1997, however, his calm words of confidence and inspiration had a different, more tragic context. A week or two after the Second Harvest gala, Joseph's health suddenly started to deteriorate. He went into hospital for tests and was diagnosed with inoperable cancer of the stomach and liver. On October 27, he died.

Those of us who knew him as a man, a friend, a mentor, have our own indelible memories of him: his impeccable manners, his unexpected sense of fun and appreciation of eccentricity, his compassion. In our house, and in many others, he was an *ami du maison*, an unofficial godfather to our children. On the day we moved into our current home, a ramshackle rental on the fringes of Leaside, he appeared unannounced with a wonderful picnic lunch. He approved when we bought two cats from the pound, seeing it as a sign that Wendy and I were finally settling down. Every summer, when we scooped up the children from school and hightailed it to Europe, meandering down to revisit the house in Corfu, he eased the journey with advice on favourite hotels and tiny perfect restaurants hidden away in the French and Italian countryside.

But Joseph's influence extended far beyond the circle of his acquaintance. His taste and his unimpeachable honesty throughout his thirteen years as the magazine's food editor gave *Toronto Life's* restaurant reviews unique credibility. Every chef who worked that much harder to win an extra half star profited from his system of values. All the restaurateurs whose ratings fell, who swallowed their indignation and set about fixing what was wrong, owed him a debt. The debts accumulated; the standards of dining rose. Joseph never took credit for the beneficial effects of his unremitting hard work. Preferring the role of staff officer to the fields of glory, he wrote under the pseudonym of Samuel Ryan. For me and for many others, he remains the arbiter. When an issue of ethics, taste, or syntax arises, the first thing we ask ourselves is, "What would Joseph have said?"

FOR YEARS I have played a writerly game, trying to find a metaphor that might capture the complex, continuous dynamic of this city's restaurant industry. Sometimes the movement seems tidal – ten steps forward and nine steps back – but tides are too linear and too predictable. Sometimes it's more like an orrery, a mechanism depicting the orbits of fashions, with each style of cuisine revolving at its own pace, bringing new combinations into the limelight, bearing others back into the shadows.

High in the sky are the fixed constellations, the survivors immutable. The first meal I had in this city was at Ed's Seafood, and

I am delighted to see that the place is still going strong. It has outlasted Three Small Rooms, Napoléon, Troy's, Fenton's, Nekah, Lotus ... Who says life in Toronto is lacking in irony? A great deal has happened in a mere twenty years. Fads have blazed like comets and faded, tastes have changed, but most of the actors from those early days are still on the stage. Our restaurant industry sometimes seems like a repertory company, with the same faces reappearing in different productions from season to season, from week to week. Recipes, waiters, wine cellars, cooks, even furniture is recycled for duty. Acrobat's bar graces the top-floor lounge above the new Winston's. Fenton's ice buckets now cool the wine at an excellent little Italian bistro called Paese.

And what of the future? For the food columnist, that is the second most frequently asked question. As magazine and newspaper editors plan their New Year issues, the telephone rings with invitations to comment on forthcoming trends. The humble writer is obliged to play the haruspex, foretelling the future from the steaming entrails of the past (a problem, with offal so rarely seen on a menu). I suppose it's a just retribution for all the perks of the preceding months, but as deadlines approach, the task becomes increasingly worrisome. It takes a special arrogance to describe events that have not yet happened. Here in Toronto, the usual practice is to scan the current scene in New York and then cobble together an article from fashions that might conceivably immigrate to Ontario – wraps and Latin-American food were recent good calls. But fortunetelling should not be lightly undertaken. Long, long ago, I wrote a facetious New Year's column in *Toronto Life* lampooning the predictors of trends. I filled it with the most outrageous, implausible prophecies I could think of, culminating in the preposterous suggestion that Fenton's would turn Tex-Mex. Within a year, Fenton's had closed and a fajita joint called Tortilla Flats had opened in its space. Ever since then, I have been wary of playing the seer.

The one question everyone asks, far more often than any other: What's the best restaurant in Toronto? Marc Thuet's Centro? Chris McDonald's Avalon? Scaramouche, North 44°, Truffles, Youki, Pastis? The proper response demands an extended psychoanalytical inquisition, ranging from earliest childhood memories of eating out to what the interlocutor had for lunch. Do you care about wine? About service? How important to you is décor? Are you thrilled or dismayed by noise and bright lighting? Do you yearn for gustatory adventure above all things, or comfort, or value for money? Does it matter that dinner will take four hours?

The eyes of the questioner have glazed over. All she wants is a name, an opinion. Restaurants aren't like that. You might as well ask what's the best painting in town, the best piece of music, the most interesting book. On any given night, someone may order the best meal in Toronto at any one of a dozen rooms. Include ethnic restaurants and a dozen becomes ninety-nine. Few places on earth offer such a diversity of gastronomic experiences. That is our strength and our glory. The city is young, it is rich, it is healthy and free with its loyalties. It still has a long way to go. You ask for the best, but how sad it would be if we didn't believe that the best is yet to come.

❧ INDEX ☙

This book is set using the Sabon family
and Bodega typefaces.

Sabon was designed by Jan Tschichold
in 1966, its inspiration coming from
the typeface Garamond, originally created
in 1532 by Claude Garamond.

Bodega Serif is a display typeface
designed by Greg Thompson in 1992.
It adopts its characteristics from the
early 20th century.

Book design by AM Studios
Typesetting by Marie Jircik
Illustrations on pages viii, xiii, 1, 26, 56,
98, 162, 207, 252, 278, and 300:
copyright Simon Dorrell